D0273924

MARK STEEL is a comedian and writer. His TV and radio series include *The Mark Steel Solution* and *The Mark Steel Lectures*. He writes a weekly column for the *Independent* and has appeared several times on *Have I Got News for You*, on *Grumpy Old Men* and *Room 101*. His *In Town* series on BBC Radio 4 won the Silver Award for Best Comedy at the Sony Radio Academy Awards in 2010, and the Writers' Guild Award for Radio. His other books include *It's Not a Runner Bean, Reasons to be Cheerful, Vive la Revolution* and *What's Going On?*. He'd have written several more if he hadn't wasted his time wandering around record shops and trying to play cricket. He lives in Crystal Palace with an assortment of people he's related to.

By the same author

It's Not a Runner Bean
Reasons to be Cheerful
Vive la Revolution
What's Going On?

MARK STEEL'S

In Town

FOURTH ESTATE • *London*

First published in Great Britain in 2011 by
Fourth Estate
An imprint of HarperCollins*Publishers*
1 London Bridge Street
London SE1 9GF
www.4thestate.co.uk

Copyright © Mark Steel 2011

The right of Mark Steel to be identified as the author
of this work has been asserted by him in accordance
with the Copyright, Design and Patents Act 1988

A catalogue record for this book is
available from the British Library

ISBN 978-0-00-741242-6

All rights reserved. No part of this publication may be
reproduced, transmitted, or stored in a retrieval system,
in any form or by any means, without permission
in writing from Fourth Estate.

Typeset in Minion by G&M Designs Limited,
Raunds, Northamptonshire

Printed and bound by CPI Group (UK) Ltd, Croydon, CR0 4YY

MIX
Paper from
responsible sources

FSC® C007454

FSC™ is a non-profit international organisation established to promote
the responsible management of the world's forests. Products carrying the
FSC label are independently certified to assure consumers that they come
from forests that are managed to meet the social, economic and
ecological needs of present and future generations,
and other controlled sources.

Find out more about HarperCollins and the environment at
www.harpercollins.co.uk/green

This book is dedicated to all the people who've lived in history, in towns or other places, without whom it would not have been possible.

CONTENTS

INTRODUCTION

What's the point in going anywhere if the place you go to is the same as the one you left? Who'd bother going on a holiday that was advertised as: 'Visit the magic of the Seychelles, it's IDENTICAL to your own house.'

Imagine if in Tunisia, instead of the background of the call to prayers, the mosques played Magic FM. Or if Paris didn't have that slightly exotic drainy smell, because EU regulations had compelled the place to be cleaned with Jif.

Once, in the New York subway, a huge woman barged into me and yelled, 'Hey, out my way asshole!' And it was marvellous, because that's what's *supposed* to happen in New York. It was as exciting as when I was nineteen and went to Amsterdam and bought a lump of dope off a man in a woolly hat but it turned out to be mud.

After taking the trouble to go to the Lake District you want it to smell of cow pats, and at Blackpool you want everything to look as if it should be in a Carry On film.

Having toured Britain plenty of times, usually to talk to an audience for the evening, I find these local quirks compelling. For example, on the way to Skipton, in North Yorkshire, I noticed a road sign to a town called Keighley. Later, during the show, I asked the audience, 'Is Keighley your rival town?' And the room went chillingly quiet, until one woman called out with understated menace, 'Keighley – is a sink of evil.'

There was something delightful about this, because it was an expression of specifically Skipton malevolence.

Similarly, I went to Merthyr Tydfil, a blighted town at the top of the Rhondda Valley that's been shut down bit by bit. After the show the manager of the theatre told me, 'People often come in and ask what time a performance is starting, so I'll tell them, "It starts at seven-thirty," and they'll say, "Oh, that's a pity. I won't be able to come to that, as I'll be drunk by then."'

And somehow there was a warmth to hearing that, because it was a story of distinctly *Merthyr* despair.

Before appearing in Stockton-on-Tees, in the North-East, I was sent a message on Twitter by a local resident that said: 'This town is where Joseph Walker invented the safety match in 1834. Before that, when we wanted to set fire to upturned stolen cars we had to rub two sticks together.'

And before my visit to Cambridge, someone sent me a message about the town saying, 'This place is Hogwarts for wankers.' It was a cosy thought, because it could only apply to Cambridge, and ought to be the slogan on the masthead of the local paper.

The elements of a town that make it unique are what make it worth visiting. But also, any expression of local interest or eccentricity is becoming a yell of defiance.

Because the aim of society now seems to be to make every city centre so depressingly identical that if our town planners were put in charge of Athens, they'd knock down the Parthenon and replace it with a shopping mall called 'The Acropolis Centre', with an announcement that there was much excitement, as the new centre would have a River Island and a Nando's.

You could be dropped blindfolded into a city centre you'd never been to before, and guess correctly that there'd be a Clinton Cards just there, then a Vodafone, Carphone Warehouse, Boots, Specsavers and Next just there, with the anti-vivisection stall there, and on a Saturday you'd hear a 'pheep' and know the

Peruvians were about to start on the pan pipes just there, and within the hour they'd have pheeped their way through 'Mull of Kintyre' and 'I Just Called to Say I Love You' and 'Ob-la-di Ob-la-fucking-da', as I believe it's now officially called.

With equal confidence you could predict that just out of town there'd be a concrete expanse containing a giant Tesco, PC World, Majestic Wine Warehouse, Comet, Dreams, and an unfathomable junction with traffic lights facing in all directions that makes no difference anyway, as every turning forces you into the car park at Iceland and there seems to be no way of escaping except by reversing through the checkout at Carpet Right.

Somewhere in this world there must be someone who is immensely proud of having invented the multi-storey car park, which is often the introduction to a new town, as you sink into the trance that allows you to endure the shuffle through traffic towards this disturbing dungeon, where you descend and descend through a chilling gloom that would make Richard Dawkins say, 'Bollocks to that, I'm sure there are ghosts down here,' to level 5, where you think you spot a space but it turns out to be an illusion created by a snugly placed Fiat Uno, past levels 5a and 5b, so you've now forgotten what natural sunlight could ever be, like future generations forced to live in a bunker following a nuclear war, until you find a gap by a leaking pipe that leads to a line of green slime. At which point you're unlikely to take a deep breath, like a nineteenth-century traveller, and exclaim, 'Aha, and this is Taunton.'

Later you'll have to queue at the one paypoint that hasn't got a sheet of paper with a wonky 'Out of order' sign Sellotaped to it, which will be two floors away and up some steps that are so grimy that if you meet someone coming the other way it seems impolite not to murder them.

It's not the ugliness of modern towns, in a Prince Charles sense, that makes them so dispiriting; it's the soullessness. You know they've been plonked there as a result of some regional coordinating business advisory committee that's copied the model of what's been built in 3,000 other towns.

It's as if they're part of a new world, of call centres and chain pubs and clubs, in which the faceless corporation dictates how a town looks and lives and even, with its scripts for the staff of restaurants and call centres, speaks.

So the shops, the customs, the traditions and accents, the hip-hop lyrics, the football chants, the absurd rivalries that apply to one area are preserved almost as an act of rebellion, in place because the people who live with them have kept them going, and not because they've been placed there following a board meeting in Basingstoke.

This book is about some of those glorious human differences that comprise the heart of each town. It follows a series I made for BBC radio. Sometimes I'm asked how I select the towns to write about, but I'm not sure of the answer. I did feel a twinge of power when a butcher told me he'd gone to Skipton with his wife for a weekend after hearing one of the shows – for a moment I knew how Nigella Lawson must feel when she mentions that she sometimes has a gherkin with cheese on toast, and by ten o'clock the next morning some idiot's bought the world's supply of gherkins.

But as far as I'm aware I choose them fairly randomly, because the main point is that you can look at anywhere at all, and within a day discover enough history, grubbiness, madness and inspiration to realise that it is a distinct and unique cauldron of humanity.

For example, one drizzly dark February afternoon as I came out of the station at Scunthorpe, I got in a minicab, and the driver didn't even look at me, but kept staring straight ahead as he said, 'I don't know what you've come here for, it's a fucking shithole.'

And that's made me remember Scunthorpe ever since.

Penzance

In a spirit of rebellion, I'll start at the end.

If you go to Penzance by train, you will get fooled, even if you've done it before. Less than three hours after leaving you get to Plymouth, and think, 'Oh, we're nearly there. I thought it took six hours to Penzance as that's what it said at the station and it's what the announcer said but it can't take that long because we've gone 230 miles and there's less than sixty left, so I'll start collecting my things together.'

Then the train squeaks across the River Tamar into Cornwall and puffs to Liskeard at the speed of a family of refugees trudging through Somalia, stops at Bodmin and St Austell and places with no discernible buildings so the only reason to get off would be to study the station platform or the nearby flora and fauna, then the buffet bar shuts and the squeaks of the wheels get louder and you expect the next announcement to inform you that at Truro the train will be replaced by a mule and a man in a poncho chewing tobacco who mutters, 'Head two days along the pass to Redruth and follow the track known as Devil's Dump to Certain Death Passage, then take the right fork past Camborne.'

Penzance station is the end. It's not like other terminals, where there's a branch line to somewhere: the train rolls exhausted into a huge shed and stops in front of a wall. And the town feels as if it's at the end, with a slight disregard even for the rest of Cornwall for making such a half-hearted effort at being west, an attitude of 'Plymouth? That's practically Japan.' I can only imagine the contempt they have for Polperro, in eastern Cornwall, which boasts on its tourist website: 'Polperro is easily accessible from everywhere in the world.' There isn't even a proper road into Polperro, so you need a couple of flights, a hovercraft and three days in a canoe to get there from the next village. So it seems unfair that a Bedouin tribesman in the middle of the desert might see this website and think, 'At last, a holiday destination we can get to.'

There's a sense that Penzance likes its isolation. Because it doesn't feel as if it's dependent on tourism, it's a proper seaside town. There's no pedalo hire and crazy golf, it carries on with its fishing and its High Street with charity shops and pubs that seem dark even in August, but then you look up and there are palm trees and a sunset over the Atlantic.

There's even an endearing disdain for tourists, as expressed in the pamphlet *How to be Proper Cornish*, that tells us for example, 'Though fish do form a large part of a Cornish man's diet, not all fish is fit to be put on the table. Some, such as scad and ling, is only fit for the cat. Or for tourists.'

I caught a similar attitude when I hired a pushbike to cycle to the very very end, Land's End itself, and the man in the shop answered my request with a grunt, but one that was in a Cornish accent, which was impressive and rude at the same time, as if he'd picked up a handful of balls and juggled with them so they spelt 'Fuck off'. Eventually he fetched the rustiest, clankiest bike in the shop, almost threw it at me and said, 'There you are – you know how to use it, do you?' The bike and I clattered across the hills the ten miles to Land's End, and it was thrilling, this sense of getting right to the far end of the country, especially as it was windy and thick with a deep sweet aroma of compost, and then everything is called the Last of its kind, so there's a Last Inn and a Last Post Office and probably a Last Nail Salon and a Last Branch of Social Services, and as I descended through the village of Sennen and even past that I anticipated the absolute end, where there'd be nothing but a blustery cliff and I'd stand on a rock for a poignant moment, but instead I turned a corner into the Land's End Experience, where there's a tiny shopping mall with a sweet shop, a clothes shop, a cinema and a permanent *Doctor Who* exhibition.

Why? Who thought this would attract people to Land's End? There's only one reason for going to Land's End, which is that it's at the end of the land. That's its unique selling point, whereas if you try to get people there for any other reason, the fact that it's so far tends to work against it. For example if you lived in Leicester and fancied looking at a replica Cyberman before buying a shirt and some butterscotch, you still wouldn't go to this shopping mall, because it's at Land's Fucking End.

I felt cheated, as Captain Scott would have if he'd arrived at the South Pole to find a branch of Caffè Nero.

But right at the end was the famous signpost, saying John o'Groats 874 miles, New York 3,147 miles, so I decided I'd take a picture of that. Except that I had a cup of tea, went out to the signpost, and it had gone. There were some moments of panic, the sort you'd have if you were at the Taj Mahal, bent down to tie up your laces then looked up and it had disappeared. Then I noticed a sign saying it's £10 to have your picture taken there, and at half past five the people who take the money lock away the signpost and leave. It's literally locked away, in a metal trunk, and secured in a hut. And that, I contend, makes it the most magnificently mean-spirited tourist attraction in the country.

It's even worse when you consider that at the other end of this expanse of sea is the Statue of Liberty, resplendently marking its territory, and not, as far as I know, above a plaque saying 'Give me your tired, your poor, your huddled masses – from 9.00 a.m. to 5.30 p.m. sharp when we close.'

In Penzance, however, there's a grudging acceptance that tourists have to be catered for, even if they're frustratingly demanding for locals who just want to get on with their normal lives. So you feel like a six-year-old at half term, pestering your dad for attention while he's trying to work. But the real disdain is reserved for those who rent a cottage in the summer and convince themselves it's so magical and far away from urban din and the sunset's so divine that they move down. Then a few months later they're screaming, 'I can't believe there's nowhere to get stuffed olives after nine at night. And the estate agents never mentioned it would get dark this early in January. Take me home!'

For many people, living in the area has a rugged romance, but it flows from a shared sense of struggle, of sticking it out despite the lowest incomes in Britain, the remoteness, the feeling that no one in the big cities is bothered about their problems, such as the dramatic collapse of the fishing industry. One expression of this disgruntlement is how some of the ways of the rest of the country haven't quite made it down there. I was shown round one of the big pubs by a proud landlord, who explained to me the origins of the ship's wheel propped against one wall, and his paintings of Nelson, and then in one bar he said, 'Women weren't allowed in this room until about twenty-five year ago – before all this PC shit.'

It's quite endearing, this unexpected sense of what's normal. On my first trip to Penzance I heard a couple of people make remarks about the snotty ways of St Ives, a town a few miles to the north. So when I was on stage I asked the audience if there was a general feeling that St Ives was posh, and a woman called out, 'It's posh all right – they've got a dentist.' As a definition of posh that is unsurpassable, and leaves you assuming that anyone with an infected tooth in Penzance ties a rope round it, with the other end tethered to the Isles of Scilly ferry so that as it sails off it yanks the bastard out.

It takes a couple of days in Penzance to become aware that almost everything is slightly out of sync with the rest of Britain. There's a celebrated pub, called the Admiral Benbow, with a statue of a smuggler lying on the roof, in memory of an early-eighteenth-century shoot-out with a customs official. During a meal in this pub, the landlord came up to a group of four of us and said there was live music upstairs, and we'd be fools to miss it as they were astounding musicians. So we went up, and there were twelve people sat in a circle, each taking turns to sing a Cornish song, except for a man in his fifties with spiky blond hair, nose studs and implausibly red cheeks like a sunburned Johnny Rotten who recited a poem about a man who divorced his wife because he didn't like her pasties.

Then a woman with no teeth at all sang a song about a Cornish woman with twelve sons, all of whom became soldiers, and in each verse another one got killed until there were none left. Then her friend sang a song about a ship setting off with a hundred men on board, and you knew those poor fuckers would be lucky to make it to the chorus. As expected, every one of them was drowned, though I'd been hoping for a twist in which they all came back with sacks full of fish, but were eaten by a runaway leopard. Then they turned to me. 'What song do you have for us, dear?' they asked, and I thought, 'What sort of fishing disaster song do I know? I'm from London.' Unless I made one up that went, 'In nineteen hundred and ninety-six old Dave went out in the rain, to buy some cod in parsley sauce but was never seen again.'

'So the moment has arrived that I've been dreading,' I said, and considered knocking out a version of Eminem's 'The Real Slim Shady' or 'The Wheels on the Bus go Round and Round', but instead we all said we were a bit tired and left, so instead they drew a raffle for a packet of biscuits. Funnily enough, a similar thing happened when I went to see the Wu-Tang Clan.

It isn't just a prejudice, this sense of being somewhere that doesn't fit in. Cornwall has a tradition of wanting to keep its distance. The most strident expression of that sentiment comes from Mebyon Kernow, the Cornish nationalist party, which has several councillors. It was founded in 1951, and by 1964 it had five separate branches. Ask someone to guess where those branches were, and see how long it is before they get the correct answer: Penzance, Padstow, Redruth, Truro and Nigeria.

For a while there was a militant wing of the Cornish movement, called An Gof. According to the official history of Mebyon Kernow, 'They claimed responsibility for a blaze at a Penzance hairdresser's, attacked in mistake for the Bristol and West Building Society.'

You might think that after a mishap like that they'd keep quiet and hope the police assumed it was revenge for a dodgy perm, but they thought the cause of Cornish nationalism would be advanced if they claimed responsibility, although it's hard to think of any other combination of shops it would be more difficult to mix up when trying to burn one of them down: not a scrap metal yard for a branch of World of Leather, or a vegan café for a place that changes tyres.

But these movements are marginal to the vague but widespread sense that Cornwall isn't entirely Britain. It has its own flag, a little white cross and the rest entirely black, as if it was designed by a fourteen-year-old boy who sits in his room all day listening to My Chemical Romance. It has a patron saint, called St Piran, and an annual holiday on which most towns put on a procession.

This semi-dislocation from the rest of Britain is probably a result of Cornwall remaining Celtic while the rest of England was occupied by the Romans. So at unexpected moments as you turn a corner you'll find an enigmatic stone monument or Celtic cross poking lopsidedly from the edge of a field, whereas anywhere else in England the Romans would have torn it down and replaced it with an aqueduct.

One consequence of this is that there remained a separate Cornish language. Penzance was the last area where it was the first language, up until the sixteenth century.

By the seventeenth century Cornish had mostly died out. But since the 1930s there's been a movement to revive it, and now about two hundred people speak it. I got a book called *Teach Yourself Cornish* from the Penzance library, and the librarian said, 'Would you like book two as well?' which seemed a bit optimistic Anyway, even a militant Cornishman only needs a few essential phrases, like 'Ogh! Ni re settyas an gempenoryon-gols gans tan dre wall,' which translates as, 'Oh no, we've set the hairdressers on fire by mistake.'

Cornish is a Gaelic language, similar to Welsh and Irish and Breton, and now there's an English-Cornish dictionary, a novel's been written in Cornish, and there's a weekly Cornish radio show, which is impressive for two hundred people. I imagine the radio show must have dialogue such as:

'And now our mystery voice competition: "Myttin da."'

'Is it Stan from the Cornish class again?'

'Yes, you've won £4.'

To make it more complicated, a row broke out because some people wanted to speak the old historic Cornish, which I'm sure was lovely but which died out three hundred years ago. Not only would it have no words for Twitter or Crunchy Nut Corn Flakes, it would only have words for things that were around before 1760, so the lessons must go: 'Repeat after me: "Yth esov vy ow merwel dres an pla" – I'm dying of the plague.'

So some people added modern words, and the two factions split apart, then someone tried to solve the problem by merging the two Cornish languages and calling the result 'Unified Cornish'. This was rejected as unspeakable heresy by both the other sides.

Maybe more pertinently, as you leave the railway station there's a large stone sign on which 'Welcome to Penzance' is inscribed in Cornish, and while few people speak the language, they all know there is one, and that it makes them just a bit different. This sense of slight difference seems to have been around for a while. For example, Cornwall's early trade unions were part socialist and part Cornish nationalist. So according to the book on Mebyon Kernow by Bernard Deacon, in 1847 the quarrymen went on demonstrations carrying the red flag, but with a pasty stuck on the end of each flagpole. (Perhaps their anthem went 'The workers' flag is highly priced, with onions, beef and carrots diced.')

The pasty is a symbol of Cornish pride, to the extent that the Cornish rugby team still begins each game by booting a symbolic inflated pasty through the posts.

But recently the town has become divided over a modern issue. In 2009 the government offered money for a new terminal for the Scilly ferry. Some people said it would destroy the town, especially the harbour, so they set up a group called 'Friends of Penzance Harbour'. In opposition, those in favour of the new terminal set up 'True Friends of Penzance Harbour'. Presumably the first lot were tempted to retaliate with 'Passionate Lovers of the Harbour Who Plan to MARRY the Harbour', to which the other lot would come back with 'Mistresses of the Harbour Who the Harbour Turns to for Comfort and Dirty Filthy Sex Between the Boats Because You Can't Give it What it NEEDS'.

Each group had demonstrations and Facebook pages and protest songs on YouTube, and wrote millions of furious letters, and there were hundreds of websites, and then the local MP proposed a compromise called Option PZ that was hated by both groups. If you think this is all an exaggeration, here's an extract from a letter written to the local paper by a councillor who supported the new terminal: 'The claim that the vast majority have opposed option A reminds me of those extraordinary claims by Soviet and Nazi propagandists. It is a colossal untruth, in the tradition of Dr Joseph Goebbels.'

Exactly. Goebbels always began his speeches: 'Jews and Communists are plotting to prevent the building of terminals so that Aryans are left stranded, unable to dock.' Equally measured from the other side was this: 'John the Baptist, you will remember, foretold the coming of Christ. He spoke fearlessly against the politically powerful of the time and lost his head in the process. Some things in life must be spoken against and resisted. The council's tawdry decision to desecrate the harbour wall is one of them.'

It seems that someone in that council must have been cackling, 'Bring me the head of the designer of the Friends of Penzance Harbour Facebook page.' Council meetings here must be fantastic. In most areas they just go, 'With regard to the proposed bus shelter, a document is to be submitted,' but in Penzance it's, 'I suppose next you'll be invading Poland,' and 'It's people like me who saw Christ was coming.'

As an outsider you have to wonder whether this is the best use of everyone's campaigning resources, and if they put that energy into other issues, they might at least get themselves a dentist.

But maybe it's right that this gloriously overblown internal row should be about an issue that seems minor to anyone outside. This is a town in which the High Street chain stores like Boots and Clinton Cards are punctuated by a shop that sells juggling sticks and playing cards, and in which there's a building, between a pub and a second-hand bookshop, that for no apparent reason is designed like an Egyptian palace, and by the sea is an oval art-deco outdoor swimming pool that had a cannon built into one side to fire at German ships during the war.

So Penzance is the ideal place to do something off-centre, like setting up a pagan snooker club or a nudist butterfly-collecting society. It's as if you can do whatever you fancy, because the authorities will say, 'They can't do *that*. Oh, bloody hell, I'm not going all the way down there, let them do what they bloody well want.'

New Towns:
Basingstoke, Crawley, Milton Keynes

The proof that every town retains a soul, no matter how concrete, corporate, shopping-malled, retail-parked and Tescoed it becomes, is in Basingstoke. Because Basingstoke is a new town, plonked somewhere in the south, though no one seems exactly sure where to say it is, even if they live there. It's renowned as the classic modern commuter town, strangled by regional headquarters for insurance companies and hundreds and hundreds of roundabouts, some of which you can only drive round and then straight on, so you wonder whether the roads were laid by a gang of workmen with an obsessive compulsive disorder, who if they go more than an hour without building a roundabout start rocking backward and forward and making deep groaning noises.

Amongst the organisations who've established their head offices there are the AA, which might be because it's the place they're most often called out to, where their mechanics arrive at the broken-down vehicle and say, 'Ah, I see what's happened. You've got so frustrated with the roundabouts you've abandoned the car and set fire to it.'

The centre of Basingstoke is the Festival Shopping Mall. As you leave the train station, it seems there's nowhere to go except be poured through the Festival Mall's automatic doors, into a city of New Look, H&M and Monsoon units in which you try to keep moving forward in the belief that eventually you must come out into open Basingstoke. After a while it occurs to you that perhaps this *is* open Basingstoke, and that when you finally reach the other side you'll pass one last W.H. Smith and emerge into countryside and past a sign that says 'Thank you for visiting Basingstoke'.

Its image isn't helped by the fact that on Wikipedia, under 'Cultural Impact', it says: 'An episode of *Top Gear* was filmed there in 2008.'

So I was surprised to find a book called *Basingstoke and its Contribution to World Culture*. I thought, 'Maybe there's some stuff I've missed, like Jimi Hendrix started there, singing, "There's got to be some way outta here, but every roundabout takes me to another fucking one".' Or Jackson Pollock's most famous painting was called *If You can Make Your Way Through Basingstoke's One-Way System, Joining these Red Dots Should be a Piece of Piss*.

The book starts off on a positive note, telling us: 'Basingstoke is one of the most derided towns in England. Its reputation is as an over-developed eyesore of numbing dullness. Its very name lends itself to mockery. Basingjoke, Boringstoke and the ironic Amazingstoke are used by its own residents, not always with affection.'

But if you look into the town's past it becomes clear that this isn't just a new town built by numbers to fill up a bit of Hampshire. Because, far from being solely a modern butt of jokes, the place has been loathed for centuries. The founder of Methodism, John Wesley, went there in 1759 and wrote afterwards, 'The inhabitants are like wild beasts, slow of heart and dull of understanding.'

'But surely,' you must be thinking, 'it was more exciting in 1669.' Well, the Grand Duke of Tuscany went there that year, and his valet wrote an account of the visit: 'His Highness, arriving betimes at Basingstoke, set out to explore it on foot, but it seemed so wretched it hardly repaid the effort of walking a few paces.'

'All right,' you'll say, 'but what about 1882?' Which is a fair point, except that in 1882 an article about Basingstoke in *The Times* said: 'About midway between London and Salisbury is a benighted little town inhabited chiefly by a race of barbarians.'

This is hugely encouraging for the town, because it means it has a past, a human touch beyond the everlasting Festival Centre and office blocks with eerily silent reception areas. To be insulted with such venom it must have been up to something interesting.

Basingstoke used to be a market town, and its current residents seem aware of this. They refer to a huge and seemingly pointless wall that sits in the centre as 'the Great Wall of Basingstoke', and the popular local website 'It's Basingstoke not Boringstoke' describes it as a 'great mass of concrete poured over the remains of the old market town'.

Also, as *Basingstoke and its Contribution to World Culture* points out, the town was the home of Thomas Burberry, a Victorian draper who established the line of clothes that bear his name, and who apparently invented the raincoat. It could be argued that Charles Mackintosh's coat, which came earlier, was the first raincoat, but *Basingstoke and its Contribution to World Culture* points out: 'But these sticky smelly easily punctured garments were a crude concept compared to Burberry's silky gabardine.' I've no idea who is right here, but it's joyful to see the town so stroppy over the issue, like when a quiet old aunty unexpectedly gets angry about an incident on a bus in 1957.

So there's clearly a pride in the town's past. One of Basingstoke's heroes, who seems to be known by the under-thirties as well as the older residents, is John Arlott the cricket commentator. Arlott was extraordinary, partly because he spoke in a series of six- or seven-word sections followed by a short pause, as if everything he said was a poem, and all in a gentle, lyrical Basingstoke lilt, with an underlying purr, as if while he was speaking he was pushing a slightly broken old lawnmower.

He'd quietly take the piss out of the other commentators. After one of them told listeners that across the ground he could see the sun setting in the west, when Arlott came on he said slowly, 'You can rest assured that if the sun starts to set in the east I'll be the first to let you know.'

Arlott was a committed anti-racist, and was instrumental in inviting Basil D'Oliveira, a 'Cape Coloured' cricketer who was barred from playing professionally in his native South Africa, to play in England. Arlott called his autobiography *Basingstoke Boy*, and his portrait is on every brochure or website that publicises the town.

There's one time in Basingstoke's history when I wish he'd been there, because the town now scorned as a symbol of suburban sleepiness was once known as irredeemably violent. One report described how 'In Basingstoke election days are occasions for joyous rioting. And even cricket matches are tediously prone to ending in violent disorder.'

You can almost hear Arlott saying, 'And there goes Fat Jimmy coming round the wicket – with a Stanley knife – while a crowd on the boundary – chant, "Who are yer, who are yer" – and one wonders if they don't know who their adversaries are – why it is they're kicking them with considerable vigour – in an area not distant from the testicles.'

This history, and the way it's seeped into the culture of the modern town, suggests that the old Basingstoke hasn't been entirely destroyed by the new, despite the impact of the 1944 Greater London Plan, which aimed to stop London becoming any bigger by building a series of new towns and expanding others, such as Basingstoke.

Houses were built for 40,000 people to move there, which must have seemed disruptive if you were already there, but might have created less tension had hundreds of people not been moved out of their homes to make way for new estates and roundabouts. Dozens of tradesmen were evicted so their workshops could be demolished and replaced by a new shopping centre. One man who felt aggrieved was Alfie Cole, who ran a stables on the Basing Road. In 1966 he drove a pony and trap to Downing Street to hand in a petition to the Prime Minister, Harold Wilson, and as Alfie put it, 'dumping lorryloads of topsoil at strategic parts of the town during the morning rush hour' as he went.

Alfie seems almost as revered in the town as John Arlott, and when I mentioned him in a show at the theatre there was almost complete recognition. The majority of people who live in Basingstoke now must have come there as a result of the expansion after the sixties, yet it appears that most of today's residents identify with the town as a whole, including its figures from before they were there, and approve of the campaigns to prevent the changes that enabled them to come.

Even in a town the citizens themselves refer to as Boringstoke, they want to feel that its traditions and quirks belong to them. It's *their* boring town. For example, there's a blue statue in Wote Street of a mother with a child, that everyone calls 'Wote Street Willy'. Even a travel website describes it by saying: 'At 7 tonnes it's the largest phallic statue in Britain.'

Almost the whole of Basingstoke seems aware that the Forum office block in the town is the tallest building on a line between London and New York, which is indeed impressive, although nearly all of that line goes over the Atlantic Ocean, on which there aren't many skyscrapers to offer much competition.

The wall, the roundabouts and the jokey image are what make the people of Basingstoke half-proud, rather than the joys of how easy it is to commute to London, or the variety of identical chain stores that have been attracted to the Festival Shopping Mall.

Similarly, Crawley in Sussex, about halfway between London and Brighton, was designated a new town in the 1946 New

Towns Act, and built to house 50,000 people. Crawley is mostly a suburb of Gatwick Airport, and it has a feel of earthiness, as if while there are the smug people who moved from London to Brighton, and who boast of how the sea air is marvellous for the kids, Crawley is made up of people who thought of doing that, but got halfway and said, 'Fuck it, I'm knackered, let's stay here.'

And it keeps growing, the employment opportunities it offers always attracting newcomers. But the areas within the town retain their quaint names that could easily fool people. There's Pease Pottage and Three Bridges, whose residents must think, 'It's lovely round here, quiet and peaceful. The only noise you ever get is from a major international airport.'

At one point during a show in Crawley I suggested that they must get used to timing conversations to fit in the moments between long-haul flights to Chicago. They all looked utterly bemused, as if to say, 'Is there an airport? Near here? Are you sure? We've never noticed it.' But it turned out I was the one misinformed, because the flightpaths are organised so that no planes fly over the town.

The airport is simply a huge workplace that dominates Crawley, making it like a giant modern pit village. And that makes it cohesive, for example with a Labour Party that's as established as that in any old industrial town, although it's only had fifty years to go through the cycle of being formed with enthusiasm, getting a Member of Parliament elected and then collapsing in a cloud of disillusionment.

The airport should make people across Crawley feel a sense of camaraderie. For example, its presence means that no build- ings in the town are allowed to be more than four storeys high. The Hawth Theatre boasts that it's the tallest structure in town, so if al Qaeda choose to attack Crawley, it's the theatre they'll go for.

And maybe the fact that so many people are connected to one workplace has enabled a local football team to become implanted as part of the culture, in a way that's taken place in few British towns since the 1920s, by which time the bases of most football clubs had become cemented. Crawley Town FC was helped along the way by the wealth of a character of the sort who, to stay legal, newspapers refer to as 'colourful', and who was suspended from football for corruption at his previous club in Boston. To get a sense of life at Crawley Town, here's a report by a visiting fan of their match with Bath City: 'Their manager, a rather large Steve Evans, spent the whole match pacing up and down the touchline, shouting abuse at the Bath players, the referee and everything else that holds existence on the planet. At half time an announcement was made that went, "There's an old man that lives behind the stadium and has made a complaint. He says there's too much noise and we need to quieten down. So let's make the bastard even more annoyed and make some noise."'

Now, the theory that all towns, however corporatised, retain an underlying soul, is stretched to the limit in Milton Keynes. There can be few places that try so hard to live up to their image. The first sign that something's not healthy comes as you drift through the Buckinghamshire countryside towards the town, and pass the first roundabout, which has a grid number. So a sign will tell you this is H4 or V5 roundabout, as if you're a Lilliputian moving through a giant game of Battleships.

What's more disconcerting is that, apart from these grid numbers, the roundabouts all look identical. The view in every direction from each of them is of a highway with trees perfectly spaced on each side, and a giant rectangular warehouse behind the trees, so you've no idea if you've been past this bit already or not.

You're entrapped in this grid with no way of working out what direction you're going; although I haven't tested this, I expect the town planners have fixed it so compasses don't work here, they just spin violently the way they're supposed to do if you're in the Bermuda Triangle.

The most sinister warehouse belongs to River Island. It stretches the whole length of one grid section, a shiny oblong block with no apparent entrances, no bobbles or chimneys or bits sticking out, just a perfect smooth geometrical structure that's far too big for River bloody Island. If all the clothes in all the world's River Island stores were put in a pile, they would barely fill one corner of this complex, and if it emerges one day that it's full of long corridors and solid steel doors that open only after a biometric sensor scans your iris and a sugary auto-mated voice with an American accent says, 'Identity confirmed – you may proceed to the excavation section,' and where an army of ex-Death Row inmates are building a tunnel to China in preparation for an invasion, I shan't be entirely surprised.

With no churches or pubs or graffiti or bridges or landmarks to plot your position you find yourself not only lost, as you can be in any town, but unsure where you are in relation to the rest of the world, as if you were in a rowing boat in the middle of the Pacific Ocean. The grid numbers only make it more confusing, as you pull over and try to calculate that if you've just passed H5, and the one before that was V6, then H7 must be to the right, which, as H9 cancels out V3 over 5 divided by x, the angle of the line H2–V8 must be equal to the sum of V1 squared.

Milton Keynes is a town that must have been designed by a mathematician, one of those philosophical ones like Pythagoras who saw numbers as the only part of the universe that embody perfection. Even the one building you can see as you pass through the town on the train is a huge cube comprising hundreds of identical glass squares on all sides that looks like part of a puzzle for super-intelligent giants.

Outside the station all is chillingly symmetrical, with even the lamp posts having spherical tops so the pattern isn't spoilt. I assume there must be bylaws to ensure that this picture is maintained, so that if you're planning to walk down one side of high-way H2, you have to get someone to walk down the other side at the same speed, to stop the place becoming lopsided. As an experiment, somebody should try something like leaving a kettle on the pavement to see whether an official would place one on the other side within minutes, maybe having emerged from a pipe that leads to the control room under River Island.

I took my son around Milton Keynes when he was twelve, and he found it bewildering, which I suppose was a good sign. Two years later I told him I was going back there to do a show and he said, 'Oh no, you'll be on stage and someone in the front row will slyly pass you a note that says "Please help us".'

Defenders of the town point out that it's a pleasant environment, with open spaces and lakes and a low crime rate and efficient schools and all sorts of activities, but the qualities advanced as positive aspects are all top-down, as if arranged by a happiness committee. They've been organised by the people who produce brochures that say: 'And if ballooning is your preferred leisure activity, then it's up, up and away with the Milton Keynes Hot Air Ballooning Association. Yes, whether it's double word scores at the Indoor Scrabble Centre on H3 or artificial shark fishing at the hexagonal lake on the corner of V7 and H5, you'll find all your desires are catered for here in Milton Keynes.'

Living there must feel as if you're part of a social experiment, with cameras following you to monitor the effects of issues such as triangular shapes on the heart rate. It was born when a Labour housing minister, Richard Crossman, announced where it would be built in 1966. The chairman of the committee set up to oversee the building of the town told Crossman he wanted a 'properly planned publicly owned town', and there was clearly an idealism driving the project. Maybe the dream owed something to the dominant socialist view of the time, that aspired to create order from above, organised by the state, as practised by the Soviet Union. In which case, on top of the gulags and the pact with Hitler, we can blame Stalinism for Milton Keynes as well.

The result is a town that's *too* clean and ordered. The state of mind of those most eager to defend the new town is shown in the book *Milton Keynes: Image and Reality*, which boasts: 'By the mid-1980s we could aspire to be almost at the same level as Croydon.'

In some ways the place has been a success, like a mini-America, built on immigration and a promise of a stable community on a new frontier. If there'd been a properly funded public-relations department in Washington in the 1800s, they'd have probably made adverts saying 'Come to America' in which cowboy children ran across Kentucky holding red balloons.

But like the police officers who run the village in the film *Hot Fuzz*, who are so determined to keep their domain perfect that they arrange the murder of anyone who transgresses the etiquette of idyllic rural life, you feel the people who arrange Milton Keynes feel uneasy if anyone does anything to threaten the place's controlled order of perfection.

It's symbolic that in order to get a Football League team, Milton Keynes bypassed the route of developing a club within the community, and brought one in, the MK Dons, a team that had been Wimbledon in South London until its owners took it as a franchise and planted it in its new home.

What you feel the town needs is grubbiness. It needs a market with kids' clothes tattily piled on a table next to a man with sideburns selling second-hand CDs by the Average White Band and Supertramp. It needs an area the rest of the town warns you not to go, a kebab shop that's the subject of rumours about missing puppies and a pub that everyone claims to have been in on the night Mad Jimmy went berserk with a cattle prod.

Where the old socialist planners and modern corporate planners agree is that society, and the towns that make a society, should be organised from above. But in time Milton Keynes will develop a soul from within. There will inevitably be bands and rappers, poets and writers who complain eloquently about the town and so help to give it a human touch. Eventually the football supporters will identify with the team enough to moan incessantly about it, and it will become part of the community.

One day the protest groups, the graffiti artists, the eccentrics and flawed shards of humanity that make a town whole will emerge. They'll shave corners off the angles and put irregular-shaped objects in the centre, and while the original architects might shudder at the unravelling of their plans, Milton Keynes will become a town at last.

Birmingham

I'm not sure why Birmingham is so disliked, but it is. People try to change its image by renovating the Bullring Centre every couple of years, and its citizens often tell you the city has more miles of canals than Venice, but it makes no difference. It's like the last year of a discredited government, when ministers are changed, and policies relaunched, but no one notices, because by now the Chancellor could give everyone a bar of gold and people would say, 'Typical of the thieving bastards.'

Maybe it's the train station that does it. It's surely the gloomiest, dingiest station for any major city in Britain. On the way there, you clatter past the airport and fields and light and the football ground, but this openness doesn't make you feel at all free and airy, because you know it means you're hurtling towards the damp darkness of New Street station, just as you wouldn't think, 'Ah, what a delightful breeze to set me up for the day,' if you were a prisoner sailing across San Francisco Bay to start your time in Alcatraz.

The layout has been carefully designed so that on the platforms no sunlight can enter, even on midsummer day, like Stonehenge in reverse. The first time you go there you think, this can't possibly be the station for Britain's second city, and assume the train took a wrong turning and went down a disused mineshaft. Then hundreds of people struggle with their cases along the unlit narrow platforms, like refugees from the Russian pogroms, though at least those lucky bastards had a crying family to greet them and put their luggage on a donkey. At New Street there's a search for the stairs to the Bullring, where, even if you've been there fifty times before, you stand and look around for several minutes thinking, 'Now where am I supposed to go?'

Because you're in a traffic roundabout you can only escape from by navigating subways and uncrossable intersections that no map can help with. So you submerge yourself into the concrete, deciding to follow a path and seeing where it takes you, becoming so confused you wouldn't be surprised if you came out opposite the Hanging Gardens of Babylon. Even in the middle of the city you're surrounded by flyovers and vast traffic islands that make you feel you're really not meant to be there, as if you've accidentally wandered into a military zone, and you expect an official to come running towards you screaming at you to get down, and launching an investigation into how you got in without anyone noticing.

Even in a car you get hopelessly, flailingly lost amidst the motorways and flyovers that govern the centre of the town. Surely motorways are supposed to link cities, not circulate around the middle of them. If you're going from Leeds to London a motorway is handy, but if you're popping out for a packet of biscuits you shouldn't need to take the M6 to junction 5 and find the seventh exit off the Aston interchange that leads to the Spar.

What you mustn't do is miss your turning. You see the bit of Birmingham you want to go to, maybe even passing right by the exact building. And you look up at the road sign that tells you to get in this lane for Birmingham east and keep straight on for Birmingham south-east and straight on then back in a loop and sort of diagonally across and round again for Birmingham east by south-east, and you scream, 'What? Which?' to yourself, and try to hedge your bets by straddling three lanes at once until you feel the whole motorway is hooting in a Birmingham accent, and you follow the lane that you decide is logical but now you're going back past the building you're supposed to be at, unable to exit the motorway. This shouldn't be too much of a problem, you assure yourself, as you can easily take the next exit and find your way back, but you go a mile and then another mile and past the city centre and there's no way off, then fields start appearing and it begins to get dark and you can only look forward to running out of petrol so you can get taken home by the RAC.

When I first had to negotiate the matrix that is Birmingham city centre it explained a scene I'd often experienced in my youth. My mum's side of the family lived in Erdington, and whenever we visited them my dad would spend the first forty minutes of our stay stood on the doorstep with my granddad discussing the route.

Bottlenecks at Bearwood and cut-throughs at Stetchford were traded with new roundabouts in Digbeth and roadworks up the Bristol Road until it seemed they must have exhausted every possible route from anywhere to anywhere without working out how to get through Birmingham, and would soon decide, 'So next time I'll go back through Longbridge, across to Edgbaston, drive across the cricket ground to deep square leg, up to New Street station onto the gloomy chilly track and get the train, 'cos I'm buggered if I know how to get here by car.'

It can't just be the inaccessible, terrifying centre that makes it so hard to sell Birmingham as an attractive city. Even people who don't have to suffer the rigmarole of getting there because they already live there find it hard to be cheerful about their town. I wanted to be positive myself, so I had to ignore websites called – and I'm afraid these are all real – 'Erdington is a Shithole', 'Bearwood is a Shithole' and 'Smethwick is a Shithole'. I think they're all independent and not part of the shithole franchise, but eventually I found one that actually promotes the city, called

'Birmingham is not Shit'. (I showed it to my son and he said, 'The sad thing is that's the official council website.')

The blurb explaining itself goes: '"Birmingham is not Shit" loves Birmingham's people, arts, animals, buildings and grass verges.' I'm not sure this is encouraging, when you're trying to promote the positive side of the second biggest city in Britain, and after four things you're down to the grass verges. 'Birmingham is not Shit' launched a competition for Brummie of the Year, and I thought, 'Ah, that's quite sweet', so I looked up who were the finalists, and it said, 'Due to foul and abusive comments this year there will be no Brummie of the Year.'

In the search for a positive view I saw a film about the city, featuring Telly Savalas, the iconic actor who played Kojak. For some reason he presented this tribute to the beauty of Birmingham, and at one point he says: 'There are so many beautiful sights, such as the inner ring road, a majestic network, miles of concrete and flyovers that link with the Aston Express.'

I really, honestly don't want to be cynical, but without question when Telly Savalas saw the script he must have been straight on the phone to his agent screaming, 'Is that the best they can do, the motherfucking ring road? Hasn't the place got a beach, a mountain range, something that links up with somewhere better than the Aston fucking Express?'

It does make the place marvellously earthy, though. Whenever I hear people talk about the wit of football fans, the poetry of the terraces, I always think of Birmingham City, whose anthem goes: 'Shit on the Villa, shit on the Villa tonight, shit on the Villa, because the Villa are shite.' You can only imagine the excitement as the author paced around his kitchen for inspiration at three in the morning, yearning for a rhyme that went with tonight, and suddenly yelling, 'I've got it – SHITE – it's PERFECT!'

Something else the town can boast is that there are apparently more lap-dancing clubs per head of the population in Birmingham than in any other city in Europe. Strange that, isn't it? You'd think that blokes in Birmingham should be able to attract women without paying for it. 'Shit on the Villa, shit on the Villa tonight' – don't tell me the women don't go for that.

And yet historically Birmingham should be as proud of its intellect as anywhere. For example, any account of the period from around 1790, when science and rational thought had to battle to win their place in European culture, gives a huge mention, alongside Darwin, Franklin and the pioneers of medicine and electricity, to the Birmingham Lunar Society.

Pathetic though it may seem, I can't help but wonder at the wisdom of calling their groundbreaking group the Birmingham Lunar Society, because I imagine them standing outside each night going, 'Yep, it's still there, that moon. It's a bit smaller than last noit, I hope it don't disappear altogether, or we'll have to close our society down.'

Another possibility is that it made sense for Birmingham to emerge as a centre for science at the time, as it was a city driven by engineering. This was a period when viewing the world with a scientific mind was still a challenge to the religious order, so Birmingham became a home for radical groups who saw the new discoveries as a political statement. To view the moon as a satellite that could be studied and analysed was an affront to those who saw it as a heavenly body driven by God's will.

Keeping with the lunar theme, the doctors, inventors and industrialists of the Society met once a month, on the night of a full moon, and set about promoting the latest scientific debates. They probably saw no distinction between their academic work and their role in establishing Britain's first anti-slavery campaign, in 1788, long before even most radicals suggested the trade should be abolished. Partly this was in response to the fact that much of the wealth of the city at the time came from the manufacture of guns, which were used to capture slaves. The anti-slavery society also organised a boycott of sugar picked by slave labourers.

The Lunar Society helped establish a tradition of radical movements in the city, though some failed in magnificent fashion. For example a women's movement was set up in 1825. According to *Birmingham: A History of the City and its People*: 'In the mid-nineteenth century a group of young females formed the Birmingham Maidens' Club, where the members agreed to remain unmarried. But the club had to close down after most of them got married.'

And there's the Bullring, so named because bulls were once tied there and taunted for the amusement of passers-by, though now despite its name it must be the most impossible place in the world to get a bull, as the finest matador of all time couldn't coax it through the underpass, round all the angles, up the steps and across the ring roads to the diesel-filled concourse where its ancestors were prodded for fun.

There were riots at the Bullring in 1839, led by campaigners for an extension of the vote. And as Birmingham became the centre of the motor industry the city became central to the trade union movement. The engineers who joined miners to shut down Saltley coke depot in 1972, in support of miners' pay claims, were responsible for one of the most celebrated union victories of the century.

Birmingham's response to calamities, such as the pub bombings of 1974 or the decline of the car factories, suggests that they're seen as traumas that have rocked the whole city, in a way that might also happen in Liverpool or Newcastle.

Perhaps more importantly in shaping a city-wide sense of community, there's a shared sense of unease over what happened to Birmingham's statue of King Kong. It used to stand by the Rotunda building in the middle of the Bullring, possibly because someone in the planning department was misinformed, and believed King Kong ended up on top of the Bullring holding a girl from Selly Oak. At one point someone set fire to his rear, which led to a disputed insurance claim, then at the end of the 1970s he suddenly disappeared.

Thirty years later you still hear theories about where he went, as if he's the city's Lord Lucan. A typical letter in the *Birmingham Post* in 2011 said, 'I remember being absolutely terrified of King Kong as the number 50 bus came around the corner of the outdoor markets and HE came into view. I also remember that it ended up on the Stratford Rd at a coach firm's depot/office.'

Another story is that he turned up outside a car dealers in Digbeth, and it's said that in 1976 he was sold for £12,700 to a Scottish company called Spook Erections, which put him in the markets it ran around the country. A recent article in the *Birmingham Post* informed its readers that the statue 'has been found lying in a car park in Penrith'.

Unlike those of Lord Lucan, you'd think these sightings would be easy to verify, what with him being twenty feet tall and incapable of moving, and I can't imagine Penrith is the sort of town where a King Kong can be dumped in a car park without being spotted, the way you might just get away with it in New York. Or maybe he'll continue to create these wispy visions, and there'll be unconfirmed reports of him living in Bolivia disguised as Godzilla, being employed by the CIA to intimidate anti-government forces in Angola, or being melted down by the Mafia after a row about gambling debts.

Another unifying fact about the city is the one about it enjoying more miles of canal than Venice, although this seems to miss the point, as you might as well boast that there's more paint in a warehouse in Luton than there is on the Sistine Chapel. The important fact is that it's quality rather than quantity that attracts tourists when it comes to a canal system. The Birmingham Tourist Board seems to think otherwise, and must assume that visitors to Venice find the place disappointing because there's only one canal visible from St Mark's Square, and might say, 'I hear there are a whopping four round the back of the Stetchford gasworks passing under the M5 interchange where the junkies leave their needles. We'll go *there* next year.'

Birmingham's canals are another sign of its influence at the start of the industrial age. They were the earliest in Britain, created to transport iron from the Black Country to the centres of engineering. Now, for all the canal miles that gives the city, not everyone is confident of their value as a tourist attraction. For example, when a friend arranged a canal boat weekend in Worcestershire, she was told by the agency that made the booking, 'We don't recommend you take the boat into Birmingham. You just don't know WHAT might happen.'

As fearful overreactions go, I'd say that beats those people in the 1980s who would give the advice 'Don't drive through Brixton,' as if the place had fallen to bandits and warlords who'd ambush random families heading for a day trip to Brighton. How dangerous can crossing the nautical border into Birmingham really be? Are these waterways notorious for pirates? Do hooded, eye-patched gangs of youths jump on board and demand at the point of a sword that you hand over your tea, coffee and potted plants? You can see how getting away from danger would be a problem, with a shout of 'Step on it!' and then a gentle 'puff puff puff puff splosh' as the barge crept towards its maximum permitted speed of four miles an hour. Maybe the whole system is like *Apocalypse Now*, with barges moodily rolling towards their destination while the captain sits on board wistfully chewing grass and keeping watch in case of ambush from the rebels of Tipton.

But Birmingham's canals give it a myth of being an English Venice, which has become a part of its identity. It also has its university, its Test match cricket ground, Cannon Hill Park and its football clubs, all unique, and all possible to cross without the use of a flyover or underpass, though this probably infuriates the planners who designed the city's layout in the 1960s, who must watch Aston Villa and think, 'That player could nip up the wing much quicker if we'd been allowed to put a bypass on the halfway line, to cut out the bottleneck in midfield.'

And Birmingham has its accent, which people are so rude about you could probably arrest them for hate crimes. But more important than what outsiders think of it is the fact that the place has its own accent. Unlike Glasgow, which has an accent not all that different from other cities in southern Scotland, or London, whose accent stretches to Southend and Luton, Birmingham's is its own. In this world of stultifying sameness where it's so hard to be genuinely original and unique, Birmingham has a one-off.

So the city defends its dialect with pride, and if it should ever be in danger of getting diluted it ought to be preserved, the way Welsh is, by insisting that all children in the city are taught in Brummie and that the road signs should be in both English and Brummie.

On top of this, Birmingham can claim to be the place where the Balti curry was invented. There are areas such as Sparkbrook that are lined with Indian and Pakistani cafés, with plastic table-cloths and lopsided portraits on the wall that may be of the owner's father or could be the President of the Punjab.

Birmingham's image probably isn't helped by its confused status as Britain's second city. Whereas that title was accepted across most of Britain until recently, in a poll in 2011, 48 per cent said Manchester was the second city, and 40 per cent said Birmingham. This only matters because of expectations, other-wise people in Oswestry would be gutted every time a new survey emerges that says it's missed out on second-city rank yet again, despite the new windows in the post office.

But something needs to be done about Birmingham's centre, because the joys and quirks of the city are hidden behind the oppressively unwelcoming concrete algebra puzzle that is its unfathomable heart. It's like writing a captivating novel but insisting that the cover smells of raw sewage.

The planners do make regular attempts to renovate the Bullring, but with delicate architectural genius they always manage to make it even uglier. It's as if there's a committee somewhere that thinks, 'Just one more flyover and then it will all be sorted,' so that by now an aerial view of the place makes it look like a Scalextric course after the dog's sat on it. The latest attempt at renovation entailed the creation of a giant, mesmerising bubbly thing in the absolute centre, that looks as if each day it's going to get bigger by eating the first twenty people who walk by.

So it should simply be abandoned. The Bullring, the station, the inner circle and the flyovers should be covered in barbed wire and left derelict, like bits of Chernobyl, and the centre should be moved two miles away, in whatever direction the locals prefer. Outsiders will then arrive in a city it's possible to walk around, and where it's possible to imagine that a park may be nearby. They'll look around for the Asian cafés and the exuberance of Jamaican Handsworth, the abundance of canals and the symphony orchestra, and will hear the accent as a lilting melody, a symbol of the pastoral effervescent jolliness, with its strange cordoned-off area on the outskirts, that is Birmingham.

Didcot, Oxford

Didcot must be the town that's least visited compared to how often it's seen in the whole country. It's in the south of Oxfordshire, and consists of two main roads on either side of a tiny pedestrianised centre, a small railway museum, a fire station, a post office and a fucking great power station with six vast funnels pumping out fuck knows what that can be seen from everywhere, including, I should think, on a clear night, outer space.

If you're travelling to the Midlands by road or rail, you might casually glance west and note a power station. That will be Didcot. If you're going to Bristol, you might at some point turn towards the north and see a power station. Didcot. Even when you're used to this you get caught out, and think, 'That power station can't *possibly* be Didcot,' but it will be, because it's on wheels and they must move it to comply with regulations regarding smoke limits in one area.

It may not be coincidence that it's visible from so much of England, because Didcot was the perfect place for southern England's main railway junction, en route to everywhere, in the middle of everything. Many towns grew up around a railway, but in Didcot the railway was the town, created to serve Brunel's vision of a network from east to west. You'll probably now be wondering how you can read much more about the impact of the railway on Didcot, in which case you may be drawn to a book I bought called *The Railway Comes to Didcot*. But unfortunately the opening line goes: 'In no way is this book a history of the railway in Didcot.' I couldn't help feeling slightly cheated by this. It's possible that another of the author's books may contain some information in that area, but I was slightly put off by its title: *The Long Years of Obscurity: A History of Didcot, Volume One – to 1841*.

Didcot owes its modern existence to Lord Abingdon, who refused to allow a railway to pass through Abingdon village; Didcot was chosen instead. Now it has around 20,000 people, and a sense that the landscape might not be something to put on a tin of biscuits.

When I asked on Twitter for comments from the town, possibly the two most poignant were, 'You can always tell on the train to Oxford who's from Didcot, from their morose demeanour,' and 'I seem to remember a character in *EastEnders* confessing they were from Didcot.' That is truly disturbing, to be considered a subject of trauma in *EastEnders*, presumably with dialogue that went:

'We've gotta talk.'

'What is it, doll?'

'Look, this ain't gonna be easy, but I'll come aht wiv it. I'm from Didcot.'

'You what? Oh no, that explains your morose demeanour, you slaaaag.'

But the town has developed a stoical sense of pride. Everyone I spoke to there was aware of the Cornerhouse Theatre, which they told me with great satisfaction had been built with money originally scheduled for Reading. And everyone was shocked, *shocked*, that I wasn't familiar with William Bradbery, who came from Didcot and was the first person to cultivate watercress.

As well as being defined by, and looked down upon from all angles by, the towers of the power station, Didcot is also defined by, and looked down upon from all angles by, the town ten miles up the road, which is Oxford.

To start with, in 1836 the Great Western Railway applied to build a branch line from Didcot to Oxford, but the colleges were the main landowners, and they refused to allow the new route. The reason was that they didn't want the grubby people of Didcot to be able to lower the tone of Oxford by merrily travelling to it on the train. Eventually in 1843 the colleges allowed the new line, but on the condition that no one below the status of an MA was allowed to travel on it. Now, when I first read this, I was certain that I must have misread or misunderstood the sentence, so to save you going back over this paragraph, eventually in 1843 the colleges allowed the new line, but on the condition that no one below the status of an MA was allowed to travel on it.

Not only that, but the university authorities were given free passes to travel along the line at any time, to check that no one was trying to catch a ride who wasn't sufficiently mastered up. So there were actually people looking through the carriages, maybe even wandering down the train calling, 'Can I see your Masters, please? Masters and doctorates, please. Thank you, Professor. Thank you, sir, that's fine. Ah, I'm sorry, sir, media studies isn't valid on a Friday, you'll have to get off at the next stop.'

If it hasn't already received one, I'd like to nominate this for the all-time snobbery award. When discussing their proposal the university authorities must have said, 'It is quite possible that not being able to speak Latin is contagious, in which case for our finest minds to be in the proximity of these Didcottian dunces could be calamitous to our nation's intellect.'

Hopefully the local youngsters found ways round this rule, by flashing a 2:1 in geography at the barrier, then running off before the inspector could check it. Or maybe they forged a BA in philosophy, and then rather than squirming as the inspector asked them for a précis on Cartesian dualism, they panicked and locked themselves in the toilet.

But it would be a mistake to think of Oxford as a monolithic body of pomposity, because the town is divided between the university hierarchy and a normal population. This has given rise to a tension that goes back to the early days of the colleges in the thirteenth century, and that erupted spectacularly in 1355, when two students complained to an innkeeper about the quality of his beer. According to one account, they 'took a quart of wine and threw the said wine in the face of the taverner, and then with the said quart pot beat the taverner'. The students then fetched bows and arrows, but these were confiscated by local bailiffs, so more students turned up and attacked the town magistrates. A complaint by residents was made the next morning, so the students, being young and full of mischief, set fire to the town. At the end of the day's fighting sixty students and thirty-three people from the town were dead. By this time I presume the landlord had cleaned his barrels and freshened up his beer.

You might imagine some sort of sanction would have been applied to the students who started this jape, such as a couple of marks knocked off their business studies final paper for every blacksmith they murdered, or something. But the government blamed the people of the town for the incident. So each year the mayor, bailiffs and sixty burgesses of the town had to attend a mass, and pay a silver penny to the university for each dead student. This penance carried on until 1825, when there was probably only the *Daily Mail* left screaming that if criminals can get away with a 490-year sentence, it's no wonder the streets aren't safe.

Today the rift between university and town ought to be less pronounced than in the days when students were almost exclusively from the nobility, but this is complicated by the fact that in Oxford the students are *Oxford* students. Some of them, though a smaller percentage even than fifty years ago, may be from working-class backgrounds, but all of them are imbued with a sense of superiority. As you head through the centre of town past the courtyards, the gothic buildings, the boys in black gowns, the quaint bridge that seems designed to tempt you to jump off it into the Thames at two in the morning, the perfect lawns, the entrances behind thick spiky chains, you feel as if you're at a gig with only a white wristband, but you need a purple one to get past the ropes and the security staff to where people like you aren't allowed.

Even so, the town is seductive, with pubs covered in ivy that make you feel as if you should sit at an oak table with a jug of ale being wise, and gentle paths by the river where you have to delicately brush away dangling lengths of weeping willow to walk along them. It's hard to reconcile yourself to the fact that this is the same Thames that charges through London all full of rage. It seems as if the river must go there to work all day, then commute back home to Oxford and relax by gently rippling past muddy banks on which there ought to be an old man showing his grandson how to whittle.

So it must seem peculiar to live there if you're part of the population that has no business with the university. Because Oxford's college's aren't to one side of town, like most workplaces that dominate an area, by the docks or on an industrial estate. They're stood, grandly, peering at you from all angles, reminding you that beyond the gables and the statues are your masters and future masters, and probably a function at which someone's carrying a tray of tiny sausages to honour a benefactor from the Wellcome Trust.

This is a world that certainly isn't dominated by the soulless and the corporate, with no room for individuality. Here they saunter across quadrangles between spires and gargoyles, every delicately designed corner of every building intricately unique.

A chancellor of Oxford University would be facing controversy, I would imagine, if he suggested that the colleges should
be relocated in a huge education park and become part of chains
called First for Firsts and Masters-rite.

Yet there is a town behind these buildings that functions
normally. Over the river and past the station are the nail salons
and pound shops, the Westgate shopping centre with its Vision
Express and Nando's. It does have a retail park, and a nearby
depleted car factory, and a football team that slid out of the
League but came back again, and postmen and a Big Yellow
Storage Company.

Occasionally the two worlds collide. Walking across the
bridge to the normal part of town, I met a professor. 'Excuse me,'
he said, in a controlled slur that suggested he'd had practice at
trying not to seem drunk. 'Can I talk to you for a moment?' He
had a tight cravat and a short sheepskin coat, and asked again,
'Could I, just for a moment?'

I said, 'Are you homeless?' and tried to give him some
change.

'Good Lord,' he said. 'No, I'm certainly not homeless. I'm a
veterinary surgeon and a professor, and I'm very sorry.'

'Why are you sorry?' I asked him. 'Did you sew up the wrong
end of a rabbit?'

'Oh, I've done that many times,' he said. I wondered if I'd
landed in an Eastern European novel, and the day would end
with me whipping a dwarf.

'Are you sorry because you're meant to be with your wife, and
you're late because you've got drunk?' I asked.

'My dear dear darling wife has come to expect that of me, I'm
afraid,' he said. 'No, I'm sorry because I have to be at a college
function and I'm not sure where it is. I don't suppose you know
where it is, do you?'

I tried to get a clue as to how I could help, but it was always
unlikely that I'd be better informed than him about the where-

abouts of a function in a college in his city to which he'd been invited.

We carried on in this surreal fashion for about ten minutes, then he put his hand on my shoulder and said, 'Well, it's been lovely talking to you. The main reason I wanted to talk to you is that I was a bit lonely, I'm afraid.'

As he walked off, I concluded two things. Firstly, if I ever have a sick pet I should look him up, as he'd probably be a lot of fun, and even if he was a little shaky with a scalpel, he'd appreciate the company. And secondly, while glorious spires, immaculate lawns and vast gothic wooden doors are inherently more beautiful than smoky putrid power-station cooling towers, I think I prefer Didcot.

Wilmslow

Wilmslow, in Cheshire, is ridiculous. It's known as 'the Knightsbridge of the North', but if Harrods tried to set up a branch there it would be refused planning permission as it would lower the tone of the area. When I first arrived to survey the place for one of the radio shows, I was slightly sceptical of its reputation as a haven for the prime of new money – its population couldn't just be soap stars, ex-criminals and Premier League footballers; there aren't enough of them to fill a whole town.

To start with I went to Alderley Edge, where the cream of the area's over-privileged twattery is said to live, and popped into the post office for a stamp. In the window, just as you might see in any post office, were dozens of little cards, which would normally advertise 'Pram for sale' or 'Carpenter – no job too small'. But in this window the first card I saw said, 'Ring me if you need a butler.'

And that seems to be Wilmslow's essence. As you enter the main street there's a vast Aston Martin showroom, which boasts that it sells more cars than any other branch in Britain, including the one in Mayfair. I went inside, and it was hard to adjust, because none of the normal car-buying etiquette applies. If you circle the DBS 6.0 Volante model, throwing it the half-interested semi-scowl you're supposed to adopt when sizing up a car for sale, kicking the tyres and scornfully looking under the bonnet as if to say, 'You'll be lucky if anyone takes this off your hands,' and ask disparagingly, 'How much you asking, mate?', you'll get the reply, 'One hundred and ninety-one thousand, five hundred pounds sir.'

The salesmen are so 'high class' they don't even bullshit you. 'They call this a four-seater, but I don't know what size of person would fit in those back seats,' one told me, adding, 'But one feature we do offer with these models is the option of customising the upholstery to match the colour of your hat.'

With not a hint of disdain, or that he was thinking 'Don't waste my time, serf, you couldn't afford the fucking wing mirror,' he demonstrated how the speakers have sensors that automatically move when you get in, adjusting themselves to the direction and height of your ears. Then he perkily told me that one of his customers keeps his car in the garage, sits in it each evening listening to classical music, and never takes it anywhere.

Mostly the High Street is full of beauty salons, dozens of the things, as if the residents leave a beauty salon, walk fifty yards and go, 'Oh my *God*, my nails haven't been done for nearly a *minute*, they'll be *corroding*,' and dive into another beauty salon.

Each of these emporia needs a unique way to market itself. One, called 'Esthetique', has a subheading on its sign that says 'Beauty – wellbeing – science'. So presumably as they're manicuring your toenails they'll tell you that according to quantum mechanics the varnish they're using has no fixed resting place in the universe. Another has a board outside that says '3D eyelashes'. I can see why that would be useful, as it's so irritating when bits of your body are only in 2D. Those normal eyelashes, you go to brush them and your hand passes straight through them, the awkward two-dimensional buggers. What a delight it must be to have eyelashes that seem like solid objects, rather than looking as if they've been projected by film onto your eyelids, though presumably when you've had the 3D eyelash treatment you have to hand out special glasses to everyone around you, or the effect doesn't work.

There's an endearing old tailor's shop on the stretch of road to Alderley Edge, full of tape measures and dummies wearing semi-sewn suits, and crisp folded shirts packed on mahogany shelves. In the window was a purple smoking jacket, seductively eccentric. Once you'd put it on, whoever you were, you would surely start flowing with witticisms about the nature of women and reciting captivating anecdotes about your trip to Bermuda with King George VI. 'I'm just, er, out of interest, asking, er, about the cost of that purple jacket, please,' I enquired of the immaculately grey, slightly theatrical tailor.

'Ah, indeed, the purple jacket,' he purred. 'That is stitched with such exquisite precision by my dear friend who goes by the name "Dashing Tweeds". Do you know him?'

'Not really,' I said.

'If you peruse the lining you catch a sense of the inner strength of the cloth, and up close you can feel it almost breathes with pleasure. It will never lose its shape, that item, sir.'

'Roughly, er, roughly how much?' I asked, as if the price was just an incidental piece of red tape I had to clarify to satisfy the bureaucrats in my office.

'That particular item is priced at £1,800,' he said. 'Plus VAT.'

'Hmm,' I said, as if I was barely interested, and if anything that was disappointingly on the low side, but he must have been able to read in my eyes that every bit of me was going, 'FOR A FUCKING JACKET!!!!!!!!!!!!!!!!!!!!!!!!!!'

But mostly Wilmslow's money is about property. Football stars such as Wayne Rooney, Peter Crouch, Rio Ferdinand, Cristiano Ronaldo and David Beckham have all bought land there, along with Andrew Flintoff and an assortment of *Coronation Street* actors. And invariably, once the deal is settled, the first thing the happy buyers do with the new house is to knock it down. Then they're free to build a modern structure in its place that doesn't have the embarrassment of being second-hand.

So along the roads that surround Wilmslow are lines of skips and teams of builders catering to this demand. Trades such as interior designer flourish in this environment, more than they probably would in Moss Side, so the place abounds with the likes of Dawn Ward, who designed the Rooneys' pad. Her proudest creation, she revealed, was a glass floor in a hallway, which enables anyone standing on it to see the snooker table in the room below. I bet one day we'll all have them, and will look back on the days when if we wanted to know the score of the snooker match downstairs we had to walk down the stairs, with the same incredulous pity we feel now when we learn of villages in Uganda where they still have to fetch water from a well ten miles away.

Every one of these properties boasts a 'media room', as if anyone needs a special separate room for when they're reading a paper or watching the darts. They've clearly got so many rooms their owners have to invent purposes for them, which all the others will then want. So there are probably arguments, with Mrs Rooney going, 'It's not fair, how come the Flintoffs have got their own particle collider? I want one.'

But it would be hard to beat the estate agent's leaflet I saw, from 'Property Confidential', that oozed pride as it announced the sale of a 'luxury bungalow' for £1.75 million. The property included, it said, a swimming pool and sauna, and added, 'This luxury bungalow also boasts an additional feature – a second floor.'

Occasionally some of the older locals initiate a spot of official grumbling about their area being converted into a Cheshire Dubai, but they don't seem to have the will to carry it through. For example, some residents complained that Cristiano Ronaldo's house was 'offensive and insensitive', and began the process of demanding a local referendum to change the area's planning rules. But the plan was scrapped because a referendum was considered too expensive, probably because they'd insist on a solid-gold ballot box.

Nowhere in Wilmslow seems immune to the pervading local ostentatiousness. The Barnado's charity shop on Alderley Edge High Street is full of Gucci shoes and Armani coats that don't have prices on them, and you have to ring the bell to be allowed in, as the stuff's so valuable.

The chip shop has a notice on the menu saying, 'We often get celebrities in our chip shop. We would be grateful if you would respect their right to eat their meal in privacy.'

It wouldn't be surprising to find a 'Grand' shop, for throw-away household items like ironing-board covers and dishcloths, where everything costs only a grand.

Even crime has its Wilmslow aspect. The *Wilmslow Express* reported: 'A mum of two turned have-a-go hero and hit a burglar for six with a cricket bat. The bat was used in the Ashes series by the England squad, and her husband bought it in a charity auction.' In Wilmslow you can't attack burglars with any old bat, it's got to be one worth thousands of pounds for its historical significance. She was probably wandering round the house going, 'What shall I attack him with? I couldn't whack him with that tatty old broom, what on earth would he think?'

The *Live Cheshire* magazine that lies on tables in the cocktail bars and beauty salons has headlines such as 'Why Mustique is a Must', and 'Justin Timberlake and Madonna Swear by it, and Now it's Come to Cheshire. It's Hyberbaric Oxygen Technology Skin Treatment'.

While the footballers and soap stars are the most prominent characters fuelling this bizarre fountain of new money, there's a sub-layer of financiers and bankers; and that, you'd think, must be that: the place is no more than a monument to the triumph of bonuses over talent, a creation of pure Thatcherism.

Except that the Wilmslow spirit goes back further than that, and its fondness for the 1980s goes back to around 1850. This was when Manchester became the heart of the most dynamic phase of the Industrial Revolution, the centre of the world's cotton and clothing industries, the biggest urban setting on the planet. But it was also squalid, the waste of its citizens slopping merrily down the streets, the smoke creating constant darkness. And the managers and owners of the factories didn't want to live amidst the gunge they were helping to create. They needed somewhere far enough away that they couldn't smell the place, but near enough that they could get to work every day. The perfect spot was Wilmslow.

Its Alderley Edge wing was virtually created for that reason. It was barely inhabited at the time, but the railway company did a deal with the Trafford family (of Old Trafford fame), who were the main landowners of the area. Anyone who bought a certain amount of land there would be provided with a lifetime first-class season ticket. Within a few years the first railway commuter town had been created.

But it wasn't just respite from the soot and sewage of Manchester that the Wilmslow residents were seeking: they wanted a separate world from the people they employed. They saw themselves as members of a new class that had made money without having to inherit it. While they may not have wanted to adopt all the manners of the aristocracy, they did want to create a cultural gap between themselves and the hordes they employed, who they saw as inferior. For example, in the 1850s Henry Gibbs wrote in *Autobiography of a Manchester Cotton Manufacturer* about a fire that burned down the factory he ran: 'The women were, of course, the first to escape. But why did they not walk out quietly, with calmness and dignity? There was really no need for them to make such a helter-skelter exit, with their rolling eyes, hair loose and arms unnecessarily used in the act of dragging each other from the place of destruction. "Shame," I cried, for the noise they were making, to which they took no heed.'

Because you certainly wouldn't get his class of person behaving in such an uncouth manner; they'd calmly burn to death, without rolling their eyes.

Throughout Wilmslow, houses were built to cater for such people, and while they didn't have media rooms, they had billiard rooms and servants' quarters and a million rules of etiquette created to distance their owners from the riff-raff. According to *Manchester Made Them*, by Katharine Chorley, who was brought up in one such Alderley Edge house: 'The downstairs lavatory, for instance, was sacrosanct to the men of the family and their guests, the upstairs reserved with equal exclusiveness to the females. Woe betide me if I was ever caught slinking into the downstairs one to save time. Conversely, the good breeding and social knowledge of any male guest who was suspected of having used the upstairs toilet while dressing for dinner was immediately called into question.'

The Manchester *nouveaux riches* settling in the area were described by the older landed Wilmslow types as 'Cottontots'. They devised a system for introducing women newly arrived in the area into the right circles. According to *Manchester Made Them*, 'A wife or daughter with nothing to do was an emblem of success, like a large house or garden.'

Perhaps unsurprisingly, Katharine Chorley writes: 'A socialist was unthinkable in Alderley Edge company, and had he got there he would have been treated with a mixture of distrust, contempt and fear.' At the very least a socialist would run into even more difficulties than normal, as the master of the house grunted angrily, 'Sir, I fear your proposition to diminish the gap between rich and poor should have been made *prior* to the serving of dessert, as advocacy of the overthrow of capitalism after the meat course is *strictly* forbidden.'

Dessert might have presented another quandary for socialists. Chorley wrote of the manager of a Manchester bank, 'When he and his wife gave dinner parties, they presented dessert on a solid gold plate.'

A special girls' school was established to teach the female offspring of this tribe how to eat off gold plates, and be a proper lady. One regular lesson was on how to keep your back straight in a ladylike fashion, so, 'After midday dinner, we had to lie flat on our backs on the floor for ten minutes, to straighten our spines so we could hold ourselves well, while the mistress in charge read to us from the *Daily Telegraph*.'

I'd like to see Davina McCall make *that* fitness DVD. 'Now, keep that spine as straight as you can and take deep breaths in time to the letters page, and ... "Sir: When one regards the hordes of feral youth that blight our city centres" – AND STRETCH – "one is forced to conclude" – KEEP THAT BACK STRAIGHT – "that the time has surely arrived" – DEEP BREATHS NOW – "when we must return" – KEEPING THAT TUMMY TIGHT – "to the virtues of corporal punishment" – AND RELAX.'

In their way, like much of Victorian Britain, the settlers of Wilmslow were establishing tradition. And none of it is different in essence from the craving for 3D eyelashes and sports car upholstery to match your hat.

But a glance beyond the shopfronts suggests that can't be all there is to Wilmslow. In the inevitable pedestrianised precinct, outside Costa Coffee stands a man selling the *Big Issue*, and he seems to be there every day. Maybe people walk past him whispering to themselves, 'Isn't it dreadful? That poor man has hasn't even got a second home.'

Or perhaps he's an art installation. But there's a side of Wilmslow that he represents, like the Colshaw estate, owned by the council before it was sold off and chunks of it boarded up, where one attempt to clean it up involved removing 104 dumped cars, discarded by joyriders. Or maybe the council misunderstood, and they were all Aston Martins that they assumed had been dumped as they hadn't moved for years, but actually they all had labourers sitting in them listening to Shostakovich.

Many people in Wilmslow worked at AstraZeneca pharmaceuticals, where three hundred were laid off in 2008, or at

Worthington Nicholls air-conditioning plant, which laid off one hundred. It's unlikely that they all had a butler to hand them their coats as they left work for the last time and say, 'Your P45, sir.' The local postmen picketed the sorting office during a strike, in which fifty of the fifty-four staff supported the action.

The young of the area can display classic small-town frustration. Frisko Dan is a local rapper who led a local march in 2010, in support of a 'Robin Hood tax' to reduce inequality. Another hip-hop crew managed to rhyme 'living in Cheshire' with 'feel the pressure'.

The average weekly wage in Wilmslow in 2007, according to a report from the Office of National Statistics, was £772, compared to the poorest area of the North-West, the Manchester district of Gorton, where the average was £403. That would seem to confirm the image of Wilmslow as an exclusive enclave for the elite. But you could also interpret those figures as suggesting that the gap between rich and poor areas is much less than might be imagined. Because while the average company director makes fifteen times as much as the average of his employees, investment bankers and the real rich can make more in bonuses in a single year than the people who clean their office earn in a lifetime. So you might expect the difference between Wilmslow's average and that of a poor borough of Manchester to be much wider.

This should be even more likely when you think that that average must include Wayne Rooney and friends. If you took a few dozen comically rich superstars out of the statistics the gap would be smaller still. Every rich area has its working-class quarter, just as every poor town has a rich bit. The divide between rich and poor is much less a conflict between areas than one *within* areas.

Perhaps an area can seem to be dominated by wealth more than it really is, because a handful of rich people have a disproportionate bearing on the look of a place. The shops will cater for them, because they're the ones who have the money to spend. A country road on which ten millionaires live is an area swimming in wealth, whereas ten people on the minimum wage wouldn't fill a single house converted into bedsits. The restaurants, beauty salons and purple-jacket shops tend to the needs of the richer section of the community. So you end up with a place that, in some ways, must be even more frustrating to live in if you're on a low income. Because on the way to work you have to pass an Aston Martin showroom and a shop selling jackets for £1,800 plus VAT, and even if you're driven to burglary you're likely to get walloped with a bat signed by Andrew Flintoff.

Wigan

A few miles from the media rooms and glass floors of Wilmslow is the slight contrast of Wigan, where I sensed that the old couple hunched in the tea bar in the indoor market didn't trust us. All around were the props and costumes you'd lay out if you wanted to make a film set in 1971, maybe involving a detective trying to get information out of a trader who sold knocked-off kettles. Above each stall was an old green or brown board with the owner's name painted by hand, in the sort of font used for Olde English Marmalade and by companies who want to convince you the stuff they stew in a vat in an industrial estate in Kent was made by a farmer's wife with a rolling pin, who says, 'Right, that's today's cherry pies for Marks and Spencer in St Albans sorted, now I'll just take round the vicar's gooseberries and I can get on with Mrs Finlay's plum crumble portions for Budgens in Exeter.'

These signs usually suggest that you'll be offered a small dish of hand-picked olives stuffed with low-fat organic Tuscan soil at £30 an ounce, or stilton mixed with conkers packed in the sort of fancy box you'd use for a wedding ring. But in Wigan they don't need to artificially recreate the chic individuality of pre-industrial shopping. These stalls really have been there for a hundred years. If any designers for farmers' markets were to wander in they'd clap their hands and shriek, 'Oh, how rustic! It's so *authentic!*'

There are countless racks of kids' dresses, and shirts for four quid, and a record stall with a range from Hot Chocolate to Bachman-Turner Overdrive and *Top of the Pops* albums. There's a stall selling sherbet by the ounce and stuck-together pear drops, and a café with rickety chairs that belong in a primary school, that only sells lobby, which is a stew with potatoes that looks as if it's been made at a camp by scouts.

And there's a tea bar, that sells tea from a huge green metal pot with the enamel flaking off, in huge white mugs. As we sat slurping in contentment the old couple, wrapped in so many scarves and hats and coats and jumpers that if a madman had gone berserk with a rifle they'd have been perfectly safe as no bullet could penetrate all those layers, glared at us as if we were occupying troops in full uniform. The man nodded in our direction and said with utter disdain, 'Manchester thespians.'

If I'd gone across and told him I was from even further away than Manchester he'd have said, 'Surely not Stockport, you pouf.'

Outside this market is the pedestrianised centre of Wigan, indistinguishable from the centre of anywhere else. The building societies, W.H. Smith and anti-vivisection campaigners are all in their designated places, and it's by a door opposite Clinton Cards that you pass through a magical vortex into the market, a world that hasn't so much resisted modern corporate life as remained unaware that it exists. Maybe that's because for a century or more Wigan fitted the notion of what was considered a working-class town better than anywhere, so that when George Orwell wrote his study of working-class life, it was Wigan he went to live in, to see what the proles get up to.

The pier that provides the title of Orwell's *The Road to Wigan Pier* is a slightly raised step, about two feet long, on one side of the Leeds–Liverpool canal, from where coal was once tipped into the barges. The area alongside the canal used to be packed with one of the greatest concentrations of mills in the country.

One of those mills, just behind the pier, became a mill museum, but now that's shut down as well. You can't get more working-class than that. Presumably the actors who had to walk round dressed as Victorian loom operators went home one day and said, 'Bad news I'm afraid. There's trouble at Mill Experience.' Now they'll have to hope that someone invests in a museum about what it used to be like working in the museum.

Opposite the pier is a factory that anywhere else would have been converted into offices or flats or a restaurant, but that turns out still to be a factory. It makes Uncle Joe's Mint Balls, the pride of Wigan. According to the logo, the mint balls will 'Keep you all aglow', and there's a picture of Uncle Joe looking like your favourite uncle in a top hat, and you think you remember skipping down the street in short trousers with the sixpence you got for polishing Mr Higginbottom's Austin Rover to buy a pack of mint balls, which were not only the finest sweets but back then were believed to prevent whooping cough.

The mint balls are defiantly Wigan, and I imagine the old couple from the market would be astonished if they met someone who'd never heard of them, as if they'd said they'd never heard of a banana.

No doubt the place is just as proud of its mint balls as it was of the Wigan man declared to be the fattest person in Britain. Eventually he couldn't get out of his specially made seat, and relied on his wife, who, once it was confirmed he held the record, boasted about it to all her neighbours – 'He's the fattest in Britain now, you know' – and showed them all the newspaper clippings that confirmed this triumph. It turned out she'd only met him after reading about his size in the local paper, and decided to make him her own. When he died the windows had to be removed so he could be hoisted through them, as there was no way he was getting through the door. A neighbour I spoke to, who'd never met him, was asked by his wife to go the funeral. When she said she was sorry, but she really couldn't make it, the wife said with astonishment, 'But he was the fattest man in Britain.'

Even the irresistible force of the Premier League has stumbled in its attempt to overwhelm Wigan as it does most places. Despite the local side having been in the top division for the past six seasons, the crowds are smaller than for the rugby league team.

So it shouldn't be a surprise that the historical local hero, commemorated with a statue in the centre of town and his picture on all the official leaflets for local events, is George Formby. If Wigan's most famous figure was a prominent physicist or an influential Pre-Raphaelite painter it would be a terrible let-down, like finding out that your great-grandfather was a pimp.

George Formby was a buck-toothed banjolele player who sang slightly saucy songs with lyrics such as 'If you could see what I can see, when I'm cleaning windows'. It's unlikely that any of his songs will ever be covered by 50 Cent, but he was a superstar who people from a place like Wigan could identify with, who they could imagine bumping into at the pub. This image went beyond Wigan, as he became hugely popular in Soviet Russia, and it was even rumoured that Stalin had awarded him the Order of Lenin. This would presumably have irritated the odd Soviet commander, who might have lived through the siege of Leningrad for two years living off earthworms and fighting the Nazis using whittled toenail clippings as weapons, only to lag in the queue for a medal behind a banjolele player from Wigan. The story of the medal was an exaggeration, but there was something about Formby that was the embodiment of Wigan, not just working-class but unashamedly so. Otherwise how could he have sung a song called 'The Wigan Express' that went 'She got some shocks in her signal box'?

In 1946, when he toured pre-apartheid South Africa, he upset his hosts by refusing to play segregated venues. As a result a black member of one audience presented Formby's wife Beryl with a box of chocolates, and George gave the man a hug. National Party leader Daniel François Malan, who would introduce apartheid two years later, heard about this and phoned Beryl to complain, to which she replied, 'Why don't you piss off, you horrible little man?'

At first the idea of George Formby and his wife as radical anti-apartheid activists seems as surreal as finding out that Bobby Davro spent five years as a guerrilla fighting with Che Guevara, but in a way it symbolises Wigan's history as an apparently jolly working-class town getting by without complaining, but with a calm commitment to rebellion underneath. In 1779 cotton workers in Wigan staged one of Britain's first riots against unemployment. It lasted for several days, until the militia was brought in from Liverpool. The area was at the centre of the Lancashire Luddite riots, and in 1842 a strike of spinners ended up in a battle with two companies of riflemen.

The first miners' strike of the twentieth century was in Wigan, in 1921 Wigan miners rioted until dispersed by the 16th Hussars, and the local pits were influential in every national strike. It feels as if a Wigan historian might say, 'Ee, I'll not call it proper decade if we've not been fired on by yeomen or suchlike.'

All this may make Wigan an unlikely setting for a vegan pagan café run by warlocks and called the Coven, but it was right opposite the main station. The warlocks greeted you with the most unsettling behaviour warlocks could manage, by being disconcertingly normal. 'Hello love, right windy today, isn't it? How about a piping-hot mug of elderflower-and-nettle tea to warm them bones up?' one of them said.

The place was cluttered with sticks of incense, dream catchers and models of black cats, and there was a cheery sign informing you they'd cast a spell for you if you liked, in that chirpy lettering that looks as if it's been written by a neat ten-year-old to be put on the classroom wall. But somehow warlocks seem palatable when they're working-class and from Wigan. They were warm and neighbourly warlocks, always likely to nip in to see old Elsie on the way home, as she's getting on and can be a bit forgetful, and one night when she'd forgotten to get any food for her cat, the friendly warlock turned it into stone until the morning so it wouldn't get hungry.

Sometimes they were disappointingly normal, just bringing you a coffee when you were hoping they'd break into a naked fertility dance. But one Saturday afternoon in the Coven, with my daughter and her friend, we were waiting for our drinks by the upstairs window while flicking through a folder of common hexes. Suddenly the girls said, 'Wow, look at that!' A group of men had rushed out onto the street from the Wetherspoon's pub next door. One of them was on crutches, and he made four agile bounds before deftly swinging them onto the back of someone he must have had a disagreement with on some issue. The street quickly became a battlefield. 'Someone should do something,' said the owner of the café. Presumably he'd run out of the potion that deals with a mass crutch-wielding brawl, or at least shrinks the fighters to the size of mice, so they don't hold up the traffic.

It was almost as if the fighters were making a statement, that you can sit somewhere fancy and pagan if you like, but you can't escape the real Wigan.

The place where the real Wigan meets the world of chain-company uniformity head on, where the greatest imagination has been displayed in the quest to eliminate imagination, is King Street, which is made up entirely of nightclubs. This isn't a seedy quarter with bands playing under railway arches, and shirtless DJs scratching from what was once an office in a converted tinned-pudding warehouse. There are twelve clubs in a row, including Walkabout, Revolution, and a fake Irish place. The road is blocked to traffic, and outside each entrance a pair of bald men in black suits act as sentries, so you feel a sense of relief and smug achievement if you get in at all. At the first one we were told sternly by the bald men that it was open until 6 a.m. This information was conveyed with the sort of chilling menace with which I expect guards at Abu Ghraib said 'You'll be in here until 6 a.m.' to prisoners as they were being shown into a room full of rusty implements.

Then we were looked up and down and searched, and it felt as if we might be taken into a small, bare room to be interviewed by an official while a man in a white shirt stood silently behind us holding an unsettled Alsatian on a short lead.

Eventually they let us pay £2 each and rubbed a blurry inkstain onto the backs of our hands. Triumphant, we marched through the huge wooden doors of a glorious Victorian building, that could have been an embassy if Wigan was ever a country, into the split-level dance floor, past a flashing semi-circular bar and a machine pumping out dry ice. Having looked round thoroughly, it was clear that we were the only people there. After a couple of club mix versions of songs I thought I recognised but probably didn't, four more people came in, but it turned out they were security.

It was tempting to stay until 6 a.m., but instead we went to a nineties club, where about twenty people danced to 'Wiggle Wiggle' and Bobby Brown, including someone dressed in a blue all-body gimp outfit with one hole to breathe through. But the most disturbing thing about the place was the overwhelming stench of cleaning products. Was this a new trend, clubs that are renowned for their excessive cleanliness, with a promise that every surface will be polished with Pledge every seven minutes? At the bar it seemed natural to ask for a pint of Jif with a Toilet Duck chaser, and the carpet oozed the aroma of an office to let that's been abused with too much Shake 'n' Vac, which was a mistake, as that was definitely a symbol of the eighties, not the nineties.

The best-known chains seemed to be the most popular. Walkabout was the sweatiest, and unlike our first venue you couldn't practise chipping golf balls across the room without any fear of irritating someone. But as we strolled up the street past the bare thighs and gelled hair, across the pavement that was ready to receive the night's vomit, I was sort of jealous. How I would have loved, when I was twenty, to have had a street where you were not only allowed but virtually ordered to drink until any time you liked, with hundreds of women in attendance enabling you to dream that at any moment *this* week you might have a brief conversation with one of them.

But there's something lacking in a street that regiments adolescent disorderliness. It's like a board put up by the council for people to graffiti on. The whole point of drinking and danc-ing late is to feel slightly seedy, to be aware that you're gyrating or slumped against a fruit machine while respectable society is fast asleep. Once it's sanctioned, contained, sanitised and run by chains that have a brand image to convey, it's lost its edge. It's predictable, as the Arctic Monkeys say. After all that anticipa-tion, 'All that happened is you drank a lot.'

Worse than encouraging binge drinking, this is a top-down, orchestrated encouragement of *corporate* binge drinking, the vodkas and tequila slammers arranged according to the demands of a study group that discussed its findings using a PowerPoint display in a room overlooking the Thames in Reading.

Maybe this is more poignant in the home of northern soul, the scene driven from the bottom up that led thousands to hitch and cajole lifts across the country every week in the 1970s to venues such as the Wigan Casino. There's no generally accepted theory as to why this started, why a lobby-eating, overwhelm-ingly white corner of north-west England became the centre of a music scene that originated in the black districts of Detroit. But northern soul became a whole category of music, as much as ska or speed garage, revolving around Wigan and fuelled by the thousands who went there, rather than by the desires of leisure-centre-industry shareholders, and who took drugs and danced and then hitched home to Essex or Devon. The trend faded away in the eighties, but there are still posters in the King Street nightclubs for monthly northern soul sessions that take place, for some reason, in the afternoon, as if it's a modern version of a tea dance, in which a lady comes round with a trolley and asks, 'Would you like an upper with your tea, Mrs Bottomley?' and is told, 'Oo no, dear, I had two doses of speed yesterday, any more will give me terrible indigestion.'

So one of Wigan's most unlikely achievements is that the town that had already contributed to international music by propelling the banjolele across Soviet Russia became the heart of a global music scene, attracting soul legends such as Edwin Starr, who sat a few yards from the pies and lobby and the mint-ball factory, across the road from the indoor market, and if he popped in for a cup of tea he probably risked the disapproval of a middle-aged couple who'll have looked him up and down and muttered, 'Student from Bolton, I shouldn't wonder.'

Horwich

The generalisation that all Londoners are grisly and unfriendly while northerners whistle all day and give away their houses to strangers is clearly a myth. But there are plenty who insist that this irrational idea is true. You could cite any example as evidence to the contrary, and they'd say something like, 'Yes, but at least the Yorkshire Ripper would lend his neighbours a cup of marmalade, even on the morning of a murder.'

But some people will work tirelessly to fit the stereotype. To sight the snarling Londoner the best method is to ride through the capital on a pushbike. The first time you hear someone lean out of a window and screech, 'Get out of my way, you fucking cunt!' you might be slightly peeved. But then it becomes fascinating. Sometimes their rage is so overwhelming you're captivated by the veins pumping out of their neck, and it seems they're physically unable to reach the end of the word, so they yell, 'Cuuuuuuuuuuuuuuuuuuuu' until you've turned right and into the next street never knowing whether they got as far as 'nt', or if they had to go to the doctors, still growling 'u-u-u-u-u-u-u-u' like a stuck CD until they're given an injection.

One morning, on the north side of Vauxhall Bridge, I pulled up at the lights next to a gargantuan lorry. One of the essential rules of cycling in London is, when you're at traffic lights, to make eye contact with the motorist behind you, to be certain they've seen you, especially if they're driving a gargantuan lorry.

Nearly always the motorist smiles or waves or acknowledges you in some innocuous way, but this time the driver wound down the window and snarled as if gravel was swilling round his voicebox, with every consonant emphasised for maximum snappiness, 'What's your fucking problem?'

'I'm just making sure you've seen me, mate,' I said, being slightly dishonest with the word 'mate'. And then he spread his frame and breathed in, as if preparing for a roar like Godzilla, and yelled, '*I* pay road tax. *You* pay *fuck off*.' Just imagine the anguish rolling around in this driver's head at that moment. Presumably he was thinking, 'Here is the ideal opportunity for me to convey my thoughts on the iniquities of our road-funding system, whereby he is considered exempt from contributions in spite of using the roads as much as me, albeit on two wheels as opposed to my 184, and that, in my view, is inconsistent and must be redressed. But at the same time, I can't wait to tell him to fuck off. Oh no, now I've combined the two, and it's come out grammatically incoherent.'

On the other hand, to spot a swarm of neighbourly northerners chatting to each other on pavements you should try Horwich, a couple of hills from Wigan and four miles west of Bolton, at the foot of the South Pennines. It's a town of about 23,000 that grew around a railway works, and since that shut down everyone seems to spend all day chatting. I became familiar with Horwich from 2007, when I first met my wife.* That meant I got to know the neighbours, which means everyone, and join them in mid-

---

* I refer here to the woman to whom I am attached, although we're not married; but what term am I supposed to use? 'Partner' is woefully poor, and could leave you unsure whether I'm talking about the woman I hold hands with while watching *Newsnight*, or the bloke I open the batting with for my cricket club. 'Missus' is wrong on several fronts, and I'm too old for a girl-friend, so to describe her as one could reasonably lead to an investigation as to whether I should be placed on the child protection register. So 'my wife' it is. In fact, I even considered getting married to solve the problem, which probably wouldn't have been the most romantic proposal ever made, to be truthful.

street chats. One day a woman called Betty tried to stop me for a chat while I was going for a run. 'Oh, hello love. How you getting on? Only, I've been meaning to ask you –' she said, as she leaned on her shopping trolley while I jogged by in my shorts.

As I called out, 'I'm going for a run at the moment, Betty,' I felt as if I'd committed a dreadful crime, as the etiquette here is always to stop and chat, even if you're fleeing for your life from a maniac with an axe. Even then you'd probably be all right, because the maniac would have to stop and chat as well, until after forty minutes he'd be told, 'Anyway, love, I can see you're busy so I shan't keep you,' and all being well you'd both set off again at the same time to keep the chase fair.

In another forlorn attempt to be physically active I went for a swim at the leisure centre, and in an inept moment I veered to one side and brought my foot down and across those plastic baubles used to divide the pool into lanes. It was enough to cause a stifled yelp and make me turn round to see what damage I'd done. I could see the foot was cut, and little streams of blood were starting to create mesmerising shapes. At that point a woman swimming towards me in the next lane stopped and said, 'Oo, hello, oh, you don't know me, love, but I've seen you on TV on, oo, what was that programme, anyway I said to my husband I've seen you round Horwich, I said to him, "I'm sure that's Mark Steel I saw popping into the grocers on Winter Hey Lane."'

By now I was a bit giddy, and the blood was getting a deeper shade, with some of it drifting her way. 'That's very kind of you,' I said, adding, 'I've hurt my foot.' She looked directly at the line of blood emanating from between my toes, which was by now forming clotted patches and fascinating patterns in the water like in a Greenpeace film about whales being harpooned, and said, 'So have you got family round this way, love?'

To anyone used to London, the instinct of strangers to talk and help is disconcerting at first. Someone you've never met smiles and says hello, and your first thought is, 'What you after?'

But after a few months you relax and start to say hello back. This is essential in Horwich, as the town appears to be set in 1957. For example, it takes an hour to buy three sausages from Arthur the butcher, as he'll go through an itinerary of discussion points that starts with local gossip, moves on to regional issues, international affairs and sport, and feels as if it should end with a traffic report, a weather forecast and a brief look at tomorrow's papers. Arthur is what Horwich has instead of the internet.

Or you can enter the nostalgic world of the Salad Bowl grocers, and wait while the customer in front takes twenty-five minutes to buy a cluster of spring onions while describing the pain he has at night in his gall bladder. Then you make your request for, let's say, two pounds of carrots, and Ted will slowly select a few, amble the three steps to the old metal scales, balance them against the round weights on the other side, take one out and replace it with a slightly shorter one to make it exact, then put them in a brown paper bag and twirl it round and write '32' or whatever the price is on a separate paper bag with a biro. If anyone ran in screaming, 'Oh my God, please help me, I've been stung by a rare insect and the only cure is to rub the wound with three pounds of cooking apples immediately or I'll die,' he'd say, 'Right. Cooking apples, you say. Well, we've got some Bramleys just in, so I'll have a look for some that are just ripe for you. Now hang on, I'll get Alf's beetroot ready first, he's always in for his beetroot on a Tuesday.'

The fish and chip shop shuts at six o' clock, exactly the time you're most likely to want to buy fish and chips, and the most cosmopolitan the town ever seemed was when I heard a group of elderly Spaniards at the table next to me in the café. But after about twenty minutes they all sighed at the same time, then one said, 'Oo, I did enjoy that,' and it turned out it was the Horwich pensioners' Spanish-speaking club. It can seem you're jammed between two time zones, caught in a space pocket where the pubs have Sky Sports but the Prime Minister is Harold Macmillan.

Some people not only love all this, they can't imagine being anywhere else. One man in his fifties told me he'd turned down a job he'd have loved when he was thirty, because 'It meant going to London, and I knew I'd get homesick for Horwich, 'cos I spent a few weeks in Bolton once, and I got homesick for Horwich there.'

Horwich people may have this attitude because of, apart from their innate eagerness to chat, the terrain beyond the edge of the town. This leads on to the Pennines, past stone cottages and something that calls itself a hotel for dogs, over stiles and fields where foals are born, past brooks and the sort of ruined follies that kids had adventures in on TV programmes shown on Sunday afternoons in the 1960s. In the other direction, at the opposite end of town is Middlebrook, the retail park attached to the Reebok Stadium, which is Bolton Wanderers' ground. It dominates the view from the hills around, looking like a giant white upside-down bug that can't get itself the right way up. Middlebrook boasts a Subway and a Nando's, a multiplex cinema and a bowling alley, and is described by Eileen in the *Bolton News* promotional video for the town as 'a place that's absolutely marvellous for shops', while the camera lingers on a branch of Carpet Right.

It may be convenient, but it's hard to see how anyone could honestly believe that Middlebrook is 'marvellous', because it's hauntingly identical to every other retail park anywhere. Maybe there are people in Horwich who feel genuinely proud of Middlebrook, as they think it's the only place like it. One day they'll drive past the one in Darlington and start screaming, like someone in a science fiction film who comes face to face with another version of themselves in a parallel cosmos. Regarding Middlebrook as somehow special makes no more sense than saying, 'I had a wonderful drink round at Bob and Mary's last night. It came in a tin and was called Coca-Cola. I must ask them for the recipe.'

Middlebrook starts with a huge car park with sections divided by pristine shrubs. Your first thought as you arrive is to remember that you've parked by the fourth bush along, five spindly recently planted trees down, in line with the 'i' of Pizza Hut. From then on your visit will be almost entirely predictable. You can't wander down a side street or try a different route from last week, unless you force yourself to get to Dixons by walking past Dixons, then up to the fifth bed in Dreams and back again. If you bump into someone you know, you can't nip anywhere for a chat unless you say, 'Fancy popping into Comet? You can tell me about your new job by the tumble dryers.'

Middlebrook must offer something, or no one would go there, and it may be that some teenagers hang about the place as it's modern and hip-hop thumps from some of the shops (which doesn't appear to be company policy at the Salad Bowl). The cinema might be charmless but it does show films, and there's nowhere else in the town that does. Even if there was a cinema in the town it would show *Singing in the Rain* every day and shut just as the film was about to start.

Horwich does have pubs, but most of them are bewilderingly gloomy. You can sit in them on a bright summer's day by a huge window, and everything still seems hazy and grey, and in the Pheasant Plucker I'm sure it sometimes drizzles on the inside.

Most nights, by nine o' clock the two main streets of the town are empty. I've heard teenagers discuss whether to go to 'Nitebar' in such a way that you think it must be a room under a railway arch where they play Nick Cave and Gorillaz and it never shuts before 2.30 and there's always a thin bloke called Zippo in the corner available to sell you grass in the toilet and the walls smell of mould, and it's claimed the Happy Mondays started there. But it turns out that it's the burger bar that stays open until eleven. Even so, at night as you glance up the deserted street, the fact this place has a yellow light that's on makes it seem like the wild untameable frontier. If the shoe shop put a blue light on at night, before long it would become a rival to Nitebar, with kids insisting the place was crazy and cool as you could see the sandals through the window right up to midnight.

One way of solving the problem of living in a place short on thrills is to start a gang. In the 1980s a group called the Horwich Casuals was formed, that boasted it 'ruled the North-West'. The fascist group Combat 18 also set up a mini battalion in the area, and it was possibly this group that led to a surreal twist in Horwich's history.

In 2005 the Loyalist ex-paramilitary 'Mad Dog' Johnny Adair, leader of the Ulster Freedom Fighters, was involved in an internal squabble within his group in Belfast which had resulted in several deaths. So he did what anyone would do in that situation: he left Northern Ireland and went to live in Horwich.

Sometimes he must have popped into the Salad Bowl, where presumably he was told, 'We've got some lovely cucumber just in, Mad Dog,' and people would stop him in the street and say, 'Hello, Mad Dog, love. I'm glad to have caught you. I've been having trouble with them blooming slugs gnawing at my runner beans. Can I pop round, when you've got a minute, to borrow your Heckler & Koch semi-automatic self-loading pistol to get rid of the little perishers?'

If the local parish council had any guts, as soon as Adair arrived they'd have declared the town independent of the United Kingdom, and applied to become a county in the Republic of Ireland, but as they rejected that strategy he lived there until his son was locked up for drug dealing, and split up with his wife in a manner not usually recommended by Relate, having an all-out fight with her in the children's park, before heading for Scotland.

Here then is a town which seems to have maintained its sense of individuality and personal chattiness, but it's not appreciated by anyone with a spark of youth, as they go mad for a bit and then leave. Yet there's no fundamental reason why the town couldn't include a club or a bar in which there might be a band or DJs or something that might attract a crowd more in search of excitement than the Salad Bowl's target audience.

There's no intrinsic reason why there couldn't be a cinema, or a café with posters for last year's Reading Festival on its wall and a screen showing MTV and that stayed open until eleven, or even later. But such a place can't emerge within the retail park, because nothing is allowed in unless it's part of a chain. There might be a Revolution bar, with a menu designed in a head office, selling onion rings designed in Basingstoke, but no one could set up a venue with an individual local spirit, any more than you could ask the Pentagon if you could hire out a room to set up a quirky little local army of your own.

But the presence of a retail park also makes it harder to set up a shop or venue within the town. Because it divides a town into two distinct areas: one where people sleep and stay indoors, and the other, a drive away, where you shop and go bowling.

But there must be some enthusiasm for maintaining a distinct Horwich spirit, because the giant Tesco and the wonderful Carpet Right haven't destroyed the 1957 town centre. Maybe that's due in part to the annual walk to Rivington Pike, the highest point in the North-West. Every Good Friday the whole town, at some point in the day, undertakes the walk of around three miles, over a series of fields and up a steep grassy slope, followed by a rocky clamber to the summit, to a stone hut called the Pike, and then back again. And everyone does it, there being no question that they wouldn't, for no reason that anyone can recall.

No one asks if you're going up, only if you've been up yet. To say you weren't going would be as if someone asked you, the week after a relative had died, if you'd had the funeral yet, and you said, 'No, we're not bothering. We thought we'd spend the time decorating the bathroom instead.'

So you stroll up amongst the stream of walkers headed in each direction, some with dogs or pushchairs, and you tell yourself that whatever people have said you've obviously misunderstood, because there must be some reason they're all doing this, like at the top there's an office open one day a year where you have to register as a resident or you're driven out by a section of the Mafia that got lost and lives in Horwich, or there's a sacrifice to the god of idle chatter or something. And lots of people you've never met say hello, then you pass a mini fairground perched on a slope, as if anyone's likely to say, 'This pointless walk is wearing me out – I'll take the weight off my feet for five minutes by spinning violently round on a waltzer before carrying on.'

Then you make your final approach, still wondering whether there's a little surprise no one's told you about, so you'll get to the top and find the Dalai Lama there, who signs his name on your buttock. But you arrive, stop for a moment, and then come back again. Once you're back, when people ask if you've been up the Pike yet you say, 'Oh yes,' slightly smug, as if to say, 'Why, haven't you been yet, you lazy fucker?' Or maybe that's just if you're from London.

No one's exactly sure how this custom started, but the reason it's maintained with such enthusiasm might be due to the events of 1896. That year the Ainsworths, who owned a bleaching mill, decided to close the gates leading to nearby Winter Hill, which was on their land. Richard Henry Ainsworth declared, 'We have heard too much of people's rights and too little of the rights of the landowner.' Because the big problem in 1896 was that political correctness had gone mad.

This wasn't his first campaign: he'd also led the opposition to the opening of Bolton's library on Sundays. Now he was concerned about his new shooting hut, built so he could take lunch with his guests during a hunt. The hut was near the path up the hill, so he closed it off. A local socialist group responded by placing an advert in the *Bolton Journal* announcing that there would be a march across this land to defy the ban on the following Sunday.

Ten thousand people turned up, marching past the bleach works and heading for the new wooden gate. According to the *Bolton Chronicle*, 'Amid the lusty shouting the gate was attacked by powerful hands, and it was said a saw was brought into requisition.' A gamekeeper attacked the marchers with a stick, so he was ducked in a stream, and the marchers tore down the signs warning people not to trespass.

According to one account, 'The events of Sunday were virtually the sole topic of conversation in Bolton pubs, mills and factories.' The next week 12,000 people turned up, and the police had to let them pass. Thirty-two of the marchers were arrested, which led to campaigns for their defence, but the right to walk across Winter Hill was established again, and the tradition of the whole town marching up to the Pike on Good Friday must have seemed more poignant after that, especially as some of those 12,000 are probably still up there, having stopped for a chat with someone coming the other way, until one day they'll say, 'Oo, my word, love, look at the time, it's over a century we've been stood here nattering, don't seem like it, do it? They'll 'ave invented flying machines an' all sorts, I shouldn't wonder. Now I've just got to nip into Salad Bowl for me marrow and I'm done.'

London

The city in Britain that's hardest to identify with must be London. There's no major sports team called London, as there is in Barcelona or Rome or the big cities of America. No one ever shouts 'Come on London!', and I suspect whoever wrote the song 'Maybe it's Because I'm a Londoner' was from Dundee, because it's rare for anyone to be proud of being a Londoner. They might be proud of being from the East End or Camden or Deptford or Fulham, but not *London*.

And the Thames is a barrier that divides London more and more the longer you live there. You come to realise that there's a deep misunderstanding between the north and the south sides of the river, and you feel it most acutely if you live in the south, because North Londoners seem to feel it's an imposition to cross the river at all. 'I suppose we *could* come down your way for a change,' they say tentatively, in the uncertain tone you might use when considering selling your house and moving onto a boat, or joining a swingers' club.

Even if they agree, you then face the horror, when you describe how to get there, as they come to terms with the fact that the underground hardly bothers with South London. 'Get a what? A *train*?' you hear them gasping, as if you've suggested they ride on a llama, and then you await the phone call when they say, 'We've looked at the map, and it's much further to your place than we realised, so it's probably easier if you came to us.'

A North Londoner honestly said to me once, 'To be truthful, Mark, I'm more likely to go to Paris than come down your way, as that's just one train straight through with no mucking about.'

From the South London perspective, I know that if I have to go to Waterloo it feels like nipping round the corner, but The Strand, which is the same distance plus the length of Waterloo Bridge, feels like having to go all the sodding way into town. Greenwich seems like over the road, but the Isle of Dogs, just four hundred yards further through a foot tunnel, is another world, and if I had a friend who moved from Greenwich to the other side we'd probably lose touch, sending a Christmas card every second year in which we'd agree to sort out a weekend together at some point but never managing it, like when the person who lives three doors away moves to Quebec.

Part of the difficulty is that London is so huge. Getting across it is a trench war, a slog in which you learn to appreciate every few yards you advance. Distances have different meanings within the capital: eight miles from Tooting to Hammersmith is the same as forty miles in Gloucestershire.

This must add to the parochial nature of London as a series of villages. No one refers to the *Evening Standard* as a local paper, because the local paper is the one that deals with your particular bit of London. Most boroughs have their own theatre and their own festivals, their own town centres, and if someone from Wood Green was told by local gangsters, 'Never show your face round these parts again,' that wouldn't extend as far as Walthamstow, surely, as that's pretty much accepted as a different manor.

One way of understanding Londoners' lack of identification with the city is to consider who might be mentioned as being associated with the city. If you ask someone in Leicester which prominent people came from the place, they might mention Joe Orton or Gary Lineker, and everyone in Wellingborough tells you that Thom Yorke of Radiohead comes from there. But what would a Londoner say? Not many would boast, 'You know the Queen? She lives here.' And whereas it might cause a stir in Aylesbury if their town was mentioned in passing by a character in *Waterloo Road*, Londoners don't get excited at every reference in the media, ringing each other frantically to say, 'Did you see that episode of *World's Strictest Parents* tonight? Well, guess where one of the kids was from? He was from London.'

Similarly, there's not a thrill because of someone's visit to London. In Derby or Bolton, if someone you were interested in was coming to the theatre or playing at a music venue, you'd buy tickets as soon as they went on sale. But in London, if Jesus announced He'd come back and was performing some miracles on Wednesday night at Tufnell Park, you'd think, 'Oh, I'm not going all the way up there. Anyway, He's bound to be around again before long.'

If I go somewhere really north, like Finchley, I get that uneasy feeling you have when you're six and you go further than you're allowed from your parents on the beach, fascinated by what's this far away, but increasingly worried that you're being silly now, and won't ever be able to get back. I don't get this in Orkney, just Finchley.

To make the city even more mysterious, we know the names of these other areas because they're on the underground system. There must be a place called Theydon Bois, and one called Colindale, but not only have I never been to them, I've never met anyone who has, or who's ever mentioned them, or read anything about them, and it's quite possible they're not really there, but are just fake names created as part of an elaborate tax dodge.

So to follow the quirks of Londoners you can't probe the history and personalities of London. You have to break the city down as locally as you can. The contradiction here is that London has become possibly the most global city in the world.

More areas of more countries are represented as communities in London than in any other city, including New York.

When the World Cup is on, you can watch any team you choose with people from that country. I've watched Japan play in a room full of paper lanterns, with a promise of free sake if Japan scored, with everyone alarmingly polite, lowering their voice as they came in, as if arriving late for a lecture. It would have seemed reasonable if the lights had gone down and someone had announced: 'We are honoured today to see the first viewing of Nagisa Oshima's powerful production *Japan v Cameroon*, the opening segment of a trilogy that undertakes to reveal the inner truth behind playing two up front with a five-man midfield, and has taken forty-five years to make. Thank you.'

I've watched Ghana in a Ghanaian pub, with maybe three hundred Ghanaians dancing to drummers throughout, and a woman in a dazzling yellow African dress who screamed across the room when Ghana weren't awarded a free kick she felt they deserved, 'That referee is a wicked wicked man.'

The area of New Malden contains, for reasons no one's sure of, the biggest South Korean community outside South Korea. I watched their matches in the midst of a huge crowd of South Koreans in a pub garden, while a man in a multi-coloured silk robe banged a thick metal gong that looked like the sort of brass pot you see in the kitchens of stately homes, as if he was either an angry butler signalling that dinner was bloody well ready, or the drummer in a Buddhist Iron Maiden.

In Battersea I spent an evening with a crowd of Serbs watching their team play Australia, and met Nims, draped in a giant Serbian flag, who had the Cockneyest accent I've ever heard. 'My ol' man came from south of fackin' Belgrade,' he told me, 'and made the best fackin' slivovic in the whole of yer fackin' Balkans.' At one point he said possibly my favourite ever Cockney Serb sentence: 'You gotta admit, Mark, that Tito, he was a fackin' diamond.'

The nearest record shop to me is Jamaican. The staff have an endearing habit of taking five minutes to respond to any request, and one day when I asked for a record from the top shelf, the assistant looked up at the shelf, looked at the stepladder next to it, repeated this process three times, then said, 'It too high,' and sent me on my way. The nearest café to me is where the Portuguese of the area go to watch Portuguese television, which has regular weather and traffic reports they study intently, presumably so they're aware that if they have to pop down to Brixton later, it's best to avoid the ring road south of Lisbon.

My children have friends who are Turkish and Brazilian and Afghani, eat food that's Thai and Greek, have conversed with Hare Krishnas, Hasidic Jews and Sikhs. By the age of nine they might have experienced an array of cultures and customs that a hundred years ago would have been available only to a missionary or an explorer.

What unifies London is its extreme lack of unity. It's comprehensively diverse, and the more international an area becomes, the more that mix is not just tolerated but celebrated. The areas of greatest hostility to settlers tend to be on the outside edges, where it's happened the least. These are the parts left isolated, where one estate can be the size of a small town, where industry has declined and the residents feel under siege. The most obvious scapegoats are the Kurds, or the Poles, or whichever group has most recently been housed nearby. Logic disappears, and they retreat into cries such as 'The country will soon be run by Islam,' whereas in fact it's probably unlikely that anyone will ever visit a Dorset tea shop and be told, 'No scones this afternoon, love, it's Ramadan.' Or turn on the radio to hear a call to prayers followed by a voice saying, 'Good morning, this is Radio Sussex.'

One of the many tragedies of this situation is that those affected are deprived of the joy of this localised global network. For example, my son once introduced me to a new friend, saying, 'This is Ernest, he's Polish. Don't worry, I don't miss any opportunity to remind him that his lot had to be saved by us in the war.'

I said, 'What?

He said, 'Every day I remind him that his country would have been stuffed without us in the Second World War.'

I said, 'Listen, you know the aeroplane battle at the start of the war, over Kent, that meant Hitler had no chance of invading.'

'Oh, right, the Battle of Britain.'

'Yes, the Battle of Britain. Well, do you know where one fifth of the pilots on the Allied side came from? They came from Poland.'

He turned straight to his mate and said, 'See, you were nicking our jobs even back then.'

Now, who wouldn't want to live in a city like that?

Outer London*

It upsets me when Croydon is derided as ugly. That's not because it isn't ugly. It is indeed achingly ugly. But it isn't naturally like that. It's ugly like a beautiful woman who got to sixty and decided to have a series of botox operations, each of which went frighteningly wrong, deciding each time to cover it up with another one that made things worse, until she was hardly recognisable, but if you looked carefully there were odd speckles of her old self shining through, reminding the world of what she'd have been like if she'd remained natural, although this wasn't easy to spot as she now has a dual carriageway down the middle of her face; that sort of ugly.

It's hard for a town not to be ugly once it's cut in two by an area it's impossible to walk on or across or over or round. I once went to Nicosia, the capital of Cyprus, and while the palm trees alongside the High Street are seductively Mediterranean, you can't help noticing that the middle of the city is blockaded by

---

* A couple of days before this book had to be completed, a few hundred residents of Croydon made the town part of the national news by burning a chunk of it to the ground. While some people lamented the apparently random destruction, and others grieved for their wrecked shops and homes, the demise of efforts lasting several generations, I watched the flames and thought, 'Aaagh, I've no time to rewrite the chapter on Croydon now. They could at least have thought to do this a few weeks ago, the heartless callous fuckers.'

the military, behind which is half a mile of abandoned territory uninhabitable since the war in 1973 except for lines of sinister Greek soldiers followed by sinister Turkish soldiers and barbed wire and sandbags. But it's still easier to get from one side to the other than it is in fucking Croydon.

The shopping side of the town became the Whitgift Centre, a principality of predictability on two floors that I've been in on probably 2,000 occasions but still have no idea which way I'm facing as soon as I'm inside. So it was decided that what the place needed was another shopping centre, almost as big and almost identical, right next door, and then a third one about fifty yards from the second one. If Croydon's town planners had gone to Haiti after the earthquake they'd have said, 'Sod clean water and a Red Cross tent, what this place needs is a replica of the Whitgift shopping centre.'

Each of these shopping centres has a team of security guards who patrol the area with the internationally recognised slow, deliberate gait of a guard, whether in a suburban shopping mall or Treblinka. And it must be possible that one day each of the Croydon shopping centres will develop into its own state, with stamps and an army and an entry in the Eurovision Song Contest.

This layout makes the whole centre unnavigable in any mode of transport, including a tank. The road system to accommodate all this is an elaborate maze that takes the experienced visitor three or four circuits before finding the escape route, which involves creeping through a series of back streets past the car park where lorries deliver stuff to the back of a warehouse by giant metal bins, so you feel as if you're in the car at the start of the *Naked Gun* films, and will soon be driving through a wedding reception and a women's changing room before emerging onto Wellesley Road, past the office blocks scattered as if grown from office-block seeds blown randomly by the wind, and out towards Purley.

And yet within this whirlpool are spots of a different land that must once have existed: a parish church with a garden looking lonely but defiant opposite Debenhams; a reggae record shop that bedunks and badooms as far as W.H. Smith; a fruit stall where the salesman's minimalist patter involves him holding up an orange and crying, 'Fifty fifty fifty fifty fifty fifty fifty!' without ever specifying whether he means 50p an orange or fifty oranges for £1 or fifty tons of oranges for £1 million or 50 per cent off an orange if you also buy something else for 40.

There's the shell of Beanos, a second-hand record shop that stretched across three floors, with rare sleeves on the walls and a constant beat of something you'd never heard before but had to find out what it was sizzling towards the Whitgift. Every trip I made to Croydon ended up in Beanos, because after the Whitgift Centre I felt I'd earned it. A visit was impossible to complete quickly. If I went in assuring myself I'd be out in ten minutes, because after all I did have to catch a plane to go to a relative's wedding, I'd end up ringing Chicago two hours later to say I was really sorry but I wouldn't be coming, as something had popped up, while thinking, 'Which should I play first out of the new OutKast and this rare Ray Charles?'

These tiny monuments suggest that there was once a different order, the way a town in Wyoming might retain an enclave of people descended from Cherokees. Croydon's subsequent problems may stem from the way those in charge of the town seem to have an ambition for it to become a second London. The council and the local paper campaign for city status, and there are often announcements of massive new business parks and vast complexes of offices, with an artist's impression in the *Croydon Advertiser* of somewhere slightly grander than Seattle, with lifts going up the outsides of conical structures connected by spirally walkways. But none of these things have ever begun to happen. They might as well announce, 'Plans revealed for

Croydon's mid-air shopping bonanza', with an artist's impression of a replica of the Whitgift Centre run by talking chipmunks on a cloud.

These projects are usually heralded as aiming to 'create a shopping paradise to rival Oxford Street', or to 'provide a major European retail destination', as baffling as if Ipswich announced it was turning the park into a space station to rival the one outside the earth's atmosphere.

But outside the central wasteland life has survived. London's biggest Indian festival, or mela, is in Croydon. The origins of dubstep are in Croydon. There's a Kurdish centre, a Zairean church, Afghan cricketers, regular protests to save libraries at which pensioners are photographed with home-made placards for the local paper, an annual Hare Krishna festival, there's laughter and love and a windmill that has open days, an area called Croydon Airport although there hasn't been an airport there for sixty years, and a hospital called the Mayday that everyone lovingly calls the Maydie. There was an old homeless West Indian man who became famous for sitting in the underpass playing his home-made double bass, which looked as if it was built from plywood and cable stolen from a building site but somehow sounded authentic.

Crystal Palace Football Club attracts astounding loyalty, although the fans almost always expect to suffer and feel slightly uneasy when we don't. (The Palace fans' website can be the most charmingly self-deprecating document you'll ever read. For example, on the morning of one vital match someone wrote, 'How are everyone's bowels this morning?' After a variety of honest replies one fan answered, 'I'm fine. I had a perfectly normal crap at half past seven. The only thing is I didn't wake up until ten past eight.')

Croydon was also home to the most impressively dedicated Stalinists in the country. When the Communist Party of Great Britain took the decision to become mildly critical of the Soviet

Union, for tricks such as invading Czechoslovakia, the Croydon group saw this as a betrayal. So in the 1970s they set up the New Communist Party, and their mission to turn Britain Communist without the wishy-washy compromised semi-Stalinism of the normal Communist Party began in Croydon. This might seem an over-ambitious project, but it was shortly after this that the grey office blocks and the dual carriageway in the centre of town were built, so it looks as if their hard-line Stalinism won influence on the town planning committee at least. All they needed was labour camps and a couple of Olympic gymnasts and they were almost there.

Despite the pretensions of those who govern Croydon, it's a small town, and you know it's a small town because when a bit of the Whitgift Centre appears on *Peep Show*, which was filmed in Croydon, everyone in Croydon says, 'Look there's the Whitgift Centre there's the Whitgift Centre there's HMV I wonder if we'll see someone we know.'

It's a small town because when I told a neighbour there was an article about me in the *Guardian* she got very excited until she realised she'd misunderstood and said, 'Oh, I thought you meant the *Croydon Guardian*. I've not heard of that one you're on about.'

So, Croydon stands as one of the places the developers have worked tirelessly to destroy but have not managed to. And one of the finest views anywhere in London must be from the roof of the multi-storey car park at the Whitgift Centre. All of the western half of London is laid out, the Wembley arch, Heathrow Airport and a proud green gas thingy that beams from Southall, almost winking at Croydon as a tower from a fellow town that either is or isn't part of London, but can't be sure.

London is such a complex mechanism that there are places you might see every day of your life and never know where they are. Though you can see one from the other, there must be thousands of people in each place who are barely aware of the other. Southall, for the outsider, is also a celebration of difference, because it's comprehensively Indian.

Southall's green gas tower, it turns out, has a huge 'LH' with an arrow on the top, to assure pilots which way is Heathrow, after one lost concentration and landed his passengers at RAF Northolt by mistake, after which I suppose he made an announcement to the passengers that went, 'Honestly, what *am* I like? I don't know whether I'm coming or going today, I really don't.'

So the sign at the railway station is in English and Punjabi, and the pub outside the station is boarded up but is covered in pictures of followers of Krishna, alongside poems written on cardboard imploring humankind to show mercy to their fellow creatures. I presume this is because it's been used by Krishna followers, and not that it's an attempt to set up a chain of Krishna theme pubs, with a slightly limited jukebox, and on your first visit you keep thinking, 'Surely it can't be last orders already,' every time someone bangs a gong.

Next is Britain's largest Sikh temple, emitting a constant smell of dhal as they provide a continuous supply of free food for anyone – that's anyone at all – who feels in need of food. It's a sign of how the human spirit isn't as selfish as is sometimes suggested that the place isn't regularly packed with groups arriving and saying, 'Our usual table for six please.' All of this is within twenty yards of the station, and even to walk past is thrilling because it's so buoyantly *different*.

The main street, known as the Broadway, could be the most unique road in Britain. Every angle is like a giant spot-the-difference puzzle. The chicken nuggets shop has a sign above the door that says 'Home of the Halal Peri-Peri Chicken'. The betting shops display odds for cricket matches rather than football matches. Several music shops still sell cassettes. Cassettes? Cassettes aren't like vinyl. *No one* plays cassettes. That's being deliberately obtuse, like trying to sell Gary Glitter annuals or sheets of asbestos.

The cafés all have about a dozen mesmerising curries in those canteen-style metal containers, so it's tempting to say, 'Can I have all of them please?', and they have a screen to one side showing either an Asian music channel or Star Gold, which when I was last there was showing a film in which a reckless lorry driver ran over and killed a pedestrian. But as he sped off a hero somersaulted onto the lorry's roof, dragged him from the speeding vehicle and punched him about sixty times, each thump making a sound like a tap cymbal. Then about a hundred people arrived and everyone celebrated because it had clearly been a wonderful ten minutes, if you leave aside the pedestrian lying dead in the road. If I spoke Punjabi I'd probably be aware that amongst the cheering crowd was the pedestrian's brother, singing, 'My sibling's been crushed by a lorry but hoorah hoorah what a somersault.'

At various points you'll be handed a leaflet, and the one I took implored me: 'Know your future and adjust way of your life. We provide you protection for house, business and personal matters, removal all types of black magisc and evil things by performing Devi Upasana, Laxmi pooja shanthi Pooja Mandala pooja (prayers) and also protection from eneminies and jealousy. 100% guarantee result.' I can only guess how often someone rings to demand their money back, complaining, 'It's been three weeks now and I've still got several evil things you haven't removed, including a demon you said you'd take on Thursday but I waited in all day and you never showed up and now he keeps grabbing my soul, I can barely sleep.'

Traders look you in the eye and ask you to please buy their mangoes, which seems such a reasonable thing to ask, but it may be there's an opportunity for a cultural exchange here, in which a bloke from Croydon ends up asking people to please buy his orange, while an old man from Jaipur holds up a mango and shouts, 'Fifty fifty fifty fifty fifty fifty fifty!'

Amongst this mêlée, between the Bollywood DVD shops and the sari stalls, is a Greggs the bakers, jostling along merrily and refusing to feel out of place, like one of these eighty-year-olds who go to a drum 'n' bass night.

And throughout is a constant beat of Indian dance and bhangra, which sounded especially welcome one Christmas Day when, for a complex batch of reasons, I found myself on my own. So I cycled to Southall, wondering if it might be the one place in London where life carried on as normal amidst the eerie still emptiness that encircles you on Christmas Day if you dare take a peek outside.

As I turned into the Broadway the street was booming and crackling, the leaflets and curries flowing and the beats pumping out of the shops with no suggestion there'd be a chorus in which jolly was rhymed with holly, or if it did at least it would be in a language I don't understand. Friends called across the street to each other, shopkeepers displayed a relaxed and helpful demeanour that's only possible when you haven't been ordered to wear fun reindeer antlers, and everybody seemed full of good will and joy. Anyone arriving from another world would have assumed they'd landed in the middle of an annual festival, while the poor sods in the rest of the country were undergoing some enforced sacrifice.

The alien might also be confused by another aspect of Southall. Because the Broadway was the scene of one of the most violent nights in British post-war history, when in 1979 the National Front organised a meeting in the centre, and the protesters were attacked by a unit of the police called the Special Patrol Group, which led to the death of teacher Blair Peach.

But in the long term the protesters won, because not only has the Indian community stayed, it remains both distinctly Indian and firmly integrated into London.

* * *

Southall is London. Croydon is London. The adverts at the airports and on the tourist brochures should boast of these areas, because most people in London don't live in Regent's Park or on the London Eye. Big Ben is imposing enough and the West End theatres emit a certain buzz, but they aren't where people live and argue, create and joke and struggle and transform their environment, to make pulsating tales of life that overcome the office blocks and the dual carriageways and the gas towers that land and grow and rip apart whole chunks of land like the more charmless members of the Godzilla family, with no more compassion than the less subtle types whose tool is the more direct petrol bomb, but somehow never seem to overwhelm the people who live beneath them.

Hereford

People of Hereford aren't quite sure where the town is, although they know where it's not. It's not in the Cotswolds and it's not in the West Country, and it's *definitely* not in Wales. In fact there's a fascination with the aftermath of the Battle of Hereford in 760, when the castle was built to keep the Welsh out, as apparently it's still legal to fire a crossbow at a Welshman in the courtyard of the cathedral. I suspect this isn't as true as they seem to believe, as it's hard to see how it sneaked past the European Court of Human Rights, unless there's someone in Strasbourg going, 'Oh, it's only the Welsh.'

Hereford has to be admired for its imaginatively diverse array of industry. Most towns with more than one industry have trades that complement each other, like steel and coal, or fishing and being a port. But Hereford has cider, cows and the head-quarters of the SAS. Careers advisors must hope that everyone who comes to see them will fit easily into one of those jobs, by saying something like, 'I'm scared of cows, allergic to apples, and my hobby is swinging through windows with a hand grenade and shooting people through the smoke. Do you have anything suitable?'

Mostly, though, the town is defined by its cows. It even has a breed of cow named after it, and every road seems to lead to the cattle market, a huge square behind the sort of brick wall you only usually see between rows of back-to-back houses in footage of scrawny kids in 1960s Manchester. Covering this wall are posters with information about cow diseases and cow auctions and the latest cow regulations. The cattle market backs onto the football ground, as if to allow farmers to keep an eye on their stock while watching the game.

So before I went I pledged not to take the obvious line of supposing that everything was cattle-related. I asked on Twitter for local people to tell me about the town, and the first three replies each said, 'Before every Hereford home game we parade a cow round the pitch.'

The town is equally proud of its cider industry. According to the official Hereford Cider website, 'It's often said it takes four men to drink a pint of Herefordshire cider: two to hold the man down, and one to pour it down his throat.' Then it informs you, 'In the King Offa distillery, the tradition of making cider brandy has been revived. Once known as the Wine of England, this mind-blowing substance can be obtained at the museum shop!'

So whereas your normal museum shops boast a variety of gifts, rubbers and bookmarks, in Hereford you can commemorate your visit by blowing your fucking mind.

And there's that cheery little exclamation mark, the sort you put after 'The tulips were delightful!' Maybe there's another section that goes, 'For a change from cider brandy, why not pop down to a back road behind our council estates to sample some of our full-strength home-grown Hereford crack!'

And yet, from the city centre you would never imagine that the cattle market and the cider distilleries were just around the corner, as the whole area is a desert of inevitable shops and wide concrete walkways, banks and chain pubs, that stretches and bends and goes on a bit more and never seems to end, and that on a Sunday is so deserted you wonder if a nuclear apocalypse took place while you were parking in the multi-storey. Even on a perfectly still day, with no breeze and the flags lying limp, you'd still hear wind whistling around the big green bins behind Iceland.

At every point around the edge of this pedestrian zone you can suddenly emerge into a town with roads and people and voices, but if you step back onto the concrete there's only an eerie whistle again.

Just as unexpectedly, I was once greeted by the Hereford Anarchist Association, which produces a magazine called the *Hereford Heckler*, incorporating the *Hereford Insurgent*, and which campaigned against a new Tesco and against job losses at Bulmer's Cider.

They took me to their favourite cider pub, where the landlord was sympathetic, they said, and had allowed them to use the back room for an anarchist film night until the police put pressure on him to ban their documentary on the arms trade. I wish I had footage of the meeting at which the police discussed this strategy, then congratulated themselves on preventing the spread of anarchism in Hereford.

The fascination of the town is that it has all these disparate elements that shouldn't go together, like a kid's picture where they've drawn their house but put a dinosaur in a spaceship in the garden.

The next time I visited I didn't find the anarchists, so I presumed they'd either gone to the right or been executed following a word from the Hereford police to the SAS. I wandered through the Sunday-evening pedestrian eeriness, in which you feel less desire to be a pedestrian than you would in the racetrack during the Monaco Grand Prix, trying to find a pub that was still serving. Seeing myself reflected in the windows of New Look and Gap, and aware of the clip of each footstep, I found myself wondering whether my presence would wake a mutant hiding in the overflowing bottle bank by the Burger King, and stepped into the outer live ring of the town. I heard a lonely jukebox, I thought, and turned the corner to find a pub.

The barman looked at his watch as he served me, grudgingly pressing a button to squirt out a Kronenbourg, while six teenagers sat at a table pouting and staring into the middle distance with expressions that told you none of them had spoken for an hour. Suddenly one of the boys stood up, and with a teenage stroll that said, 'Why is walking so BORING?' he meandered to the karaoke machine, calling out, 'Shut up Jamie, you arse!' managing to elicit boredom and aggression from a Hereford accent, and then put a coin in the machine. Then he snapped his fingers and sang 'Fly Me to the Moon' in a silky baritone with perfect jazz syncopation, rolling the last but one 'I love you' to a 'Yoooooo-oo-ow-ow-ow', with perfect pitch and in a throaty but creamy crooner's lilt, all the while staring straight ahead looking utterly bored while his mates sipped pink drinks through straws and the barman collected glasses with a scowl.

He sauntered back to the table, even slower than he'd gone, then one of the girls shrugged her shoulders, looked around and stumbled to the machine. On came the backing for Amy Winehouse's 'Back to Black'. The girl poured out every sinew and vulnerable creak of the original. It would surely have reduced everyone in earshot to tears, except that she performed the whole song while chewing gum and staring in the vague direction of the air vent.

One by one they all took turns to look clinically bored while belting out breathtaking versions of classic ballads, as the barman emptied the till and went round the tables spraying Pledge.

The explanation for all these weird goings-on, if there is one, evades me. But maybe they're connected to Miles Smith, the Hereford canon who translated parts of the King James Version of the Bible in the early seventeenth century. That's an investigation that should be undertaken by Dan Brown, especially as I seem to recall one verse in the book of Exodus which goes, 'And Moses did question GOD as to how he would lead his cows through the market. And GOD did say, "Take thy rod and cast it into the ground," whereupon the rod did turn into a special paratrooper fully prepared for combat operations. And Moses did lay his drink upon the ground and say, "Never again, this stuff's mind-blowing.'"

Norwich

The accents of East Anglia are possibly the most expressive in Britain. They destroy self-importance: it's impossible to be pompous in reply to an East Anglian accent.

When an actor is throwing a backstage tantrum, screaming, 'How can I *possibly* work in these conditions?' there should be an East Anglian nearby to say, 'Calm you down. You can't carry on playen' Widow Twankey if you's all het up and carryen' awn.'

When a contestant on *The Apprentice* says, 'I can taste success in my spit,' the Norfolk woman should be on hand to reply, 'That's a rum ol' do. Yew wan' see doctor 'bout that, yew do.' And Bono should be made to live there, so every time he announced he'd taken another huge step towards solving the problem of the world's food supply there was a gap of fifteen seconds while people around gently supped their pints, then someone said, 'You had a good year on the allotment, have you?'

When I asked on Twitter if anyone had a comment to make about Norwich, someone sent me the message, 'I heard a woman in the market with an umbrella with a push-button thing say, "Do it do that? It do."'

The first time I witnessed this demeanour was in a house in Lowestoft, with a friend and his uncle, who had a degree in English literature as well as a full-bodied stammer. The uncle set off for the shops, then came back two minutes later and picked up the keys he'd left on the table. As he put them in his pocket he said with a gently lyrical Lowestoft lilt, 'I I I I'd f-f-f-f-f-f-f-f-forget my balls if they weren't in a b-b-bag,' and set off again.

The accent has an added impact in Norwich, as it fools you into thinking the town is a rural lolloping plain, but Norwich defies its image on every front. It's got hills, an identikit pedestrianised area, clubs that advertise MC battles, and two central multi-storey car parks, both called Castle Mall car park, so you park there, and on your way back through town you see a sign saying 'Castle Mall car park', and then wander round and round and up and along and past every single space four times until a local comes over and says, 'I 'spect you's in a wrong Castle Mall car park is it?' Presumably when they named the second one, rather than opt for one of the infinite arrangements of letters that are different to 'Castle Mall' to distinguish it from the first one, they decided, 'Castle Mall's worked well enough for first, so's no need to pick nuffin' different for second.'

Norwich seems to appreciate its distance from London. Whenever there's a suggestion that the A11, the main road south, should be widened from its one lane in each direction, there's an uneasy disquiet, as if the town thinks, 'If buggers are goan come up here we can at least make 'em suffer a bit on way.' This is understandable, given the attitude of some who buy second homes round there. The town of Burnham Market is known as Chelsea-on-Sea, and in May 2010 the new residents endeared themselves to the older community by taking legal action against the owners of some cockerels that were crowing too early. It's easy to imagine them over their sautéd noisette of sea lion boasting, 'It's so exquisitely delightful to enjoy this retreat of rural splendour, but I just wish they'd widen that ghastly road so the ghastly yokels wouldn't hold us up all day.'

So the true adventurer to East Anglia goes to Norwich, which is one of the few places where the main central shopping mall has one unit that gives away the identity of the town it's in.

Because opposite H&M and behind Waterstone's is the Colman's Mustard Shop.

Apparently the Norwich mustard industry was started by Jeremiah Colman at a water mill in the village of Bawburgh. The Mustard Shop is magnificently dedicated to mustard, with normal jars of Colman's mustard, jars of powder for you to make your own mustard, mustard pots, mustard recipe books and industrial-sized tubs of mustard that could only be used to terrify inmates at Guantánamo Bay, or for strongman events that come on Sky Sports 3 in the middle of the night.

It was outside this mustard shop that I heard a woman of about fifty, from somewhere south, say to her friend as they gazed in the door at 103 mustard-related objects for sale, 'I wonder if *this* is the mustard shop.'

Altogether, the rural image of Norwich must have made it the only town with a university, a ring road, a series of industries, shopping malls and multi-storey car parks, whose football supporters still get taunted for behaving in an illegal manner with sheep.

This might be particularly galling if you were three hundred years old, as you'd recall when Norwich was England's second city. Having access to water that led out to the East made it a major trading centre from the twelfth century until the Industrial Revolution.

The accounts of the town from this time are unusually complimentary, although George Borrow, in his translation of a German version of the Faust legend, adapted a passage about hell to read: 'They found the people of the place modelled after so unsightly a pattern, with such ugly figures and flat features that the devil had never seen them equalled, except by the inhabitants of an English town called Norwich, when dressed in their Sunday best.'

At the time of the French Revolution radicals set up the Norwich Revolution Society. According to *The French Revolution* *in England*: 'By the spring of 1793 Norwich was covered with a network of small branches, of the lower class meeting in public houses. One of their secretaries, Isaac Saint, afterwards told the Privy Council that at their meetings "they received books as loans from a middle class group that met at The Bell,* and held country meetings at which the village constable would interrupt them to say, 'Explain this or that word or the people may be misled.'"'

This is possibly the most unlikely revolutionary scenario ever to have come about, that a Norfolk village constable, presumably sent to spy on a local meeting of seditious neighbours, was interjecting with comments like, 'I think that'd be clearer if you said SMASH the state rather than crush the state. Just a thought, carry on.'

But at the time Norwich was the second city, the accent can't have seemed so innocent. It would have been a dialect of authority, of importance, of confidence, whether spoken by a landowner or a rebel, as a London or a Manchester accent is now.

Over the last three centuries the attitude of Norwich's residents towards their town must have altered to reflect its slide down the nation's hierarchy. Like an old musician accepting that he's unlikely to have any more hits but who still enjoys playing to a small, appreciative audience, Norwich appears content with its quirky image. Most people seem happy for it to be out of the way, up there on one side of the country, with no reason for anyone from a major city to pass through it or be aware of it until it pops up on the news because one of its MPs gets sacked or Delia Smith gets drunk, and the rest of the country thinks, 'Oh yes, Norwich. I forgot that was still over there.'

Martin Bell and Stephen Fry support Norwich City FC, which is as it should be, whereas if Noel Gallagher or David Mellor

---

* The Bell is now on two levels, one still a pub, the other a branch of the Santander bank.

supported them they'd have to be asked to leave and support someone else.

It's a place enough at ease with itself that when I asked people in the town to send me their thoughts about it, they sent messages such as, 'Norwich is the New York of East Anglia. There's even a sit-down Greggs the bakers.'

Everyone in Norwich seems gently proud of the town's major achievements: mustard, a radical tradition, the country's first ever lending library, *Sale of the Century* and the seats at Greggs. It's a place comfortable enough that someone there could tell me, 'Norwich is the home of one of Britain's only two full-time puppet theatres. Fuck knows where the other is, mind you.'

Boston

When Norwich was at number two in Britain's important-town chart, the unlikely holder of the number four spot was Lincolnshire's Boston. One of the *In Town* shows was recorded in Boston, and its most instantly striking aspect is that it's too flat. I imagine the residents must all travel out to Mablethorpe on a Sunday to marvel at the slight incline that leads to a post office.

As you cross the steppes from Grantham or Peterborough, past miles and miles of unchanging flatness, you keep thinking, 'I'm sure we've passed this bit already,' and wonder if you've become trapped inside a cartoon.

Driving instructors in Boston have complained to their authority that there's nowhere in the town to teach learners the hill start, except for one spot which they all queue up to use, as it's the only place where a car might roll if you take the handbrake off.

Maybe the town ought to apply to host the Winter Olympics, to give the tournament some variety. Commentators would gasp, '*What* a toboggan run from the Swiss team, completing the course in three weeks and four days.'

And presumably on the days when there's heavy snow the kids have a thrilling time, getting in their sledges, sitting there for an hour and then getting out again.

Yet Boston boasts the most magnificent homage to height, a vast church called the Stump, the tallest in Britain that isn't a cathedral, from the top of which you can see the whole of south

Lincolnshire (although you could probably do that from the top of a postbox).

H.V. Morton, in his celebrated 1927 travelogue *In Search of England*, described his sense of wonder at first seeing the Stump. He wrote: 'About ten miles away I saw a curious tower standing among the fields. "That's Boston Stump!" said a man in a cornfield.

'"And what is Boston Stump?" I asked.

'He said, "It's Boston Stump, thickhead."'

The Stump doesn't just dominate the town, it dominates everything vaguely nearby, a massive, crumbly-looking tower that's peered over the vicinity since the 1400s, when any peasant in a cornfield ten miles away must have felt constantly awestruck by this reminder that God and His people could see you all day long, even from a distance of a day's journey. It would be like a Londoner today flying to New York, then looking up to notice his line manager saying, 'I can still see you.'

When the Stump was begun in the 1300s it was expected that it would take 150 years to build, with all the vision and patience required to undertake a project that would be completed by the originators' great-great-great-grandchildren. Maybe in 1456 the people of Boston all threw their hands in the air in exasperation and grumbled, 'It was supposed to be finished this week. Typical bloody builders.'

One function served by the Stump is to be the obvious place in the area from which to commit suicide. It doesn't face much competition as somewhere to jump off as a final act, so the vicar of the Stump has to keep a watch for anyone who looks as if they're heading up the steps to dive off the top. At one point the vicar was Richard Coles, ex-member of the band the Communards. He remembers an occasion when he spotted a bedraggled soul creeping up the stairs, and asked him what had brought him to this state. The bloke said, 'I've spent all morning listening to Communards records, mate.'

But the Stump reveals another side to Boston, and indeed to the universe, which is that there is no natural order. Because when Boston was chosen as the site for this monument, it was the most important port in England after London, and the fourth biggest town in the country. Its position on the River Witham, up which ships could sail to the sea and across to Holland and the centre of international trade, gave Boston an importance it must have believed would last forever. Its inhabitants must have been no more able to imagine that status evaporating than someone in Manchester now could think of a day when most people in Britain would say, 'Manchester? I think I've *heard* of it.'

Apart from the Stump, there are other reminders of the town's roots. The middle has retained its original medieval layout, all thin alleys and slightly wonky buildings with wooden beams. In different hands it might have become twee tourist Boston, oozing cream teas and markets selling olives stuffed with woodpecker. But instead the town is known throughout the region as being under the rule of 'chavs'.

A website dedicated to exposing Boston as a chav stronghold runs for page after page, with such prose as: 'You will have the pleasure of seeing many a pregnant fourteen-year-old with the obligatory poverty pack of ten Richmond fags. Nightlife revolves around Saturday nights in Eclipse. If you like cheap gold, Richmond fags, wheeling a baby in a manky pushchair with a bottle of tea stuffed in its mouth through the marketplace then Boston could be the place for you.'

It would be hard to overstate the quantity and venom of the comments on sites such as 'Chavscum'. Those devoted to Boston alone must be the product of thousands of hours of labour, possibly a pyramid's worth, much of it from people who write simply 'I FUCKING HATE BOSTON CHAVS', while others propose solutions to the problem such as, 'Boston chavs must DIE!', making you wonder if you're reading one of those diaries that are discovered in someone's bedroom after they've gone berserk in a bowling alley with a chainsaw.

Much of the contempt for 'chavs' appears to be a simple modern snobbery. Someone could behave in exactly the same way as a 'chav', but be deemed a colourful rakish japester if they expressed themselves like Noël Coward, sitting at a piano saying, 'Here's a little ditty I composed for your delectation about my days in Boston:

> 'I recall with some divinity
> My earliest ever hump,
> At fourteen I lost my virginity
> Against the south wall of the Stump.'

The contempt is not for drink but *cheap* drink, not for fags but *cheap* fags. Much of the disgust for, and fear of, chavs in their Boston version revolves around Saturday nights in Eclipse, the nightclub down a medieval alley in the centre of town. 'Oh my God, don't go down there,' you're warned. So I went to Eclipse, where the second oldest person after me must have been nineteen, and I set myself some rules about not making eye contact and what to say when I was threatened.

As I reached the front of the queue to pay and get my hand stamped purple, the stubbly T-shirted doorman looked at me, slightly bewildered, slightly sympathetic, and said, 'Are you sure?' as if he was a counsellor at a euthanasia clinic.

'I'm sure,' I told him.

'It's *banging* in there, mate,' he said, as if he was thinking, 'Ah, this sweet old fool must be an amateur astronomer and thinks he's coming in to see an actual eclipse.'

Inside were about two hundred teenagers, drinking cheap lager from plastic bottles. They were much politer than we ever were in the punk days. 'Sorry, mate,' someone said every few seconds as they accidentally barged into someone else.

'Rewind, rewind,' called out the spiky-haired teenage DJ in a south Lincolnshire accent, which sounds as if a bit of Yorkshire is straining but not quite managing to break through the East Anglia. Then he did that DJ trick of turning down the record and calling, 'All right, let's have a big shout-out from BOSTON!' to which a few people muttered 'Yeeugh.' So he stopped the record altogether and yelled in exasperation, 'Oh for Christ's sake, Boston, that was fucking SHIT!'

But by two o'clock, when there was no sign of the police being called for the slightest reason, I felt I should ask for my money back.

Boston doesn't always do itself any favours with regard to its 'chav' image. In the middle of the High Street there's a shop selling electrical goods called 'It Must Be Stolen'. On the shop front is a picture of a burglar in a stripy shirt carrying a bag.

A parallel tension in the town is between some of the people brought up in Boston, and the several thousand Poles who have come to the area to work on the farms. Even in the Indian Queen, a rock pub where indie bands play and there's an imposing statue of the Native American Pocahontas in one corner, the charming and eloquent landlady told me, 'The trouble with Poles is they walk in groups of four on the pavement, so you fall in the road trying to get round them.'

I said, 'I'm sure just as many English walk in groups of four on the pavement,' and she said, 'Yes, but at least they do it in a language I can understand.'

Which at least is an original way to be annoyed, to snarl, 'I don't mind falling in a puddle, as long as it's with the right mix of vowels and consonants, but when it's with three or even FOUR Zs it's time we took a stand.'

There have been mini-riots in protest at the Poles, and one area of the town, called Fenside, elected a British National Party councillor. The vicar of the Stump, as he was showing me round the tiny walkway at the summit of his church, told me with splendid liberal vicarness, 'If only they could see that the wealth that created this city, and indeed funded this very Stump, was provided by gentlemen of the Hanseatic League, made up of thirteenth-century traders from the very Eastern European countries they're now blaming for taking our wealth.'

But the hostility may not be as overwhelming as it can appear. The Polish bars where you sit round chunky wooden tables drinking chunky bottles of beer called something like Gryzdnyzck are packed with a mix of Polish and Lincolnshire-raised teenagers. And on the farms, the experience of spending twelve hours a day picking Brussels sprouts together is bound to create a certain camaraderie, no matter what language someone walks in a group of four with.

I spent a morning picking these sprouts, and what I learned above all was that there are bloody millions of sprouts. Normally with manual work, you can see your progress. You look round after an hour and think, 'I've moved that amount, and there's that much left to do. I'm getting there.' But on a sprout farm you pick all the sprouts off about fifty plants, look around to survey your achievement, and beyond the pathetic insignificant patch you've picked are Brussels sprouts in all directions for miles and miles and millions of miles, way beyond the horizon stretching into infinite space, so you feel as if you're in a story from ancient Greece about a man who defied the gods and was condemned to pick Brussels sprouts for all eternity, like Sisyphus who was ordered to spend forever pushing a boulder up a hill and watching it roll back down again, except at least he had the variety of seeing a hill, the jammy bastard.

The picking session was broken up a bit by a conversation I'll recount word for word, between the farm owner and one picker:

'Hello, Ted. Are you all right? Haven't seen you for a while.'

'No. I had a heart attack.'

'Oo er. So, are you all right now?'

'No. The doctor said I had to cut down on my fry-ups.'

'And have you stopped smoking as well?'

'Well, I did, but now the bloomin' doctor's said I've got to stop *again*.'

In the packing plant I met Sandhra, whose job is to weigh the sprouts so that the same amount goes into each box. She's so skilled in this art that she could probably use it to get to the semi-final of *Britain's Got Talent*. 'I've been working here twelve years,' she told me, 'and I *love* sprouts. I write poems about them. Would you like to hear one?'

She agreed to come to the radio recording the following evening and read out a sprout poem. Then she introduced me to Alex, a Pole in his twenties who worked alongside her, and he agreed to come to the show and say a bit about being Polish in Boston.

During the recording I introduced Sandhra the sprout bard, and she waved her arms manically like a contestant trying to appear wild and crazy on a game show, and yelled, 'HERE I AM!' Then, holding a brown envelope on which she'd written her poem, she clambered onto the stage, yelled, 'I LOVE SPROUTS!' fell over while grabbing the microphone, causing a screeching moment of feedback followed by an alarming dull clump, and said, 'I've had a bit to drink.'

For the next five minutes I tried coaxing her back to her seat, with the inadequacy of someone who's had no training trying to persuade a paranoid schizophrenic to put down an axe, and the audience wept with unsympathetic laughter as she made a series of attempts to recite her poem. The only time any sounds emerged that could realistically be categorised as words was when she said, 'Sprouts make you poo.'

So I introduced Alex, with a 'Follow that.' And Alex stared back at me. I tried to introduce him again, more slowly, aware that he may have been overawed or be having trouble with the language. Then he stood up and screamed, 'I am from POLAND!',

and it became clear he'd achieved the impressive feat of being even more drunk than Sandhra.

'What do you like most about Boston?' I asked, pathetically.

'I love SANDHRA!' he yelled. 'I LOVE her!'

'He don't mean like that. I'm married,' said Sandhra, rediscovering her ability to speak.

In a way it was a beautiful example of friendship across the cultures, of potentially diverse ethnic groups finding more to unite them than divide them, and as such should be celebrated as a homage to the Hanseatic League.

As well as its economic importance in the fourteenth century, Boston became one of the world's most important towns in the seventeenth century, as a centre of the rise of Puritanism. The radicalism of the Puritans was their insistence that rather than inhabit the earth in a hierarchy ordained by God, all men were equal before Him. This idea found an audience amongst the poor of Boston.

A local aristocratic family, the Penns, complained that 'no gentlemen, none but mean persons' were Puritans. A landowner agreed that most poachers were Puritans, because 'it's as if they wish no King to command them'.

The Church needed preachers, and the most enthusiastic people applying for the job were sympathetic to the Puritans. In 1612 the new vicar appointed to Boston was the Puritan John Cotton.

Cotton was called before the Church courts for preaching 'non-conformist' ideas, but he was so popular they didn't dare sack him, and hundreds of Puritans came to Boston, attracted by him. The King and the heads of the Church must have been furious. The man preaching every day in the biggest church in Britain was someone opposed to their very existence, and there wasn't anything they could do about it. It must have been as if the government today suddenly realised that the BBC weather reports were being read every night by George Galloway, who stood there going, 'Now, let me be abundantly clear. The on-going precipitation and relentless cascading of fluids from the heavens remains as inevitable as the obsequious lickspittle bleatings of Mr Cameron before the forces of murderous, rapacious imperialism. Now here's Alison with *tomorrow's* forecast.'

Eventually the royal family and the Church suspended anti-establishment preachers, and Cotton was sacked, 'upon special complaint to the King', for not kneeling during communion. It was around this time some Puritans decided on a change of tactics, which was to set up a new country in America. Between 1620 and 1640 about a fifth of Boston's population, including John Cotton, sailed to Massachusetts Bay, where they set up a new community which they called, imaginatively, Boston. One of the first batch to arrive was John Winthrop, who announced, 'We have been divinely ordained to build in New England a city upon a hill.'

Maybe all they really wanted was to live somewhere with a bit of a slope, where they could have their own driving lessons.

The Puritans who stayed behind became more rebellious. In the year before the Civil War began, the House of Lords ordered that landowners around Boston should evict people who were living on land that had been regarded as common. The people living there rioted for three days.

The Sheriff of Lincoln, Sir Edward Heron, tried to suppress this rebellion, but the commoners drove his people away, and filled in the dykes that had been built to enclose the land. When two of the rioters were arrested, a crowd of a thousand people besieged Lord Heron's office and threatened to demolish it, at which point the prisoners were released. It was reported that Lord Heron had to flee 'while the mob followed along the street throwing stones and dirt at him'. Local juries refused to convict anyone on trial for the riot, and the people were allowed to carry on living on the common land.

In 1642, when King Charles I declared war on Parliament, Boston was one of the most enthusiastic towns in the country for resisting him.

One of the most important battles took place when some Royalists came over from Holland to help the King, but troops from Boston seized them in Skegness and took them prisoner. The King went berserk and ordered Lord Heron to recapture them, but when he got to Boston he was arrested as well, and sent to the Tower of London. At this point the King made it 'illegal to aid Boston'. In some ways the people to feel most sorry for here are the Dutch Royalists, who arrived in England and saw two things – jail and Skegness.

Boston's history leaves a magnificent irony at the heart of the town. Here is a place struggling to settle an immigrant population, yet it gave its name to a city that was created by the planet's most famous wave of immigration, and that is a hundred times better-known than the original place.

There are other contradictions in a town that seems to alternate between global importance and Isthmian League obscurity every three hundred years or so. Few people outside the area visit it, maybe because it's stuck out on the east coast, so it's not on the way to anywhere. This has left Boston with a distinct feel, an endearing grubbiness, so the river is a proper river, with a filthy, muddy bank littered with broken rowing boats, and not a single square pink-gated riverside apartment. The town feels as if it has a past, and not just because there's a framed photo of a local mill owner in the Wetherspoon's. And everyone there adores the Stump. Because it's theirs, and only theirs.

There may be one more irony yet to play itself out in Boston. The early settlers made their homes by selecting patches of land marginally higher than everywhere else, so they would just avoid being ruined with every flood. Left to nature, the whole area would be marsh, but the incoming sea was drained by dykes, then kept out by windmills, then sluice gates and now vast pumps. But the water engineers who showed me round the pumping station acknowledged that rising sea levels will mean that in around a hundred years, 'We'll have to take a decision as to whether it's worth saving Boston.'

And when that happens, all of Lincolnshire will be wanting to come to the place, because while every other town is under fifty feet of water, in Boston they'll be able to cling to the top of the Stump, shouting down, 'Not laughing at us now, Spalding, are you? Shall we flick you down a packet of Richmond fags?'

Surrey

The first problem with Surrey is that no one knows what or where it's meant to be. Whereas Sussex, for example, is the bit between London and the sea, Surrey's a bit here and sort of towards there, the bits south of London that don't fit anywhere else, as if its real name should be Miscellaneous. Then it could include other chunks of the country that don't fit anywhere, like a bit sticking out of Leicester and the odd island off Northumberland. There's no sense of a connection between, say, Epsom and Farnham. It's just a pile of places that don't know each other. It's unlikely that any crowd has ever shouted, 'Surrey 'til I die, Surrey 'til I die, super Surrey super Surrey Surrey 'til I die.'

Even the cricket team plays at The Oval, by Vauxhall Bridge in central London, so that it would be just as accurate to call the team Denmark.

And the county stands for smug suburban comfort. Reggie Perrin lived in Surrey. The area known as the 'Stockbroker Belt' is in Surrey. It's not just wealthy, it's appallingly safe: if you hear police sirens wailing, they've probably been called out to deal with an incident in which someone cheated at bridge.

I went to Dorking one Saturday afternoon, and in the centre of the shopping area, where you would normally expect the Christian group and a bloke sent by the job centre to sell balloons, there was a poetry stall, a performance by the Dorking

Folk Club, a belly dancer, a gardening club and a Rachmaninov stall, staffed by the local Rachmaninov Society. If you wanted to stage a massive celebrity moment in Dorking you wouldn't get Britney Spears or George Clooney to wave at the crowd in the main square, you'd book the panel from *Gardeners' Question Time*. People would push feverishly forward for a glimpse, throwing gladioli and screaming with hysteria until they all hyperventilated and the St John Ambulance people had to put everyone's heads between their knees.

There's a skateboarding shop in the High Street, and even that's called 'The Boardroom'. There's a road called West Street that consists of one antique shop after another, and they're not the sort of places where you barter for a second-hand chest of drawers that might be handy for keeping your parking fines in one place. They're full of old globes and strange curvy uphol-stered things that turn out to be something like a chaise longue specially built by Prince Albert for his mistress who was a midget.

I found a quote from a Louis J. Jennings, who wrote of Dorking in 1877: 'Who could stand the weary strain of the small and narrow tone and depressing social atmosphere of such a spot? A man who came to live in Dorking would perish miser-ably of utter boredom and dry rot. The town is at all seasons one of the dullest in England, and for young people it must be intol-erable. There is scarcely anybody of their own age to associate with, no amusements, just the narrow influences that always grow in small gossipy places. Life is altogether stagnant.'

Which seems a little harsh for a place that within 125 years would have its own Rachmaninov stall. The centre of Dorking presents itself as proudly Victorian, so even the branch of Millets is in a curvaceous, elegant building, as you can still make out if you look above the display of hiking boots. After a couple of hours there you find yourself thinking, 'It's actually delightful. The posh, endearingly tactile women in the upmarket charity shops, the delicate cafés, the cosy ambience, the abundance of community projects – it's all thoroughly pleasant. For Christ's sake, let's go before it drives us nuts.'

South and a bit west is Cranleigh, which boasts that it's the biggest village in England. It's such a village that the spotless shops with their small square dainty windows look as if they're freshly painted every morning, and all of them have immaculate names such as 'Mr Seeley the opticians' written above the door in a font that looks as if it's been inscribed by Samuel Pepys. The main road feels as if it should be in a TV programme made for toddlers in 1965. The exquisitely presented butchers ought to be owned by a chortling man called Mr Brisket, and the quaint camera shop be run by Mr Aperture the photographer.

There's a pub called the Richard Onslow, with a board outside that would normally tell you that this Monday it was showing Fulham v Blackburn, but in Cranleigh it says, 'Every Monday is networking night. Free canapés, build your business contacts 6.00 to 7.30.'

There are several noticeboards in the village, to accommodate all the activities: there are announcements about choir practice, bridge evenings, a 'shabby chic clothes sale' which is Surrey-patois for jumble sale, a poster telling you 'Please park better' and an advert for an 'occult comedian' appearing at the village hall.

It must seem unfair that Surrey is labelled as dull, when Cranleigh Arts Centre puts on a series of Indian dancing classes. Surely that's the peak of community spirit, when someone can rush into a hall and splutter, 'Sorry I'm late everyone, darned sales conference overran and I missed my usual 5.48 from Waterloo,' and then step in line to place their hands together and move their head from side to side as if they're peering out from behind a tree.

And Surrey provides the visitor with dozens of specially crafted settings, rivers and herons and ambassadors' houses reflecting off sleepy ripples, with patches of trimmed grass by the bank that make you want to search for a chequered table-cloth so you can lay it down and have a picnic while laughing at the antics of a shaggy dog.

Walton-on-Thames has all this, and is where E.M. Forster lived, and some of *Three Men in a Boat* is set there, and it also has a claim to have been the location of the cricket match in the eighteenth century during which a ball went between the two stumps without dislodging the bail, so the rules were changed and the middle stump was invented. And none of this is surprising. When you first arrive you think, 'I wonder if this is the location of the cricket match where a ball went between the two stumps, resulting in a change of the rules. Ah, it is.'

But the shinier the surface of a place, the more certain there'll be an oily, grubby underneath. Thus, in the 1970s Walton-on-Thames provided enough teenage boredom not only to cultivate a punk scene, but to produce Jimmy Pursey and Sham 69, the most hard-core, rawest, punkiest punk of all, which had some of the most paid-up, zipped-up punks of all saying, 'Oo no, that's a bit *too* punk.'

Similarly, if more tunefully than 'Borstal Breakout', Woking, Surrey, created Paul Weller. And the copy of the *Surrey Advertiser* I bought on the day I visited Dorking contained a list of the fifteen most-read stories on its website, of which fourteen concerned violent crimes and the other one was 'Vandals Leave Guildhall Clock Chiming out of Time'. Surrey appears to contain a grumbling element that protests not despite the cosiness, but because of it. To put this another way, if Jimmy Pursey had been told, 'There's no need to be anti-social. If you're bored, why not join a gardening club or help out with a Rachmaninov stall?' it probably wouldn't have made much difference.

Adding to the sinister undercurrent rumbling beneath the shabby-chic clothes stalls is the advert that comes on every few minutes on the county's radio station, Jackie FM, which says, '107.8 – sponsored by Surrey Aquatics and Reptiles.' Presumably they've done their research and this has some effect, so that as a chief accountant's wife drives to the shops to pick up a Tudor commode she hears it and thinks, 'Oh yes, I could do with a lizard.'

In H.G. Wells' *War of the Worlds* a wounded Martian with a heat-ray lands in the Thames and warms up the whole river before escaping in a boat to Walton Bridge, where he was lucky not to have found himself captured by Surrey Aquatics and Reptiles.

Wells must have chosen his venue for a reason, and it may be he'd noticed that the flawless suburban landscapes and jolly communal activities hid a grubbier, but more fascinating edge to the vicinity.

It's got a history, this edge. In 1830 starving agricultural labourers rioted in Dorking until they were dispersed by cavalry, who could have directed them to the gardening club if they'd used their imagination. In Victorian times a town-wide game of football was played each year in which the object was to get the ball into the most unpleasant place in the town, such as the slaughterhouse offal heap in West Street, then brawl to get it out.

But most spectacular was the role of Walton-on-Thames during the English Civil War. As questions arose concerning the nature of monarchy, democracy and property, the religious reformer Gerrard Winstanley formed a group called the Diggers, who planned to set up a commune with the aim of sharing the land and its produce equally. They chose Walton-on-Thames as its location, partly because the town's population had over-whelmingly supported Parliament against the King.

The Diggers dressed as soldiers, as they had been in Cromwell's army, and marched into St Mary's parish church in Walton, announcing that in their society the Sabbath, tithes, ministers, magistrates and the Bible were all abolished. Then they moved onto common land on St George's Hill and set up their new world. They insisted that the land belonged to everyone rather than to the landowners, so a general was sent to disperse them, but the Diggers upset him by refusing to remove their hats because 'He is not superior but a fellow creature.' Anyone who's studied conflicts will be aware that if they couldn't reach agreement on the hat issue, there wasn't likely to be much progress on the matter of them taking over the land.

The movement sparked off similar communes, which were seen as a threat by Cromwell, so troops were sent and the Diggers' commune was demolished. But they're often seen as the first communists, and Winstanley is remembered in plays and songs and sometimes in exam questions.

The Diggers weren't just making a lifestyle choice: they saw their protest as an attempt to redefine how we see land and property, and to create a new world in which society produced goods collectively and owned them jointly, with all the rules of that society made in common as well. Winstanley's pamphlets about these issues still seem poignant and radical, and Walton-on-Thames remembers his contribution with a statue you are directed to by a blurred map you can get from the town hall. I drove up the road as directed, and past the spot where it looked as if it should be, and stood with the map at all angles and experienced that sensation you have when you can't find something on a map of feeling utterly stupid and saying, 'Or is this road that road and that road this path and we passed it and we're now in the river?'

Eventually I noticed a tiny structure, the size of a fire hydrant. I brushed aside some stinging nettles, and there was a lump of concrete on which was depicted a spade and some parsnips. Because that's how he should be remembered, as someone who, whatever his opinions, always turned out a lovely parsnip.

I tried to get to St George's Hill, but it's now a gated estate, and big gates as well, made of forbidding iron which suggests that if you rattled them a series of searchlights would come on and Al Pacino would appear on the roof with a sub-machine gun.

In 1999 some fans of the Diggers commemorated the original group's 350th anniversary by camping on the heath as near as they could to the original site. But their attempts to recreate the events of 1649 were made all the more authentic when a resident from the gated estate emerged from a black four-wheel-drive vehicle, punched a camper and then reversed at high speed towards a group of people by the entrance to the site.

So Surrey isn't at all one-sided and twee, it's still locked in a conflict that's lasted 350 years. If Gerrard Winstanley was to come back today he'd realise straight away that a great deal has changed, and that if he wanted to grow parsnips on St George's Hill now he'd need a division of fucking great tanks or he'd never get on there in the first place.

Merthyr Tydfil

Oh dear Lord, Merthyr Tydfil. There was one building I knew about in this South Wales town before I went there, which was the Wyndham Arms. I'd seen it on Sky One's *Britain's Roughest Pubs*, in which a group of men in their seventies were shown arguing about which of them ran off from a fight against a gang from Dowlais in 1959. 'I've never bottled a fight in my fucking life!' bellowed one of the pensioners, and to prove his point he did some press-ups in the middle of the floor. So to visit Merthyr without seeing the Wyndham Arms would be like going to Stonehenge but not bothering to see the stones.

Merthyr is about twenty-five miles from Cardiff, but the journey by rail takes two hours, as the train creeps through the valleys, stopping for unexplained periods, groaning as if it's mumbling, 'Oh bollocks, me back's gone again,' and defying the terrain like a truck built out of stolen lawnmower parts used by escapees from a Japanese prisoner-of-war camp as it clanks through the jungle.

But the journey does offer a comprehensive view of things that have been shut down. Pits, factories, shops, concrete huts that must have served some purpose before their metal door became a sheet of brown rust and the windows were ritually slaughtered. It's a shock when you see a stream, as it feels it ought to have barbed wire alongside and boards nailed over it.

The train eventually approaches Merthyr, and heads towards a Tesco that looks uncomfortably gigantic even by Tesco standards, as if it's got that disease that makes people unable to stop growing so they end up eight feet tall and used in adverts for *The Guinness Book of Records*. It appears at one point as if the train's descending into the Tesco, and that you're arriving at a version of Disneyland, where low-paid immigrants skip in line all day dressed as Tesco carrier bags, and students subsidise their education by dressing as tins of custard powder and waving at children while singing, 'We're three for the price of two because each penny counts for you.'

To start with I went to the library, where I'd been promised a selection of books for research on the town. But when I arrived, at around eleven in the morning, the woman I was supposed to meet was dealing with a lad of about twenty with a wispy semi-moustache who was shouting loudly into his mobile while walking in a circle. 'I'm – fucking – no – hang on – I – I haven't got his fridge, I told him I hadn't got his fucking fridge – who said I had his fridge?' he slurred between sups from a dark-blue tin, then collapsed onto the counter.

'No mobiles in here, love,' said the librarian, but she might as well have read out the clues from that day's *New York Times* crossword. So she gently grabbed his mobile and he shook slightly, then said, 'That's my you got took give me back I haven't got his fridge.'

'Sorry love, you're not allowed to talk on your mobile in the library,' she told him. Suddenly he looked slightly regretful, said, 'Oh, sorry, I didn't know I was in the fucking library,' and left. If Merthyr was a film it would have to be congratulated for establishing a style and characters right away, so you know what you're getting right from the beginning.

Over the road a woman was leaning against a wall shouting 'Bollocks!' over and over again, though she was clearly a social-minded sort, as she wasn't doing it in the library. Then, after a tour of the bus station and a closed ironworks I stepped into the Wyndham Arms. It consists of two connected rooms, one of them slightly raised, and around the walls are posters for the countless bouts fought by Merthyr's many champion boxers.

I couldn't help thinking, 'Wow, it looks just like it did on the telly,' as you might if you visited the Sphinx, except that a woman who looked eighty was in the middle of the room dancing to 'Dancing Queen' while a dozen others ignored her. Then 'Freebird' came on, and she was replaced by a man of around twenty-five in a denim jacket who howled, 'I'm as free-ee as a bi-ird now, and this bird you cannot tame,' then picked up one of his mate's crutches and used it to mime the guitar solo, getting down on one knee and biting his lip and rolling his head while moving his fingers rapidly up and down the holes in the crutch. No one appeared even to notice he was doing this. The barman carried on arranging boxes of crisps, although his mate did occasionally yell, 'Give me back my fucking crutch!'

A few weeks before, the local Hoover factory had shut down. It had employed 5,000 people in 1973, before reducing its work-force to three hundred over the next thirty-five years, each reduction accompanied by an insistence that the town must reluctantly accept the redundancies now, otherwise there could be even more later. Now the factory is the last shut object you pass before arriving in Merthyr, a vast wilderness of scattered washing machines destined to go nowhere, like a high-security prison for electrical appliances.

One consequence of crippling levels of unemployment is that a lot of people get drunk, but another is a fierce camaraderie amongst those who stay upright. So there's a popular website called 'Merthyr's a Toilet But We Love It', where you can read comments such as, 'I'm excited. I've heard Merthyr's getting a Nando's.'

And yet it was Merthyr that created modern Wales. From being a hamlet in 1750, it became bigger than Cardiff and

Swansea put together, the fourth largest town in Britain. In fact, at the start of the nineteenth century it was growing quicker than anywhere else in the world, because of its iron industry, fed by coal deposits to the south. People moved here from across Britain, and in around 1810 2,000 Spaniards moved over from Bilbao.

Merthyr's four huge ironworks were among the earliest monuments of the Industrial Revolution, and the regular wages they promised sucked in a mass of humanity from rural areas across Europe. But the owners of the ironworks, known as the masters, weren't so keen on providing the facilities that might make the place more like a town than an illegal rock festival, so they rejected the idea of installing luxuries such as toilets. According to one of the major landlords, Josiah Atkins, the reason the houses had no toilets was 'I do not think the people want toilets.'

One in five babies didn't survive; there was a cholera epidemic, then typhoid. One book about the history of the town, *Iron Metropolis*, has a chapter titled 'Disease, Debility and Death', that graphically describes the details of disease, debility and death, and then says, 'Before moving on, we should first mention some of the darker sides of life.'

Merthyr's squalor was something new: it wasn't the common rural poverty of the past, but a new urban, industrial poverty that wouldn't reach its peak until 170 years later, when cities such as São Paulo, Mumbai and Mexico City attracted millions who could no longer make a living on the land, and left many of the new arrivals to fester in slums, as if in touching homage to Merthyr.

Two institutions thrived in this congestion and filth: the pub and the Church. One in six houses became a pub, and among the town's characters were men such as Thomas Thomas, who was barred from the Farmer's Arms because, according to the landlord, 'He has an artificial limb, and if refused beer he smashes the tables with his iron arm.'

113

The Church was not so keen on the inhabitants finding the odd moment of pleasure. For example, a choir leader was disciplined for 'taking his children for a walk on a Sunday', suggesting that if Osama bin Laden had met the leaders of that Church he'd have said, 'The trouble with you is you're *too* religious.'

But the Church split, between the official body, which urged acceptance of authority, and a dissenting branch that questioned whether cholera and a refusal to give people toilets was entirely in keeping with the teachings of Jesus. The new Church encouraged its followers to read the writings of the revolutionary Tom Paine, whereas some in the congregations of Merthyr's established Church had their bootnails arranged in a 'TP' shape, so that with every step they would 'trample the infidel Tom Paine into the dirt'.

In 1831 one ironmaster, William Crawshay, cut the wages of his employees. The rumbling discontent that erupted was centred around the issue of the truck system, whereby ironworkers had to spend most of their wages buying stuff from the company store. These stores relied on a body called the Court of Requests, which could refer anyone who owed money to the company store to a bailiff, who would take away your furniture, then your watch, then your bed.

The events that followed should be studied by whoever sends out those letters that arrive if you don't pay the gas or electric bill or your council tax within forty minutes of it arriving, with a sinister red and black heading in bold capital letters saying 'DO NOT IGNORE!!! PAY NOW!!!!' and then informing you that as well as the unpaid bill for £28.76 you must also pay £6,376.89 for bailiffs' fees and court costs 'IMMEDIATELY!!!!! *DON'T THINK WE'RE JOKING, SHITFACE, LOOK OUT THE WINDOW – RECOGNISE THAT HAMSTER? IT'S OUR BITCH NOW UNLESS YOU PAY UP!!!!!'*

The Merthyr bailiffs went for the property of Lewis Lewis, a miner from Penderyn. His neighbours blockaded his house and the bailiffs could only grab one trunk of his belongings, but the crowd grabbed it back and lifted Lewis Lewis onto it to make a speech. From there they marched to the office of the Court of Requests and threw firebombs through the President's window.

The next morning, a crowd met up near the Castle Inn, and set off to visit the town's bailiffs and get back all the stuff that had been confiscated. They went to a hundred bailiffs and pawnbrokers, and then to the house of an old shoemaker called Phelps, shouting at him to come with them and get back his watch and Bible that had been confiscated. But Phelps, in one of those moments at which individuals refuse to roll with a historic moment, told the crowd he couldn't come as he was finishing the repairs to a shoe.

Eventually his wife persuaded him to go. They smashed down the door of the offending bailiff and Mrs Phelps grabbed the bailiff's wife, screaming, 'Bring me the watch or the mob will come in!'

Mrs Bailiff said she didn't know where the watch was, so the crowd ran in, found it, and the Bible, and everything else that had been confiscated. The magistrates arrived and read the Riot Act, and sent a message to Cardiff appealing for 'every soldier we can get hold of'. Highland troops were dispatched. By now the crowd was up to 10,000. They elected delegates, who went to the magistrates to put in a series of demands, including an end to the Court of Requests, higher wages and for the price of bread to be reduced by half. They flew a red flag, which became the symbol of the labour movement across the world, and chanted 'We want cheese with our bread,' which didn't catch on quite as much.

The crowd surged forward and seized the muskets of the front ranks of soldiers. Troops positioned in the Castle Inn started firing, killing over twenty demonstrators. As word got out, the whole of Merthyr formed into mini regiments, raiding shops for guns and ammunition with which to try to take over the town.

The army sent for the Swansea division of the yeomanry, but as the troops arrived the rebels stood on the hills above the road and rolled huge rocks down on them. The commander of the government troops, Major Penrice, was captured. For four days these battles went on, with the rebels taking control of the town until the army was reinforced by enough troops to win back authority. At the end of it all, maybe there was a knock on the door of Mr Phelps, and someone said, 'Is my bloody shoe ready yet? You said you'd have it done four days ago.'

Afterwards the authorities were wary of being too vicious with their retribution, in case they sparked off another uprising, but they did charge one of the crowd's delegates, Richard Lewis, with bayoneting a soldier, who wasn't killed and couldn't identify him. But Lewis, who was also known as Dic Penderyn, was hanged.

The rebels didn't feel they'd been crushed, and Dic Penderyn became a local hero, because as the historian Gwyn Alf Williams said, 'His was not a face *above* the crowd, his was the face *in* the crowd.'

In the weeks that followed the hanging, some of those who had taken part in the battle organised the first secret trade union meetings, and so Merthyr's uprising played a part in shaping the Britain of the next 170 years. It also created a problem for Wetherspoon's.

When the Merthyr Tydfil Wetherspoon's was opened it was to be called the William Crawshay, after the ironmaster. But a campaign began, launched by the local historical society, demanding that the pub should be named the Dic Penderyn. The company employed the usual arguments dispatched from head offices when their routine is challenged: 'Dear Sir/Madam, We thank you for your letter regarding something we did that has angered you and everyone you know, but we are unable to change what we did as that is the way we do things. However, we value you as a valuable customer and look forward to ignoring you again in the future.'

Letters were sent to local papers, protests promised, a campaign of furious messages sent to Wetherspoon's, and the result is that you can now drink cheap bitter round a shiny table in the Dic Penderyn.

Since the initial explosion of industry Merthyr has been devastated regularly, like an economic version of one of these places in the South Pacific that's always getting knocked over by a hurricane. The 1936 Means Test reduced unemployment benefit from fifteen shillings to five shillings for many people. In response, women in Merthyr organised a march of 3,000 unemployed to the unemployment benefit office, Iscoed House. When they got there, according to one marcher's account, 'They smashed all the windows. The police came but they were helpless. The demonstrators went inside, pulled the stairs away, and all the records were flung in a heap.'

Maybe they should have made an advert afterwards that went: 'Benefit offices – we're closing in.'

This led to some of the new rules being scrapped, but it didn't endear the town to the authorities. So in 1939 a think tank called Political and Economic Planning proposed 'the evacuation of the whole town to the Glamorgan coast. It does not seem reasonable to ask the rest of Britain to pay taxes to give large numbers of people the doubtful pleasure of living in one of the least habitable districts of England and Wales.' This, I would imagine, is unique: that plans are drawn up to shut a place down entirely, not as a result of ethnic cleansing or to turn it into a military base or a site for drilling for oil, but because the government considers it a dump.

Maybe the officials visited the pub I went to, where the landlord told me proudly, 'See that piano? I found that in the fucking road, I did.' Three lads were singing 'We Will Rock You' on the karaoke, holding each other up the way an old car can be held together by rust. 'Bigerbeg disgerace waving over perler perlace', they sang, and then one collapsed, bringing down the rest. From there I went for a curry. The waiter took my order for poppadoms and asked, 'Is this your first time in Merthyr?'

'I've been once before,' I said, trying to sound familiar.

'This is a terrible place. Please take my advice and don't stay,' he said. 'Starter?'

The recording for the radio show was in the only place available, a room in one of those further-education colleges built in the 1970s that looks like somewhere you sit all day before claiming invalidity benefit, and has walls you daren't lean on in case they're made out of cardboard. The café was an empty white room with one yoghurt, a very old banana and a till. But the audience was from the stoic wing of the town, with boxers and singers and the local history group among them, as this wouldn't be where someone would come to get smashed and sing a medley from Queen.

Until I mentioned Tesco. Before I'd said anything about it, just the word itself set off a cry from the middle of one row of 'Don't you fucking knock Tescos. That's saved this town, that place, I love that place, I fucking love Tescos,' from someone waving a tin of beer in random directions, as if using it to imitate the flight path of a bluebottle.

'Not now, Steve,' said his friend.

'What? Fucking Tescos, there's a fucking Tescos,' was the next cry. This carried on for ten minutes, during which time we were never to return to this level of coherence. Occasionally there'd be a yell of, 'Saved this town, Tescos has fucking saved this town,' so in the end I said, 'I tell you what mate, you've convinced me.

Tesco has saved this town, and I shan't mention anything bad about it again.'

'What?' he said. 'I fucking hate Tescos.'

As a punchline it was flawless. 'Fucking Tescos,' he went on to explain, 'didn't have any fucking beer-battered chips. I wanted beer-battered chips and they didn't have any beer-battered fucking chips. I fucking hate Tescos,' he confirmed.

Eventually his mate persuaded him to leave the room and pursue this line of thought somewhere else.

But Merthyr can't just be a shithole, or everyone would have left. Even Dowlais, the bleakest section of the town, with record-breaking levels of poverty, the only place in the world where if you tell them you're from the centre of Merthyr they'll say, 'Ooo, there's posh. I suppose you spend your evenings at the Wyndham Arms, Mr La-di-da Merthyr,' has a resilience within. Part of this is expressed through singing: the Dowlais Male Voice Choir displays the vigour and competitive edge of an American football squad. They train and practise almost every day, and perform at international festivals that seem to be the equivalent of the Olympics in the world of male voice choirs. At one point they performed in a concert with Donny Osmond.*

And there's the attachment to boxing. There's Howard Winstone, who became world featherweight champion despite losing the tips of three of his fingers, and poor Johnny Owen who was killed in the ring, and Eddie Thomas, European welterweight champion, who said, 'When boys in Merthyr are born they come out with clenched fists.'

But they all stayed in Merthyr. It seems that the prouder someone is – and few people exude more pride than either a singer in a male voice choir or a champion boxer – the more adamant they are about remaining in the town that was threat-

---

* I know you don't believe me, so look it up on Google.

ened with being shut down, and that seems to have gone down-hill from there. Eddie Thomas, who became a boxing manager and earned the description 'successful businessman', became mayor of the town rather than move.

The dominant attitude of Merthyr Tydfil seems to be, 'How do we pull together through this?' rather than 'How do I escape this?' So the librarian will evict the drunk intruder with firm compassion, rather than yell at him or call the police.

There are statues of the prominent boxers from the town, and of Dic Penderyn, and there's always a chuckle of contempt at the word 'Cardiff', as if to say, 'That's not proper Wales,' and a sense that Merthyr might be a dump, but it's *our* dump.

When I went to Merthyr for the radio show I stayed at the only hotel, called the Castle, on the site where the worst of the shooting took place in 1831. The smell of chip fat seeped into every corner of every room, and in defiance of the laws of geom-etry every window looked out onto the 'Everything a Pound' shop. Next door was the pub with the found piano, from where the sound of the evening's entertainment would drift through the hotel, the low rumble punctuated by cries of 'Yabafuckaragabolloxinbereber!' as something or someone fell and crashed, leaving you to ponder what or who had fallen over and broken this time.

But the young women who worked in the hotel were foun-tains of cheery assistance, perky apologies for the place's failings pouring out of them. 'Oooo, sorry, I'm afraid we've no eggs left. If you like, when I've got a minute I can pop up the shops and get some,' said one of them, displaying the teenage girl's sympa-thy face that can also be used when a stranger in a nightclub toilet tells them their boyfriend has run off with their dad. 'I can try and get someone to fix the TV for you,' they'd say, and you could see they were thinking, 'Who do I know who's ever fixed a TV? What about Gareth, my aunt's next-door neighbour? He's a car mechanic, it can't be that different.'

Merthyr jolliness is possibly the most hardened jolliness in Britain, a superjoy that an army couldn't overcome, but instead would scream, 'We keep firing misery, sergeant, but it bounces straight off them.'

Edinburgh

Edinburgh is a city built on two levels, at every level. It's the city of twee kilty woollenness, of quaintly tiled cafés and Morningside ladies with their catchphrase 'Ye'll have had yer tea?' And it's the city of *Trainspotting*, of poverty and the highest rates of drug addiction in Britain, where maybe, on the Muirhouse estate, the dealers stand by the stairwells asking passers-by, 'Ye'll have had yer crack?'

The genteel side has beaten the grubbier side to be the dominant image. So even Burke and Hare, the nineteenth-century grave robbers and murderers who supplied anatomists with corpses are seen as a fun pair, the sort of kindly knockabout grave robbers and murderers you only get in Edinburgh, not like in Glasgow, where the grave robbers and murderers can have quite an unpleasant side.

Edinburgh has witnessed vast convulsions and great heroes, writers, rebels, warriors and pioneers that transformed the world, so its most celebrated figure is Greyfriars Bobby, a bloody dog that apparently visited his master's grave every day after he died for fourteen years. Because if Alexander Graham Bell wanted to make a contribution worth remembering, that is what *he* would have done instead of wanking about with telephones.

From the 1500s the Grassmarket and Cowgate were built lower than the rest of the city, in a valley where cows could be led, and the poor bustled around at this level, nicely contained where those above could look down at them from the bridges and hope there was some sort of powder they could put down to stop an infestation of them creeping up to their level.

Edinburgh is a city with a prestigious university, which makes the student population a mix of those delighted to be there, and those whose parents dropped them off saying, 'Look, we *tried* to get you into Oxford and Cambridge, darling, but the beasts said your results weren't good enough. Now here's your spray, cover yourself in it all over if any of these working types brush past you and you shouldn't suffer a reaction.'

It's almost unnecessarily stunningly dramatic, with a huge castle and a mountain in the middle of the town. You emerge from Waverley station and look up at the cobbles that lead to the castle, and it feels as if you're in an adventure that won't end until you've found a relative long since believed to be dead who lives in a room in an alleyway called Cribbet's Close, making sporrans for the Edinburgh Woollen Mill Company, and you have to inform him that you've received a letter stating he's the new King of Bulgaria.

Current town planners must wonder what vandal designed the place like this, when castles are so obviously supposed to be on the edge of the town, with maybe just a wall surviving as one side of the Castle Shopping Centre.

It's not just the castle, the middle of the town is all dramatic. Every few yards off the main streets there are musty alleys rumoured to be packed with ghosts, and at various points there are flights of chunky concrete steps with no sign of where they lead, that seem likely to pass through a cloud and emerge into a world of goblins run by a talking squirrel.

Opposite the station is the Walter Scott Monument, a mesmerising structure shaped like Thunderbird 3 and the sort of building through which Harry Potter escapes from evil lengths of bindweed.

Most of the accommodation in the centre seems to be in flats in grand stone terraced buildings with old solid buzzers for each apartment outside on the wall, firm and slightly green through corrosion. You press them with the assumption that they can't possibly work, as they're hundreds of years old, or that they will cause a nearby bookcase to swivel round and reveal steps leading to a cavern full of treasure.

Inside the building is a flight of steps with two flats on each floor, all with kids' bikes outside chunky doors set in thick immovable stone. There could be an earthquake in the centre of Edinburgh and these places would barely creak.

From a road by the main swimming pool you can walk up Arthur's Seat, the dormant volcano from where you can look across the city like a Greek god. This is especially exhilarating because climbing a steep, rocky mountain releases a chemical in the brain that makes you a smug self-righteous bastard for the rest of the day. So the woman in Scotmid grocers might ask, 'How are you today?' and you'll reply, 'I've been up Arthur's Seat.' Or if instead she says, 'Have you got anything smaller than a £10 note?' you'll say, 'I haven't had a chance to get much change. You see, I've been up Arthur's Seat.'

Everything in the town is ridiculously sturdy. Buildings such as Fettes College and the Assembly Rooms are mighty, solid, permanent landmarks, made up of chunky pillars and vast black doors that will still be there long after a nuclear holocaust or if the sun collapses.

Every town has its rich and poor, but Edinburgh has the highest concentration of millionaires in any city in Britain, and in some areas the greatest levels of poverty. The United Nations judged it to be one of the ten most dangerous cities in Europe. From the centre of town this seems inconceivable, unless sometimes a team of archers emerges from the castle and fires arrows randomly into Princes Street Gardens.

If you're not part of the level that's dangerous, Edinburgh offers a constant cosy revelry. Whatever the time, when a bar closes, someone will call out the name of one they think is still open, and a few people wander round there. When you arrive it's packed, with thirty people squashed over the bar waving wads of Scottish pound notes, and a guitarist playing in a corner while his drummer's sat on the table with a conga.

I tested this theory once when I was at the festival, with results that have almost certainly guaranteed that whenever it is I expire, it will be two years earlier than if I'd stayed in that night.

I met Mark Lamarr at the Assembly Rooms in George Street at six o' clock in the evening, and we stayed at the bar until it closed, when a stranger shouted the name of a pub in Cowgate that was staying open late for anyone willing to take part in the céilidh, a Celtic country-dancing evening. This is the sort of thing that's normal on a night out in Edinburgh. Word spreads that there's a bar at the aquarium on Dundas Street and they're having an all-night tadpole and cider party, so everyone drifts up there and carries on. It seemed the most obvious response to go to the new venue, without considering that it would be part of a harrowing documentary if the narrator said sombrely, 'At one point things became so bad, to get another drink they were willing to humiliate themselves by country dancing.' So we country danced until the place shut, then got a cab to Leith.

Leith used to be a separate town, a mile or so down the road from the main city. People from Edinburgh would walk there with their families and suitcases for their holiday. Now it has bars that stay open when the country-dancing pub shuts.

That night, it got to four in the morning and I felt that strange sense of achievement, that while all those lazy bastards are asleep it was lucky *someone* put in an effort to keep drinking. The drunkenness gives way to a murky tiredness you mistake for being philosophical, and when it starts to get light you think, 'I've done it. I've stayed up all night, I've *done* something with my life.' But the bar shut at five and someone shouted the name of a pub back in the centre that opened early for the postmen.

There are a few pubs like this in Edinburgh, most famously the Penny Black, and for years I accepted that they did indeed open early for postmen, until I realised that this made no sense, as postmen may get up and start their round early, but that doesn't mean they need a pub open, unless they've got a very strong union that's negotiated a working day in which they all get up and immediately go to the pub.

Still, these places are famous for being neighbourly and lively at five in the morning, so when we got there I put some money in the jukebox, but instead of my choices seven consecutive Eagles tracks came on. I stood up defiantly and called out, 'Who keeps putting on the bloody Eagles?' Because if the Civil Rights movement taught us anything, it's the importance of having the courage to make a stand.

'I did,' said a huge man, with a shirt that suggested he was a lumberjack. And by way of an explanation he added, 'I – LIKE – the Eagles.' He walked over, looked me in the eye with one eye while the other pointed at a variety of random points in the room, as if it was a laser on a rifle searching for its target. Then he squeezed me and insisted I sang the chorus to 'Hotel California' with him, although the jukebox was now playing 'Take it to the Limit'.

We sat on the fag-burned plastic seats that were perfect for the situation, and a man on his own in the next seat fiddled in his pocket, maybe for his wallet, or some tobacco, but it clearly mattered a great deal to him, and we were intrigued. Eventually he pulled out a voice machine, a box that enabled him to speak, which he put to his throat, and in the tone enforced by his condition, that metallic 1960s robot sound, he said, 'Wanker.'

'What? Me?' I asked.

'Wan-ker,' he said.

Now I was glad he'd found his box as quickly as he did. Imagine how awkward we'd have been feeling if we'd had to crawl round the floor, poking under seats and making sure he'd checked all his pockets, then eventually found it had fallen inside the lining in his jacket, and I'd patronisingly said, '*There* we are, I knew we couldn't have lost it. Now, what did you want to say?' And he'd put it to his throat and said, 'Wanker.'

I asked what had upset him, and whether he was a fan of the Eagles, but he just spoke drunken gibberish, through a voicebox. I realised that one of the problems of speaking through these things is that it's such a palaver to get the box in place, with everyone watching and waiting, that what you've got to say has to be something dramatic and poignant to justify the tension. I don't suppose people in need of those boxes ever put it to their throat and say, 'Dearie me, I keep thinking it's Tuesday.'

There is a world where this is all normal, and the portal to that world is only accessible in the all-night drinking sessions available in Edinburgh.

From there we clocked up all the ingredients of the all-night drink. We chatted to a woman who burst into tears, then a student threatened us with a fork. By now the people of the town were at work, having a whole new day, whereas for us it was still yesterday, creating the philosophical dilemma of whether we were in tomorrow.

We moved to an Italian bar that served breakfast, and then on to the filthiest, most squalid bar we could find, on the Lothian Road, where no one else was in, there wasn't and never had been any light, and which was possibly part of Edinburgh's contribution to science as the place where someone invented TB.

And the landlord came over and told us off for swearing. It was the nearest I've ever got to the feeling I expect you have if you get to the top of Mount Everest. I'd gone as far as I could go. I was in one of the most uncouth places in the universe, and had been told off for being uncouth.

Later on, at around four in the afternoon, everything went fuzzy and my head collapsed on the table. I was probably like that for two minutes, until the landlord grabbed my hair and pulled me up, and said, 'We don't have many fucken rules in here, son, but the one we do have is if you canna stay awake you have to fucken leave.' So we decided to be sensible and call it a day, as it's always healthy to have an early night.

While I take a small amount of responsibility for this debauchery, the main culprit was Edinburgh. It does it to you. There's an undercurrent of bohemian ribaldry that's always trying to lure you, as if it's saying, 'You can't go to bed yet, not when I've gone to all the trouble of getting a mountain and a castle in the middle of the town.'

And there are the festivals, for theatre, television and books, and sometimes you discover one you've never noticed before, like the International Sword-Swallowing Festival. They last through all of August and dominate everything, so every bus and taxi and wall is covered in adverts for shows, the main streets are clogged with enthusiastic performers trying not to look desperate as they offer leaflets for their show, and every back room is turned into a theatre. I went to a show once in the basement of someone's house, in which there was a set of cricket stumps and an actor in cricket whites delivering a monologue that started, 'The Ashes – a cricketing prize, and yet they remind me of the ashes of my poor departed father.' Then he played a shot and ran to the end of the room and back for two runs, and then did a bit more. Throughout it all he must have been terrified his wife might come in and say, 'Sorry love, I'm looking for the weedkiller.'

Thousands of people in the city rent out their homes in August, to performers and tourists. It must feel as if the soul of the place is let to the festivals. For some people it must be like being parents who have let their teenage son have a party in the house, as they hover about trying not to get in the way, but can't help peering round the door occasionally to check that no one's tipped up the Scott Monument.

And there's another level of Edinburgh in August, that exists alongside but in a different dimension from any of those others, which is the international tourists, thrilled by the Tattoo and the bagpipe players who play all day at the station, as ridiculous as if all London rail terminals employed someone to play 'My Ol' Man Said Follow the Van' on a broken piano, and tell everyone who got off a train that Reggie Kray was a diamond.

These visitors filter down the Royal Mile that leads from the castle, and presumably buy the dolls in kilts and tartan jumpers that pack every shop in the road. A friend who lives in the city told me she'd actually heard an American say, 'You'd think they'd have built the castle nearer to the shops.'

Edinburgh pulsates again with all these layers for New Year. From the day before New Year's Eve the centre of the town is redesigned, with barriers and cones placed along the edge of every road, signs telling everyone where they can't go springing up in all directions, and official-looking trucks drifting by and stopping every few yards for twelve men in uniform to get out and do something important with a red and white plastic portable wall and some tape. If anyone wanted to stage a coup in Scotland they should do it on New Year's Eve, as you could demolish the Parliament and everyone would assume the tanks were part of the preparation for Hogmanay.

These rules were introduced in 2005, when the event ceased to be free and you needed a ticket to get into Princes Street, and a special ticket to get into the gardens. Early in the evening stewards clear the whole city centre, unless you're in the sort of uniform that entitles you to place cones in the road, and no one's allowed back in without the appropriate ticket. Edinburgh becomes like a giant rock gig, with everyone entitled to move about only as far as the colour of their wristband allows. One

year my family considered hiding, as firework-display stowa-
ways, by locking ourselves in the toilet in Starbucks overnight,
or knocking a truckload of cone operatives unconscious and
stealing their uniforms, because otherwise when the festivities
start, if you haven't paid to stand in the street you have to
leave.

You can understand how the corporate world must be infu-
riated by Edinburgh, as so many of its main attractions are
natural and free. You can enjoy a wholesome Edinburgh experience by admiring the castle, the Georgian architecture, the
cobbled crescents and eerie alleyways, and no one makes a
penny. There must be all manner of think tanks and committees dedicated to correcting this injustice. They've probably
considered electric fences and a tollgate on Arthur's Seat, a
'vista charge' by which cameras spot anyone looking up while
in Princes Street and send them a bill (although as a gesture of
goodwill anyone being carried into an ambulance on a stretcher
will be considered exempt), and an atmosphere supplement,
involving seven bands of charges payable as you leave the
centre, which depend on how genial the atmosphere is in any
given two-hour period, ranging from £4.50 when there are
three or more bagpipe players out, down to 30 pence if there's
an incident with a student and a fork.

The clone-town process that dominates most cities has found
ways of seeping into Edinburgh. The Waverley Shopping Centre
is a classic gloomy and generally disliked huddle of depression
attached to the station, which drones to the beat of Magic FM
oozing past the Vodafone store and between the paninis, so it
always seems like late on a Sunday afternoon in there, and when
you emerge into the street in front of the station it will be the
only time in your life that you mouth the words, 'Aah that's
better – bagpipes.'

Similarly, the new cinema complex in Leith Walk looks as if
it was put together in a factory on an industrial estate by the

branch of MFI that builds cinemas. Then it was slotted into the street by a couple of blokes who delivered it in a van, after which the local manager had to put together the giant Bugs Bunny, using an unclear diagram and a packet of bolts, and build the counter where you buy a bucket of lemonade.

Or there's the issue of the trams. If anyone in the city speaks to you about trams you become aware that the full phrase is 'tram fiasco'. To say, 'Edinburgh tram' without the 'fiasco' is a grammatical error, like referring to the world's most famous painting as the *Mona*.

By the start of 2011 the scheme had used up 78 per cent of its budget in completing 26 per cent of the system. The main route appeared to be from the airport to Leith; the adverts would presumably say: 'From the airport a few miles outside the city centre, the new super-efficient tram system will take only 40 minutes to transport you deep into the heart of somewhere else only a few miles from the city centre.'

£600 million was paid to contractors to little effect, while the whole town was dug up and left with holes all over it. A typical letter in the *Scotsman* said: 'If they go ahead and finish this project we should have the trams painted white and named after different elephants, such as Nellie and Dumbo.'

It would be hard to imagine a more universally hated local policy. If a town council insisted on tigers roaming loose in children's playgrounds, or contracting out car-parking enforcement to the North Korean army, it would be more popular than the upheaval of the half-built wreckage of the tram project.

It could be argued that this is fitting, as it was Edinburgh that laid out much of the ideology of the modern world of business. In the eighteenth century Adam Smith began lecturing in the city about economic theories to explain the workings of profit. David Hume wrote his philosophical outlines for this new world of business there. Then Edinburgh figures such as James Watt and Alexander Graham Bell made their crucial breakthroughs, that can appear as classic capitalist success stories, so making a few bob with little regard to how it affects the poor might seem central to the city's spirit.

But the scientists, physicians and theorists of this time were known as the Edinburgh Enlightenment, a part of the European movement to explain each aspect of society in rational terms, rather than relying on the view that anything could be reduced to God's will, or that power was due to whoever was born into a higher rank of nobility. The city flowed with their notions of this grand new world. Adam Smith wrote that part of the working man's wage must give him access to adequate leisure, and they held a vision of a society in which everyone would admire and participate in the ingenuity and artistry that underpinned modern humanity.

If they returned to Edinburgh now, they might imagine that the city had resolved its human problems. They could look down at the Grassmarket and instead of the poor, they'd see restaurants and theatres. They probably wouldn't realise that you need a taxi or an infrequent bus to get to the outer ring of the city, where they would see the estates, the danger, the other Edinburgh, renowned as the 'AIDS capital of Europe', the junkies, the inspiration for *Trainspotting*, the layer that has been carefully placed on the outside, hidden from view with such care.

I'm aware that this may be romantic nonsense, but I suspect that Adam Smith, David Hume, James Watt and Walter Scott would still love Edinburgh, its view of the Forth Bridge, its imposing crescents and pillars and balconies and Morningside ladies asking, 'Ye'll have had yer tea?' But they'd ignore the Vue cinema, and Walter Scott would write a stern letter to the council about the bagpipe man playing opposite his monument. Then they'd sneak into beautifully awful plays in the festival and get pissed in squalid pubs in the Lothian Road, being ordered out for swearing during an argument about the nature of gold as a global currency, or barred when the landlord growled, 'We don't have many rules in here, but if you fall asleep while Mr Hume's opining on the separation of mind from body ye have ta fucken leave.'

Orkney

The top of Britain seems like a fault in the design. It's a huge long extra bit that goes on and on for no reason, taking up eight unnecessary pages at the end of your national road atlas. Surely Inverness is far enough to have anywhere, isn't it? But then there's another 120 miles that's pointless.

It's not that the top bits are too far or too north, they're just empty. That might be excusable if they were on the way to somewhere, but as they're the last bit they're a waste of mountains.

You feel slightly uneasy once you pass Inverness, as if your insurance won't cover you up there. There are miles and miles of nothingness, punctuated by odd villages made up of a farm, a stream, a grey housing estate and an industrial building behind a padlocked green gate. As you approach the very end of the country there's a vast wind farm covering the hills, from where you expect to hear whoopy sirens and an echoey voice booming, 'An intruder has entered the Kingdom of Highlandius,' as robots surround the car and march you underground to meet their leader.

Then comes Thurso, the small town that sits near the top of Scotland like a night-time security guard, keeping lookout in the stillness, and just past there is Scrabster, which is a cliff and a place to get the boat to Orkney. A blue bus trundles up to the port, and you imagine that if you asked the driver where to get the ferry, he'd say, 'Ferry? But it's Christmas Eve 1935.'

A couple of trucks join you in the queue for the ferry, which is next to a hut with one of those visitor centres that's not only shut but has clearly never ever been open. After twenty minutes in the queue as the rain gets heavier you realise you've no guarantee this is the queue for the ferry, you've just assumed it. You get out to peer through the downpour at a nearby sign which you imagine will give you some information, but it's full of regulations about transporting pigs, so you walk back drenched, and wait a while longer in the car.

Once you're on the ferry you feel like a proper explorer, leaving the top of Scotland behind, as if you're breaking all the rules and there ought to be people calling at you, 'Stop – no one's ever been up there and come back.' That's the glory of Orkney: it's a place where the directions are to get to John o'Groats and then do something else. When someone from Orkney reads about those people who cycle from Land's End to John o'Groats they must think, 'Lazy bastards. They never made it to here.'

You can seek comfort by the bar, or try to play a fruit machine as it tips up with the waves, but for the true experience you must go out on deck and see strange, uninhabited islands emerge through mist and rain, and as the foam and sleet merge into a combined assault on your ability to stand or see, you feel an urge to write a diary entry that starts: 'It was six days since we last ate, at the base camp at Inverness, and we began to discuss eating the weak ones.'

After the ferry had swung into Stromness I drove past treeless watery fields to the capital, Kirkwall, where I was welcomed with a distinctly Orkney greeting three times in the first hour: 'So you made it to the island then?' The wonderful implication is that many people who try are never seen again. It's a sentiment that carried itself into the radio show, where I got the biggest ovation I've ever received at the start, which was clearly nothing to do with the show but acclaim for having got there.

I expect the reviews of shows there go something like, 'It was a virtuoso five-star performance, in that he turned up. This was so much more powerful than last week's production of *The Crucible*, which gave up and did the show in Scrabster.'

Kirkwall has a population of about 5,000, but it fools you because you know it's the capital, and the biggest town in the entire geopolitical region. So you start at one end, get to the first shops and think, 'Ah, we're getting near the centre,' then there's a farm and a country lane and you realise you've been through it. Its character isn't so much determined by being small, as by being remote. Normally in a town that size you can get in a car or train and go to a place so populated it has two sets of traffic lights, but Kirkwall *is* the big town. If there's something you can't get there, you won't get it by nipping up the road to the peat bog where they've got a much wider selection.

There are two main roads in Kirkwall, one that passes the harbour and a parallel one with the few shops, some of which improvise by taking on more than one role. For example, the pram shop, which exhibits an impressive array of prams, buggies and baby baths in the window, has a sign above the door saying the premises is licensed to sell beer, wines and spirits. I went inside, past the sterilisers, cots and nappies, to find a fully stocked off licence.

'Are you looking for anything in particular?' I was asked.

I said, 'Hmm, I can't make my mind up between a pram and a bottle of whisky.'

'Well, we've got both here,' said the shopkeeper, as if this was a normal request, and people often wander in for a bottle of rum and then say, 'I tell you what, while we're here we might as well conceive a child, as we're in the ideal place for a pram.'

It takes a while to acclimatise. I naïvely asked in the newsagent for a newspaper, and the man said, 'No papers before 11.30,' with the disdain of someone who runs a provisions hut in the

Tibetan mountains responding to a tourist who's come in demanding a decaffeinated mocha coffee with semi-skimmed milk.

Tom, who runs the museum, told me he was taking his kids out shopping the next day. I assumed he meant taking them off to the shops, to a shopping centre that had shops. A while later I said, 'Hang on – where are you taking them shopping?'

'Just along here,' he said, gesturing to the High Street. Maybe in Kirkwall kids get excited about a day out in the street where they spend their entire life anyway, stringing out the process of buying a baby's car seat long enough for the *Daily Express*es to arrive.

There are about twenty shops in the town centre, but not only are there few chain stores, the type of shops they have make you wonder whether it was designed at a mad planning conference where everyone had a cupful of magic mushrooms as they went in. Apart from the pram and whisky shop, there's a wool shop, a toy shop, three cafés, a bank, the almost pointless newsagent, a record shop, a shop that sells hats and Airfix models, and a wireless museum. I can imagine one sober official suggesting, 'I really feel we need a greengrocer,' and everyone shouting him down with, 'What? And not have a wireless museum?'

The wireless museum is one room of mostly broken wirelesses, run by a couple you can't imagine were ever younger than eighty. The natural length of time you'd spend in the place, to allow for prodding the exhibits of interest, turning the odd dial and reflecting on the poignancy of the transistors you remember from your youth, would be just under a minute. But it would seem rude to wander in, say hello, then fifty seconds later say, 'Thanks very much, that was marvellous,' and leave. So you stop and look for ages at an aerial, then the man comes across and says, 'You can turn that one on.' So you turn it on, and sure enough, there's a radio station coming from it. 'Yes, it's definitely a wireless,' I said, and thought about adding, 'I can see you're not trying to cheat by sneaking in a kettle,' but thought that might confuse him.

There was a huge map of Orkney on the wall, covered in little red pins. The man lifted up his stick and said, very slowly, like a snooker commentator, 'There were troops stationed here – and here – and some here – and some more here – and here – and troops here – and here, with some here, and here,' each time pointing at a red pin. It was really hard not to say, 'Tell me if I'm wrong, but is it that the red pins mark the places where the troops were, or is that just coincidence?'

This went on for about fifteen minutes, until I broke the spell by buying a tea towel with Second World War aircraft on it and left.

But at points in this tiny street you could imagine you were in the centre of London or Manchester, as the cafés and shops are littered with leaflets and posters for jazz evenings and folk nights, cinema clubs, festivals and bars. It's like a party you find in a barn at the end of a desolate track, and Kirkwall seems unusually youthful for somewhere so isolated, driven by an unexpected quirkiness. For example, the library has a website that states: 'Our slogan will be something like "Stop doing that crack and heroin, read a book instead." I cannot believe that no one has thought of it already.'

Maybe this is the sort of dialogue that takes place in Kirkwall library: 'I'm afraid this Catherine Cookson should have been back last week, Mrs Sinclair. There's a nine pence fine.'

'Oh, sorry dear, only I went back on the crack, you see. Off my tits I was, thought I was reading the final chapter but I was looking at the side of a paint pot. For two days I thought the chef's daughter had married a warning to wash your hands after use. Thank goodness I'm off it and back here again.'

Or there's the town hall, which has an unusual figure on its roof, of a gargoyle with his tongue sticking out. This is a result of the council recently needing to repair a section of the roof, including the gargoyle. They asked one of their labourers, who was a trained stonemason, to do the job, but refused to pay him any more than the normal labouring rate for this skilled work, so he retaliated by making the gargoyle poke his tongue in the direction of the council leader's office.

Several people told me of the Orkney wedding custom of drinking from a huge wooden bucket, that's passed round the way you imagine would have happened at a party held by King Arthur. Each resident has their own recipe for the drink that fills this bucket, and Tom was especially proud of his. He steadied himself before running through it, the way Nigella Lawson pauses for a moment before recounting what she's done so you can write it down. 'I use a bottle of rum,' he said, 'with a bottle of whisky, a bottle of vodka, a bottle of gin and then some beer.' Presumably there are heated debates about the most effective recipe, and others will be adamant that their method, which includes adding a bottle of Bacardi and a bottle of brake fluid, is essential to bring out the true depth of flavour.

After a day in Kirkwall you find yourself bumping into the same people over and over again. A woman who helped show me round St Magnus Cathedral turned out to work in the pram and whisky shop. The receptionist in the hotel was running a bar I went in. It's as if they're like a student play at the Edinburgh Festival, and haven't got enough people to play all the parts in the town, so everyone has to take more than one role.

This makes it seem even more strange that to the rest of Orkney, Kirkwall is a mighty urban dragon, the São Paulo of the region. Altogether Orkney consists of twenty inhabited islands, of which the biggest has the imaginative name 'Mainland'. One of the smaller ones, Eday, has a population of 121, and relies for supplies on an inter-island plane. This is a world-record-breaking service, because the journey from West Ray island to Papa West Ray island is the shortest scheduled flight in the world, taking two minutes. It must be a magnificent experience, especially if they do all the normal procedures, so from the moment the plane takes off you hear a garbled, 'Welcome aboard this is your captain we will be flying at an altitude of fifteen feet please listen to the safety announcements exit's over there somewhere flying conditions are expected to be fine, there might be some turbulence after thirty-five seconds but it should clear up after forty chicken or mushy vegetable thing there you are no time to eat it can I clear it away we have begun our descent thank you for flying with us bye.'

No one lives in Orkney as a retreat from the chaos of the city, the way people rent a cottage in Norfolk, insisting, 'And it's only two hours from London so we can pop up every weekend and pretend we're country folk by calling out, "Oh, look, that's a bird of some sort."'

People who live in Orkney accept that it's where they will work and live and have friends and they can't nip to anywhere, except from West Ray to Papa West Ray. Similarly, as a visitor you feel privileged. This isn't somewhere you can pop up to if you fancy a restful Sunday, so you feel a small sense of achievement after almost every activity, because you've not only done something, you've done it in Orkney. For example, 'I've just been to the toilet – in *Orkney*,' or 'I've just had a row with my girlfriend about bugger-all – in *Orkney*,' which is an altogether different accomplishment.

The people of Orkney's most impressive effort at proving they're spectacularly off-centre is a sport they call the Kirkwall ba'. The ba' is a specially made ball, and to start with the process of team selection in this sport is fascinating. It's played every year on Christmas Day and New Year's Day, between Uppies and Doonies. If you're born between the Mercat Cross in the centre of town and the shore, you're a Doonie, and if you're not, you're an Uppie. The ba', made from cork and leather, is thrown up at the Cross, and all the men of the island try to get hold of it. The Doonies have to get it to a goal uptown, and the Uppies have to get it in the harbour. And that's all the rules there are.

A reporter from a newspaper in Ohio described it thus: 'Once thrown, the ba' seemed to disappear into the swirling, pushing, steaming, kicking, groaning mass of humanity in which the male population of Kirkwall is knitted into a giant knot. In the eye of the storm the fighting is merciless.'

But the merciless fighting is all in good fun, so a local book called *The Kirkwall Ba'* says: 'There's an amusing story of how, during a tough game, a battered and dishevelled player lurched up to an innocent bystander and smote him a resounding blow on the ear.'

And that's an amusing story. There was a game in 1951 when the ba' went into the Peedie Sea, which was ice-bound, so the players all piled in after it. The ice broke, but they carried on. Some players cut their legs open on the ice, and according to my book, 'They were stitched in the surgery, but so cold were the players' limbs that no anaesthetic was required.'

Or there's the account of a game in 1998 in *Scotland on Sunday*, that described the Uppies' team-talk: 'There was a hushed silence as the captain gave his tactical analysis. "Look," he implored, "I don't want to see any of you sneaking off during the game. And if you're going to have a fag, have it in a place that can do some damage."' I think Alf Ramsey used to say much the same thing.

You can tell the sort of game it is because the book about it has a little sub-chapter called 'Through a Hotel Window'. For a moment I thought, 'Is this some clever prose?' but no, it's an account of the day someone was thrown through a hotel window.

There is a strategy to winning, that includes the art of smuggling. This is where a few members of one team sneak the ball away without anyone seeing, and get it towards their goal while everyone else carries on scrapping, unaware that the ball's gone. One year someone even got in a car with the ba', drove it to the goal, and went to the pub while most of the other players were still creating amusing stories by ripping each others' livers out in the harbour while trying to find it.

The goal at the opposite end to the harbour is the wall of a house, so the people who live at this house can find themselves under siege if the ba' comes near it, with dozens of men fighting mercilessly in their garden, preventing any living creature from getting in or out as they put their fags in places that can do some damage. As the Christmas-dinner conversation is lost beneath the cacophony of yelps as limbs are dismembered, the family inside must be thinking, 'I *wondered* why this place was thirty grand cheaper than identical houses in the rest of the street.'

This is not just an unorthodox world, it's the people of Orkney's and theirs alone. Even the climate, which Orkney scholar Hugh Marwick described as 'the vilest under heaven', makes them proud. They'll boast of not having had a day without rain for four months, and you get the impression the tourist board would be happy with a slogan that went, 'If Hurricane Katrina came through here, we'd say it was mild for the time of year.'

Unlike other remote parts of Scotland, there's little sense of Scottish nationalism in Orkney. Not out of affection for England, but because Orcadians barely feel part of Scotland. Even the accent confuses the novice, as you're expecting some variant of Scottish, but instead it's clipped and musical and Scandinavian, so the first time you hear it someone will be telling you they're looking forward to your visit, and you feel the urge to reply, 'Well thanks, but how am I supposed to take down your address with you putting on that stupid voice?'

There's a reason for such an accent, which is that Orkney was ruled by Norway until the fifteenth century. So Norway is in the names and history, and the culture. For example, one of the Norwegian earls who ruled the islands in medieval times was Thorfinn the Skull-Splitter. Fascinated by someone with this title, I looked him up in my copy of *Who Was Who in Orkney*, where it says, 'Little detail of his rule is known, although his nickname suggests it may have been violent.'

Or maybe it was a trick, and he was a pussycat, and it was James the Laid-Back Buddhist Vegan Hippy who kicked everyone's head in. But, as you might expect with the home of the ba', whereas most places might think, 'Hmm we'd best draw a veil over that Skull-Splitter chap,' in Orkney they celebrate him. There's even a beer called Skull-Splitter that, I can testify, lives up to its name. It's so strong the Portman Group, which regulates drinking guidelines, insisted it shouldn't be classified as a beer, to which I hope the reply was, 'Oh, if only there was some sort of warning we could give people that a beer called Skull-Splitter might be on the strong side. IT'S CALLED FUCKING SKULL-SPLITTER. Do you think anyone's going to go, "Ugh that's unexpectedly potent. I thought it would be mostly lime"?'

I found an account on a website called 'Gays out in Orkney' that went: 'I enjoyed a stay at Woodcock House in Evie where your gay-beckoning hosts were lovely young James and his snow white cat, Thorfinn.' So even the gay cat-loving community's hero is a bloke who split skulls. I bet Orkney Buddhists believe that if you live a truly good and spiritual life, creating only positive karma, as a reward you're reincarnated as a psychopath. Then you can do what you like.

The story of the first Norse settlers isn't what I expected, as the Vikings settled in Orkney quite happily, then used it as a base from which to attack Norway. So the Orkney Vikings were known as nutters, even amongst the Vikings. Ordinary Vikings presumably said, 'Don't go near the Orkney Vikings, they're fucking mental.'

Apart from Thorfinn there was Sigurd the Mighty, grandson of Ketil the Flatnose. With Thorstein the Red they fought a Pict called Tusk, who got his name from a huge protruding tooth.

Sigurd cut off Tusk's head and brought it back home on his horse, but on the way the tooth pierced his leg and he died from blood poisoning. Incidentally, Thorstein the Red's mother was Aud the Deep-Minded, whose daughter went on to marry Thorfinn the Skull-Splitter. Maybe they complemented each other: Thorfinn would split someone's skull, which would help Aud to contemplate the nature of dying in screaming unimaginable agony.

In the twelfth century there was a claim on the islands by someone called Erland, son of Harald of the Poisoned Shirt. And there was Palnatoki, who once trained his men by chopping off the heads of thirty of his enemies in a row.

Most of this is known as a result of the Icelandic Sagas, which have a branch of sagas specially about Orkney. It feels as if every page goes: 'Sigurd tricked Clontarf and plucked out all his men's eyes with a crow but then was ambushed by Knut the Mental who'd drunk a field of fermented thistles and after killing Sigurd's men fed them all to Olaf the Light Eater, whose name may have been ironic.'

Orkney stayed Norwegian until the 1460s, when the islands were pawned to Scotland in exchange for a dowry for the Norwegian king's daughter. Since then they've cultivated their own world, but their distinct history is what's kept their society in existence at all. Because it seems strange, when you're enjoying the merriment within this setting, that there's much here at all. Why is it that after Inverness there's very little human life, but when you get right to the top of the country and then over the sea, in a place even more inaccessible and rainy, there a community that's survived and is growing? The answer revolves around the property booms of the eighteenth and nineteenth centuries. Land became more profitable if it was used for sheep or industry than if it was farmed by people, so the owners of the Highlands, most notably successive Dukes of Sutherland, decided to go along with the free market and drove out tens of thousands of people who were living there. Thousands were forced to live by the sea, many emigrated, some refused to go and were starved.

Starving people can be a laborious process, so to hurry things along the landowners burned down the houses of their tenants. One Sutherland crofter recorded that 'Little or no time was given for the removal of persons or property; the people striving to remove the sick and the helpless before the fire should reach them.'

Until this episode the top half of Scotland wasn't seen as an empty, desolate region of natural beauty, but as an area populated by people who had their quirks and customs like any other. Without the Clearances, the north of Scotland wouldn't seem a remote hideaway only visited by ornithologists and Tornado jet fighters on training exercises, but another vibrant region with the usual arguments about whether it needed yet another Tesco. Now, due to the Duke of Sutherland's efforts, those pages in the road atlas are nothing but a series of contour lines. But Orkney, due to its different historical roots that stemmed from Norway, wasn't part of the Sutherlands' domain and wasn't trashed in that way, so there it remains, looking down on everyone, except for Shetland.

And according to Orkney, that's not a place to go. Because my first lesson in Orkney–Shetland relations was during an interview on Radio Orkney, when the presenter asked me, 'How do you know ET is from Shetland?' And the answer was, 'Because he looks like he is.'

It could be rapidly addictive, this combination of quirky liveliness and utter remoteness. Even as I was leaving from the cuddly Kirkwall airport, I had just placed my bag in a tiny, token security machine that might as well have been a chest of drawers when the pilot came over to say he'd been at the show the night before, and wondered when it would be going out on the radio. I was slightly surprised that he didn't have some boots and nails in one hand, and say, 'I mend these while I'm flying, you see, as the plane doubles up as a cobbler's.'

Dumfries

On the face of it the Scottish have cause for complaint against the English. It can be summed up in the verse of the national anthem that goes: 'May He sedition hush, And in a torrent rush, Rebellious Scots to crush, God save the King.' Apart from anything else this is clearly out of date, and should be amended to: 'Each World Cup you're dreamier, But your odds couldn't be teenier, You always lose to Armenia, Or somewhere with a population of nine.'

But the relationship between England and Scotland is complicated, because Scotland wasn't just a victim of the British Empire, it helped to run that empire, sometimes against other Scots. These complexities are embodied in the hero figure of poet Robbie Burns.

In Dumfries, for example, where Burns spent the last five years of his life, they seem to have agreed on one issue of how to remember him, which is to stick him up everywhere. So there's a huge statue and a smaller statue and a mausoleum and a statue of his wife and a Burns memorial and a picture of him on every road sign and a Burns Street and in every pub they say 'Robert Burns drank here' even though it was built in 1969 and you daren't ask for the public toilet because it's probably called the Robert Burns Dumpery and I bet in Dixons they go 'Robert Burns spent many hours here, he wrote "Ode to an iPod" – "O ye wee doonloadin' beastie".'

If a shrink was to analyse Dumfries, he'd say, 'I think it's time you let him go.'

All this is because Burns spent the last part of his life there, until a local doctor advised him to deal with his fever by walking into a freezing river and he died soon after.

Dumfries is called a 'Borders town', because it's only a few miles inside Scotland, west of Carlisle. It's part of a region called Dumfries and Galloway, and it's not always sure what it's meant to be. Outside the town you can ramble in any direction to a stately home or a castle, and the solid, magisterial tourist book of the area has a grand mansion on the cover, so you get the impression you're not allowed inside the parish boundary unless you're at least ninth in line to the throne; but the town itself is grey, mostly working-class and properly Scottish.

There are thousands of grey stone houses either side of a fast-flowing river, and dozens of pubs with a yellow light telling you they sell Tennent's beer, and hills in the distance and a shop that sells fishing rods, and unlike outside Waverley station in Edinburgh, no one plays the bagpipes.

This combination of urban and rural heritage was illustrated in a story told by the writer Frank Cottrell Boyce, who said: 'I discovered this stately home – Drumlanrig Castle – which has a Da Vinci, a Brueghel, a Rembrandt. The opening hours were a little eccentric, but you could walk right up to the paintings. I kept telling people about this place and somebody obviously listened to me, because this person drove up in a Vauxhall Nova, took Da Vinci's *Madonna with Infant* off the wall, threw it in the back of the van and it's never been seen since.'

There's a Facebook page for teenagers to discuss Dumfries, and it's called 'I know Dumfries is wank but it deserves a page on Facebook'. It includes a lively youthful discussion about the facilities there, that goes: 'There's nothing to do except kick the seagulls,' to which someone has replied, 'Hee hee, that reminds me of when I was with my young son by the side of the road and a lorry ran straight over a seagull.'

This is something not mentioned on the tourist website, that one of the main forms of entertainment seems to be watching seagulls suffer. Mike Russell, the Scottish Environment Minister, even announced a plan of action in Parliament, saying, 'Dumfries has a particular problem with seagulls, with regular reports of divebombing.' To which you can't help thinking, 'Oh for God's sake, they yell, "We are mighty Scotland, home of the brave, our blood runs blue and white with the spirit of Braveheart, ooo a wretched seagull, it's fair divebombed doon and pecked my wee sandwich, I'm frightened."'

The centre of the town is yet another predictable row of familiar outlets, with a lost-looking building called the Midsteeple sat in the middle, and an eighteenth-century toll-booth and jail whose elegant clockface and delicate brickwork seem to be saying, 'Do you want to hear my story again about when the Jacobite Rebellion came through here?' to a bored Vodafone and Boots the Chemist.

But leaning over the edge of the centre is a unique token of local pride, the football club called Queen of the South. How can you not love such a club, when its name is not even the town but a poetic description of it. It makes you wish all clubs were named like this, so if Liverpool played Middlesbrough the announcer would say, 'Port of the West 2, Dump of the North 0.'

An example of the esteem in which the club is held locally is the book I bought, *Queen of the South: The History*, a solid, anvil-like structure, with surprisingly few pictures and very close type and much longer than your average history book that deals with relatively minor concerns like the eighteenth century. It's brilliantly full of pointless obsessive detail about every game ever. For example: 'In the second half Stenhousemuir pressed forward and won a corner, but the Queens withstood the pressure,' which would be too much detail if it was happening now and you were at the game, never mind that it was in a pre-season friendly in 1928.

But the book was worth reading for this magnificent sentence: 'In 1939 there wasn't just concern for the future of the country, it was also a troubling time for Queen of the South.' I'd put that alongside the opening of *Nineteen Eighty-Four* as one of the great sentences in the English language.

The book contains other nuggets of genius, such as: 'Queen of the South left Forfar having clinched the title, with a goal average of 1.9714285 compared to Stirling Albion's of 1.772.'

Say what you will about Queen of the South, they're not like those half-hearted clubs that only work out their goal average to six decimal places.

Everyone in Dumfries seems to take at least some interest in supporting Queen of the South, maybe because the club is so eccentric. When I asked the audience if there was a song or chant for when the players ran out of the tunnel, someone shouted, 'It's, "Oh God, *he's* not playing again is he?"'

Also, for all the talk of nothing happening, the history of this area seems to be one long series of feuds and battles. According to *The History of Dumfries and Galloway* by Herbert Maxwell, in 1286 'Dumfriesshire was dragged into civil war, the Earl of Carrick attacked the Castle of Dumfries with fire and arms and banners.' Then, 'In 1297 the eleven wretched men of Galloway were confined in Lochmaben Castle and from that terrible fortress only one left alive.'

Then Robert the Bruce met rival landowner John Comyn at Greyfriars church in 1306. So he stabbed him, obviously. But Comyn was still alive, so Robert ran out of the church, where he met Sir Roger de Kirkpatrick, and said, 'I must go, for I doubt I have slain Comyn.' Kirkpatrick told Robert the Bruce to wait a moment, went inside and plunged another dagger into Comyn, saying, 'I'll make sure,' the way you might help an old person with their shopping – 'Excuse me, love, are you having trouble with your stabbing? Come here, I'll help you out – what are neighbours for?'

This is a celebrated incident now, a tourist attraction. If someone working class stabs someone it's 'Broken Britain's Sword of Shame', but if you're a noble the whole incident's painted on a commemorative box of shortbread and sold in the gift shop.

Page after page goes on like this, informing us, for example, that 'In 1353 William, Lord of Douglas, had devastated the country before him so completely that he had to withdraw to save his army from starvation. In revenge he burnt every abbey, church and town on his line of retreat.'

It seems that living in Dumfries has been like wandering through a play in which everyone gets stabbed, and you only have to pop out for some teabags to run into the murderous McAndrews laying siege to Poundking.

At one of the touristy old ruins, called Sweetheart Abbey, I thought, 'Ah, there must be a nice story behind that.' But it's called that because after John Balliol was killed by Robert the Bruce, his lover Lady Dervogilla had his heart embalmed and kept it in the abbey in a casket of silver and ivory. You can't even have a love story in Dumfries without it involving internal organs in a box.

All this explains why the website called 'Information Britain', a very serious affair, tells some of these stories and then says, 'The long history of Dumfries isn't all murder and bloodshed, wars and treachery. There were also hangings, witch trials and executions.'

Yet it's now a chatty town. Not only do people talk to you in the pubs, they come out of the pub to talk to you if they see you walking past. 'Hey, come in here. This is the best pub in Dumfries,' I was advised by drinkers from three separate pubs, a local version of the waiters who ask you to come and eat in their restaurant when you're in a European holiday resort, except that in one case the man shouting erupted into a coughing fit half-way through, so his plea went, 'Best pub in achremaha, best pub, aHEEEYUGH, best, ahawAAAKKKKKKKhremhrem ikkk aHOO,' while I waited for him to finish so as not to seem impolite.

In the Globe I immediately struck up a rapport with the barmaid, when I said I'd noticed there was a shop over the road that only sold accordions, which seemed slightly out of the ordinary. She snapped, 'It *doesn't* only sell accordions, it sells bongos as well.'

The Globe is the pub that Burns used to drink in, and they've preserved his favourite room. You need permission to get in, and there's a chair in the corner that was apparently his favourite, and a letter in which he mentioned the Globe in a frame on the wall.

Burns now seems to represent the three founding blocks of modern Scottish nationalism: the pride, the distortions, and the desire to take money from daft American tourists. For example, a spokesman for one government tourist agency was asked what it wanted to achieve with Burns. He said, 'You're always looking for a unique selling point. If you look at what he did in his life-time, you see he's a very attractive product. Burns was ahead of his time. I came across a phrase in one of his poems that said, "Welcome, welcome again," and that captures exactly what we're trying to do. And we're very careful about who we allow to use his image, so Crawford's biscuits is fine, but not manufacturers of cheap pens.'

He's clearly the right man to be put in charge of Burns's legacy, a bloke whose favourite poem is probably 'Once you pop you can't stop'.

The feeling amongst most Scots is probably more respectful: that he's a symbol of their achievements as a nation, and of defiance against the English. Scottish nationalism is a difficult force to work out. It doesn't seek to preserve a language, and the country it feels is holding it back has had four Scottish prime ministers since 1900.

An English person can live merrily and safely in Scotland, but almost the entire country will vehemently support any opponent of England. If England were drawn against Al Qaeda in the World Cup, the pubs would be full of crowds yelling, 'COME on you fundamentalists, GET INTO these infidels!'

Burns finds himself in the middle of this contradiction. It's often assumed that he just wrote about loving anything Scottish, and that his poems are full of stuff like, 'I love fair bonnie lasses, And full whisky glasses, And shoving huge thistles up Englishmen's asses.'

But he was a child of globally radical times, and one of his earliest pieces was a ballad supporting the American War of Independence. He also wrote that 'The man whose only wish is to become great and rich, whatever he may pretend to be, is but a miserable wretch.'

This was in the 1780s, when radical thinkers were disputing the notion that people with noble blood were most fit to rule. As the son of a poor farmer in Ayrshire, Burns started a debating society, and wrote a poem to celebrate it that started, 'Of birth and blood we do not boast'.

He never made much of a living from writing, which is why he went to Dumfries, where he took over Ellisland Farm, on the banks of the River Nith, and also became the Dumfries excise officer, tracking down smugglers and illegal distilleries. During this time he was transformed by the French Revolution.

He tied his support for the Revolution to his job as an exciseman when, in February 1792, armed smugglers sailed up the Solway Firth in a schooner. Burns became suspicious, and went to meet it with two colleagues. When they realised there were twenty-four men on board, all armed, the others went to get help while Burns stayed on shore observing the ship. Forty dragoons arrived, but when they and Burns boarded the ship they found it had been abandoned, although all the illegal goods were still on board, including four cannon. The law at the time was that anything captured in this way was sold at auction. Burns went to the auction, bid for the guns he'd captured, bought them and sent them to France to be used by the revolutionaries. Maybe that's his 'unique selling point', and next to his picture on a biscuit tin it should say, 'Campbell's revolutionary gun-running shortbread insurrectionary assortment'.

Burns went regularly to the Dumfries Theatre, which today remembers this modestly with a plaque on the outside wall, and inside with a six-foot statue in a special alcove lit as if he's Jesus in a Renaissance painting. Once Burns was at a benefit night for the Dumfries and Galloway Hunt, and at the end of the play the audience was asked to sing 'God Save the King'. Burns was among a group that tried to drown it out by singing '*Ah! ça ira*', the anthem of the French Revolution.

Eventually, Burns's failing health meant he couldn't work. He ran out of money, and had to beg from his friends to stay out of the debtors' prison. In 1796 he died in poverty, at the age of thirty-seven.

They're immensely proud of their Burns connection in Dumfries, with much more than the glow of celebrity a town feels from a connection with someone like Charles Dickens. A hint as to the reason may be found in the attitude towards a series of floods that took place in the town shortly before my visit, when dozens of shops and houses in Dumfries were destroyed. But the thing that annoyed people most was that the national news was all about the floods at the same time in Cockermouth, in the Lake District, while theirs were hardly mentioned. It might seem irrational, when you're clambering out of your upstairs window to be rescued by a fireman in a dinghy, to yell, 'The worst thing is we haven't even made the six o' clock news!' But maybe this was a symbol of a sense that no one in authority cares about towns like it.

Similarly, issues such as high unemployment and the Poll Tax have been seen in Scotland as problems inflicted on them by the English, and a greater proportion of Scottish people rejected Tony Blair's reforms of the Labour Party than in England. So if you're in a town that's had to put up with all that, you can understand if they get irate, and celebrate the man who died in the town who wrote, 'We're bought and sold for English gold, Such a parcel of rogues in a nation.' Maybe the modern interpretation of the works of Burns for a town like Dumfries is that he makes them feel they matter.

Andersonstown

There's a strange achievement claimed by Belfast, that everyone in the town seems keen to tell you. 'Just up there is the Europa Hotel,' they say, adding, 'That's the most bombed hotel in Europe.'

It's said with a certain pride, the way inhabitants of another town might point out the place where cotton buds were invented. Even the commentary on the open-top tourist bus that remarks on places of interest around the city says with an air of superiority, 'Over there is the *most bombed hotel in Europe*.' A part of me always feels like saying, 'Yes, all right, but what competition was there? Is there likely to be some Jury's Inn in Helsinki that's forever getting blown up by paramilitary opponents of the Finnish national insurance system?' Maybe during the war in Yugoslavia the Belfast Tourist Board were informed by *The Guinness Book of Records* that there was a bed and breakfast in Srebrenica only two explosions behind, and the IRA were given council funding to make sure the Europa stayed in front.

The issue creates a rare unity between the communities, as Protestants are as keen as Catholics to share in this record-breaking success. It's as if they want to say, 'I didn't agree with many policies of the IRA, but credit where it's due, without them the Europa wouldn't be the most bombed hotel in Europe.'

The boast is part of an admirably dark affection for the city's past. The bus tour must also be the only one in the world with a commentary that starts, 'Unfortunately the first building we pass is this ugly insurance office, and you'd think with our history we could get someone to blow it up.'

Ten years into the ceasefire, the people of Belfast seem keen to emphasise what makes their city different, which is its association with explosions and gunfire. And they probably wouldn't be able to change that image, even if they wanted to.

In the 1980s, I told my mum I was going to *Dublin* for the weekend and she gasped, 'Ooh my goodness. Well, you be *careful*.'

I said, 'Mum, Dublin's in *Southern* Ireland, a country that hasn't been at war since 1923.' And she said, 'Well, be *careful*,' making no more sense than if I'd told her I was going to Spain and she'd said, 'Well, don't go swimming, because if the Armada catch you, that'll be your *lot*.'

The Tourist Board has made some effort, with brochures and websites encouraging visitors to come and enjoy the Waterfront Centre, which has hosted various international choirs and so on. But there are places like this in many towns, vast glass soulless constructions that look like the international headquarters of a pharmaceuticals company, except there's a huge poster on the door of a bearded Russian baritone wearing a crown and bellowing.

And they promote the new St George's Market, in which you can buy stuff like sausages spiced with Maltesers, and crêpes with kiwi-fruit liqueur and necklaces made out of dried rabbit pellets. Strangely, in the right mood, these places can be disarmingly seductive, but they're cropping up everywhere, and hardly convey a spirit identifiable as Belfast.

So then the city marketed a neglected element of the town's history: that it was in a Belfast shipyard that local people built the *Titanic*. The whole of the shipyard area has been officially renamed the 'Titanic Quarter', there are *Titanic* festivals and exhibitions, and in 2009 the *Titanic* dominated every Tourist Board brochure and website.

At what point did the local chief of tourism declare, '*I* know how we can project the pride and ingenuity embedded in our past – we celebrate the ship we built that sank. You see, our ship became *famous*, not like those built in other shipyards that boringly arrived at their destinations and came back again. No one makes films starring Kate Winslet about those nondescript "all get there alive" vessels, do they? So our history isn't just about tragedy and suffering, it's also about the role we played in a thousand people drowning in freezing water.'

But the Harland and Wolff shipyard, where the *Titanic* was built, is and should be at the centre of any projection of Belfast. Firstly this is because, unlike most shut-down industries, it still dominates the view of the town. The vast yellow cranes bearing the H & W logo, standing like goals in a giants' football match, seem to be two streets away from wherever you look. They're now officially preserved as historic buildings, and it was rumoured at one point that the cabins at the top were to be converted into restaurants.

Maybe the brochure publicising this restaurant will begin, 'Hi. We were once the famous shipyard that built a ship we called unsinkable that hit an iceberg and sank on its first voyage. Now we want you to try our restaurant that dangles precariously on a crane 300 feet in the air. What could possibly go wrong?'

A glance at the shipyards, like anything in Belfast, also reveals much more about what has driven the city. Edward Harland and Gustav Wolff were members of the Protestant and Unionist establishment. They set up the shipyards in the 1860s and recruited a workforce from the Protestant Shankill Road, and from then until it closed in 2000, the workforce was almost exclusively Protestant. In 1971, for example, there were four hundred Catholics working there, and 10,000 Protestants.

For most of its life the shipyard was extremely profitable, despite the mishap with the *Titanic*, and this was especially important during Ireland's war for independence from Britain. Because while the British government could reconcile itself to losing the south and west of Ireland, it couldn't bear the thought of giving up industrial Belfast. It was helped by Unionist politicians in the city, who stashed weapons and threatened civil war if they were placed in a United Ireland, and who hoped the shipyard would be a main source of recruitment for their soldiers.

The result was partition in 1921, when most of the country became independent, except for the six counties that became Northern Ireland. This new country could only work if Protestants remained convinced it was in their interests to stay British. So they were assured that it would be their country alone. The first Prime Minister of Northern Ireland, James Craig, announced, 'We are building a Protestant land for a Protestant people,' which was at least honest.

And so countless human stories are invested in those dramatic and beautifully ugly angular yellow structures. Almost every street, building and pub has a tale to tell of its role in that conflict, although the centre of Belfast now appears to be a typical British city centre: unfathomable roadworks, pubs advertising the next Premier League game showing on Sky Sports, huddles of smokers outside office doorways, slouched pensioners staring grimly out of a Wetherspoon's window. There's the George Best Airport close to the centre, which must make it awkward on a flight to Belfast when a passenger needs restraining for being chaotically drunk, as he can shout, 'George Best was much worse than this, and you named the fucking *airport* after him.'

There's the Botanic Gardens that host concerts and food festivals, and in every direction are the misty hills that start at the edge of the city, suggesting that there must be something mysterious and best left alone on the other side of them.

But once you're out of the centre there's no disguising the delicate issue of the city's dividing lines. They're illustrated on every available space in the form of vast and, to the layman like myself, beautifully constructed murals. When you consider that, throughout the rest of Britain, graffiti amounts to scrawled statements such as 'Arsenal are shit' with all three words spelt wrong, Belfast appears to have a thriving production line of talented young artists.

The Tourist Office actually promotes these now on its website as an attraction, urging us to join their 'tour of magnificent murals', and the tourist agency 'About to Go' assures visitors: 'Sectarian strife has become a tourist attraction.' Maybe they hope that eventually hundreds of visitors will stand in the Falls Road muttering, 'I love the use of light and shade here, the way the eyes shine through the balaclava, and the clever use of perspective as the Armalite merges with the dead volunteer's coffin.'

The most popular element of the open-top bus ride is the section that takes in these murals, and you wonder whether the plan is to employ actors to run up the Shankill Road firing missiles over the bus from hand-held RPG-7 grenade launchers as part of an exhibition called 'The Paramilitary Experience'. They could get characters from the time to make the commentary you listen to through headphones as you go round, saying, 'Hi. My name's Mad Dog, and I'd like to take you on a journey back in time to a period known as "The Troubles". If you see any suspicious-looking bags, this means you're going the right way through the tour. And don't forget to keep your belongings with you at all times, including your kneecaps. Heh heh, I'm only kidding with you so I am.'

Something that is clear from the artwork by either side is how the conflict was much deeper than simple gang rivalry. The Loyalist Shankill Road is packed with Union flags, and Union Jack pennants hang by the hundred. The edge of the pavement is even painted red, white and blue, presumably in case a member of the royal family with curvature of the spine who can only look down happens to be passing through, so there's no chance of them thinking, 'I can't see any outward expression of affection towards the monarchy here. They don't seem to appreciate us much up the Shankill Road at all.'

As well as depictions of King Billy, and eulogies to paramilitaries, many of the murals are of the royal family, including one of the Queen Mother in which she looks extraordinarily drunk.

None of this, however, is the gloating of a dominant people, akin to the taunts of white South Africans during apartheid. I've sat in a pub at the city centre end of the Shankill that seemed, at first, like any grimy inner-city dive; just two old men in opposite corners sipping bottled beer while wearing their caps, another man at the bar studying the racing page through his illegal smoke, and a silent craggy barman with hands outstretched on the bar, who makes you want to ask which crisps he's got so you can see him snarl the words 'Cheese and onion' with understated menace. But across every wall were framed photos, hundreds of them, showing the Shankill Road in its glory through the ages. And in every photo was evidence of the determination to be British, not Irish, as banners celebrated a succession of monarchs, men marched for the Orange Order and fought the Papists. One in particular was from 1912, and showed a crowd of around thirty of the poorest people you'll ever see, shoeless and literally in rags, as if they were auditioning for a production of *Les Misérables*. They were marching under a huge banner, itself ragged and barely holding together, that said 'No popery'.

Of all the problems in these people's lives, you had to wonder, was this really the priority? They must have spent their evenings, nine to a room, huddled together, saying, 'We don't need to go worrying about luxuries like clean water and warmth and food for our starving child. It's keeping transubstantiation out we've got to be careful of.'

Loyalism could never boast that it gave its followers much in terms of material wealth. After partition it could offer them the right to work in a shipyard, and now even that's gone, unless they can sauté a scallop at height.

Coming back down the Falls Road, the engine of the Nationalist side, are portraits of the hunger strikers who died in prison in 1981, as well as harps and starry ploughs and other symbols of Ireland beside poetic pleas for a free nation, often in Gaelic. But occasionally there's one that stands out for its ability to peer over the Belfast hills. Along one stretch of a disused building is a portrait of Frederick Douglass, the ex-slave who helped persuade Abraham Lincoln to make the abolition of slavery the central issue in the American Civil War. Then there's a smoking Gaza, and a picture of Romanian refugees, with a message supporting their right to safety, evidently put up following an incident in which their hostel was set alight a few weeks earlier.

Perhaps because Nationalists see their battle as not mainly against Protestants, but against governments and armies, this allows them to identify with other groups doing the same across time and space.

But there remains a disconcerting flaw at the heart of their philosophy, which *is* similar to the Loyalist view, that while they may not see 'the other community' as a natural enemy, nonetheless they do view them as separate. And so, strangely, ten years into the ceasefire, there seems to be a greater multitude of flags and bunting criss-crossing the roads on both sides now than there was during the fighting.

For example, there's the leisure centre situation. Halfway up the Shankill Road is the Shankill Leisure Centre, with a modern glass front, so you can see people in leotards puffing on those step machines through the window, and you get a whiff of chlorine as you pass the door. Then you turn down a side road, past a car park full of rubble and into the Falls Road, where five minutes' walk from the Shankill Leisure Centre is the Falls Leisure Centre, identical in every way except that it's for Catholics. To the outsider this is a ridiculous surplus of leisure centres, but the ceasefire isn't a process in which the two communities learn to live peacefully with each other, it's one in which they learn to live peacefully apart from each other.

Otherwise, the worry must be that a mixed swimming pool could lead to a row about whose turn it is to use the water slide, and then it will all kick off again. This is the philosophy accepted by all sides in charge of post-ceasefire Belfast. The peace will be kept by each 'community' living separately, but each being entitled to identical resources. So presumably if the rowing machine in the Catholic leisure centre breaks down, someone from the council has to go and break one in the Protestant one, until they can both be repaired at exactly the same time.

This means that in many ways segregation has become even greater since the fighting stopped, so there are fewer children in mixed schools now than before. If anyone should doubt this trend it appears in concrete, in the shape of huge walls, known as 'peace walls', that snake their way between Catholic and Protestant areas, not just between estates but through them, sometimes bending round one particular garden and back again to complete the ethnic division. Presumably if there are any mixed marriages surviving on these estates, the wall continues through the middle of the house, after officials have been round with a clipboard to work out who sleeps on which side of the bed, so the wall can go right down the centre.

And yet, however fragile, the ceasefire remains intact and will do for the foreseeable future, for the uncomplicated reason that most people prefer not to have to dodge gunfire, or pass through four checkpoints on the way to buy a bag of crisps, especially when there appears to be no prospect of the paramilitaries achieving their aims.

The transformation of the city under the ceasefire is illustrated by the nature of its festivals. In August 2009 I was asked to do a show at the Andersonstown Sports Centre, as part of the West Belfast Festival, an annual event that first took place twenty years earlier as a cultural wing of the Irish Nationalist movement. Andersonstown, at the far end of the Falls Road, is the most unyielding of the Nationalist areas, and back then an evening of culture was almost certain to end with a room full of people standing, with moist eyes and glasses aloft as they sang along to a ballad that went something like:

'Twas in the year of eleven seventy-three that brave ol' Tomas
    O'Hara
Was shot with an arrow fired from the men sent o'er by Henry
    the Second,
And the spot where Tomas lay slain
They still call today
The Tomas O'Hara car accessory shop.

But since the ceasefire the festival has become an event involving glossy pamphlets and literary figures, tickets booked through agencies and chicken tikka wraps in the dressing room. To emphasise the point, the patron of the festival is Danny Morrison, a leading member of Sinn Féin, believed by many to have once held a senior position in the IRA. At one level you have to assume this means he gets his way, and that if there's an argument on the committee it ends with Danny lowering his voice and saying quietly, 'I say we put on *The Taming of the Shrew*,' and the decision is agreed.

I stayed with a Protestant friend in East Belfast, someone with no allegiance to Unionism, who told me she'd never been to Andersonstown, and wasn't sure of the way, pointing vaguely and saying, 'I think it's over there somewhere,' as if she was guessing the direction to Libya.

So I booked a taxi, and the driver said, 'Are you sure you want *Andersonstown?*' with such astonishment I wondered if I'd said 'Atlantis' by mistake.

The Andersonstown Sports Centre, it turned out, hadn't been designed with comedy shows in mind. It's one of the most unsuitable venues possible, slightly worse than a bottling plant, and a long way behind a hospital's stroke unit. The sound bounces and echoes across the volleyball courts like Tannoy announcements in a supermarket, and there was a constant chatter of people squeezing past tables to queue at the makeshift bar. On this night the queue for drinks consistently hovered at around a hundred people, and groups sat around tables getting drunker and louder as a variety of problems meant that the time I was due on got later and later. Eventually the room was awash with a tsunami of chatter that was so slurred, by the time most words had ended their beginnings had already bounced back off the wall to where they started.

As the compère began to introduce me, three hours after most people had arrived, around two hundred people sat in the middle of the room, looking as if they were waiting for me to start, while the other eight hundred shouted, 'Hey, Kieran, they've run out o' fucken' Grolsch' across the tables, threw peanuts at each other, and shrieked with laughter as they fell over, as if they were in a Hollywood depiction of eighteenth-century sailors on a night in a tavern.

I went on stage and surveyed this splendid testimony to disorder, aware that I might as well try to do a show to a flock of geese. A few of them shouted, 'Fuck off you fucking Brit.' I battled, pointlessly, for maybe three or four interminable minutes, while a small core of supporters yelled at the rest to keep quiet, and the rest made it clear that they wouldn't and probably couldn't. Maybe, I pondered, the two groups would start fighting, it would spill out onto the street, the troops would be called back, and this comedy show would result in the breakdown of the ceasefire. For the next hundred years rival factions would fire at each other and paint murals of me sloping off the stage. Then historians of the future would debate why it was that the Northern Ireland peace process appeared to break down at a comedy night in Andersonstown.

Although some of the Protestants of the town might have advised me otherwise, I surrendered. I sloped away, and went backstage to collect my things. As I left the dressing room I was greeted by someone I vaguely recognised. 'Mark,' he said with a ripe Belfast baritone, 'I'm Danny Morrison, trustee of the festival, and I can't apologise enough for what went on tonight.'

'It's fine, Danny,' I said.

'It's not fine,' he argued, adding, 'Mark, I'd like to speak to you about what happened there. Will you come into this room with me for just five minutes.'

It was hard not to smile at the thought that some people in the past might have been nervous if Danny had made a similar request.

We went in the room, and Danny said he was disgusted by the behaviour of the audience, who had no discipline and were '*racist*, there's no other word for it – *racist* against you for being British'.

'Maybe a few of them were,' I said, 'but I think mostly they were just drunk.' But secretly I thought, 'Of all the people asked to follow Danny Morrison into a room, I bet this is the only time the reason's been to receive an apology for the Irish being anti-British.'

Politely, with great charm, Danny offered to organise a taxi to take me back, and to stay with me in the car park until it came, so I didn't face any more revelry from the crowd, who were now stumbling outside.

'*Where* are you going?' said the taxi driver, incredulous that anyone from Andersonstown could possibly suggest the journey to Protestant East Belfast. He puffed and said 'Jesus' a few times, and tried to figure out which way was east.

But eventually I got back, and relayed the events of the night to my host, who just said, 'Oh dear, that's a bad night, when the safest option is to stand alone in a car park with a murderer.'*

---

* I should add that Danny wrote to me afterwards and invited me back to do another show, and to enjoy a few pints, which seemed the best part of the offer. And he was never convicted of murder, which I'm glad about, although I wouldn't want that detail to spoil a bloody good line.

Colchester

Surely the most gloriously undervalued resident in most towns is the local historian. There can't be a task in the community that brings less of a boost to the ego than compiling books with titles such as *Tring Between the Wars* or *When Andover had Three Fishmongers*. Most authors can at least dream that their book will become a national success, but you'd have to be very optimistic to ring up the Newcastle branch of Waterstone's and ask how many copies they'd sold of *Guildford: The Harold Macmillan Years*.

Now most towns have a historical society that puts articles on a website. Of these my favourite so far is the one for Wellingborough in Northamptonshire, which has a series of links for each century. I clicked on the first, for the sixteenth century, and it said, 'Nothing of note happened in Wellingborough in the sixteenth century.'

The care and detail displayed in history society pamphlets is dazzling. They list everyone in the town who fought in the war, or every film shown at the old Empire Cinema. If you wanted to play a cruel trick you could send a local historian a letter claiming it was Ted Billinghurst and not his brother Arthur who fought at El Alamein, as stated in Chapter 9, and he'd spend the rest of his life in the town hall's basement checking every record in the filing cabinets until he was satisfied he was right.

Where this thoroughness becomes a problem is when it's applied to local events that were shaped by great historical issues. On such occasions the big picture can be lost in the swamp of fine detail. For example, 'The Battle of Evesham' covers events in the thirteenth century, when Henry III decided to reverse the principle of the Magna Carta, which established the right of barons to prevent the monarch ruling entirely as he pleased. The nobles formed an army and captured the King, and the Battle of Evesham was the royal court's attempt to rescue him.

But the account is so clogged up in detail that it ignores how amazing it is that the King was taken hostage, and instead concentrates on the debate about the route taken by each army. So we're given the splendid sentence, 'I accept Carpenter's theory, that the Royalist army marched along the line of the current B4084.' This is followed with, 'After the fork at Fladbury, Edward's troops may have quit the line of the B4084 and marched north to cut the Alcester Road just short of Norton.'

Maybe when the armies arrived the commanders met before the battle and went, 'Next time try coming off the B4084 to Littleworth, cut through Drakes Broughton and take the bypass at Besford Bridge, which will cut out the bottleneck at Pershore.' Then whoever survived the battle could take the A3657689B through Diddlebury, which is slightly longer but scenic, and they could stop off at the Little Chef.

What the local details often show is that it's rare for one area to buck a national trend in history. So most accounts of British towns over the last 2,000 years tell a broadly similar story, with the same critical turning points. The Romans came, built stuff and left; the Normans swiped the land; Henry VIII sold off the monasteries; the town was besieged in the Civil War; around 1800 it became industrial; it was bombed in the Blitz; and the Arndale Centre was opened in 1979.

Among the most important towns in the history of Britain is Colchester. In fact, it claims to be the first town in the history of Britain, as the Romans established a headquarters there in the first century AD, with a grid of streets, a city council and a temple. It had a population of 2,000, and they called the place Camulodunum. Most impressively, the Romans brought what everyone in the town insists were the first elephants to visit Britain.

The Celtic tribe that ruled the area before was the Iceni. The Romans used them to police the area, which meant the Iceni were well armed. But when Nero became Roman Emperor in AD 54 he changed policy, decided the Iceni were now the enemy (does any of this sound familiar?) and had their land confiscated, their leader Boudica whipped, and her daughters raped. At which point she raised an army of 120,000, took them to Camulodunum and burned the place to the ground. But the main point is she took her chariot up the A12 as far as Kelvedon, and joined up with the A120 at Marks Tey to avoid the roadworks on the B1256 from Braintree.

These days, the town seems unsure how to treat Boudica. On the one hand she's a celebrity, so at every parade there's someone dressed as her, and the council vans have a picture of her on the side, which must make Colchester the only town whose council's symbol is someone who burned the place to a cinder. But she isn't seen universally as a heroine. When a newborn baby was on the front page of the *Colchester Gazette* for being named Boudica, a series of angry letters was sent in, such as one that went: 'I am disgusted a baby has been named after a criminal who murdered people. A pox on her memory.' This suggests that there may still be a Roman contingent in the town, that never quite left, and dreams of taking over again one day.

You sense the difficulty of coming to terms with such an ancient past in the book *Colchester: A History*, which ends its Roman section with: 'After Claudius and Boudica, Colchester would never be so important again.' It must be awkward to accept that your finest moment was 2,000 years ago, and that now you're just a place on the way to Ipswich. Maybe it's like being a former child star who now works in a pet shop, and occasionally someone says, 'Didn't you used to be that bloke on *Opportunity Knocks?*'

But Colchester was to be an important town again, only 1,600 years later. As the cloth trade grew in the area, it became the home of hundreds of self-employed craftsmen and merchants, exactly the types who followed the radical Protestant ideas current at the time. In the Civil War a Royalist army captured the town, and Cromwell's men surrounded them in a siege that became a major episode in the late stage of the war. The Royalists had a huge round cannon at the top of a wall by St Mary's church, which was blown up by Cromwell's troops, who made a rhyme about the direct hit. They named the cannon Humpty Dumpty, and referred to its fall from a wall.

That's the bit of history that everyone in the town knows. Such is the obsession with celebrity being attached to your town, the fact that's most remembered about the Civil War in Colchester is that it connected them with a celebrity nursery-rhyme character. But the town also has a claim on 'Old King Cole', who was a King of Colchester in the third century, and 'Twinkle Twinkle Little Star', which was written in a chapel there in the 1800s. It's as if the place is like a record label churning out hits, but in the difficult and competitive area of nursery rhymes.

Today Colchester is a classic spot for television crews to film drunk teenagers at the weekend. It may have given a false impression, but it's the only place I've ever seen a couple jacking up heroin in the High Street, which I suppose is a junky version of a romantic morning in bed with coffee and croissants.

Colchester seemed to struggle with its 2,000-year slide from fame. For example, there's an account of how elections were conducted in 1892 in the book *Colchester Voices*. Apparently, 'At election time the Liberal supporters would congregate down the bottom of the High Street, and the Conservatives at the top of North Hill. Then someone would blow a whistle and they'd start to march towards each other. I used to be there and got involved all right, pushing and kicking. They were the good old days. All the roughs of the town who wanted a fight joined in, about fifty on each side and the police didn't mind as long as there was no damage to property.' Immediately afterwards there was probably an excited reporter from Sky yelling, 'Our polls show the Conservatives won the fight, breaking sixteen ribs to the Liberals' nine. Let's see if we can hear what Mr Gladstone has to say about that.'

But at the heart of the town there's a sense that something of note must have happened here before. The town centre is yet another town centre, but the dual carriageway along the side passes an old stone wall, the sort that would cause my mum to say, 'Oo, that place has got a lot of history.' There's a huge water tower and odd bits of stone emerging from multi-storey car parks, giving rise to an expectation that everyone from Colchester must be brought up with some sense of their town's distinct place in history.

So when I performed at the theatre there, I wondered if there should be a more historical angle to the show than usual. And it might have gone that way, except that I mentioned the zoo, in which, it's claimed, there's a creature that's a cross between a zebra and a donkey, called a zedonk. I said that this seemed a handy myth with which to attract people to the zoo. I'd have got away lighter if I'd told them I spat on their gods and their mothers were whores.

The whole audience seemed to shout back, 'It's TROOOOO!' so I asked if anyone had seen this thing. 'YEEEEEEEES!' they all screamed. I felt as if I'd been sent to investigate reports from some remote part of the world about a man-eating yeti. 'When you saw this stripy donkey, or "zedonk",' I said, 'did the stripes tend to wash off in the rain? Did anyone notice used felt-tip pins lying nearby?'

The howls that this was an authentic zedonk became shrieks, and the audience seemed to elect someone to tell me calmly that this beast exists and is in their zoo. Although he was measured in his description I did feel he was about to finish, 'So ALL HAIL THE MIGHTY ZEDONK!' and everyone in the room would lie on the floor crying 'Ee-aw!'

For a moment I couldn't make up my mind. They'd seemed a rational bunch, but so do people who tell you they've been taken for a ride in a flying saucer, up to the point they tell you they've been taken for a ride in a flying saucer. I agreed to keep an open mind, but every couple of minutes from then on someone would lose control and shout, 'There IS a zedonk!' and someone else would give their account of meeting the bloody thing.

Every time I found myself becoming convinced, something would cast doubt. One person might announce that it died last year, then another would say it was still alive, and I'd wonder if someone was about to say, 'Oh, and something else – it flies and it holds up the sun.' While all the talk of Romans and Cromwell, of Boudica and weavers and sieges had largely slipped by, this issue seemed to cause uproar.

When I got home I discovered that Colchester Zoo has been noted, by various reputable institutions, for its work in breeding zebra/donkey hybrids. Darwin himself commented at length on the issue of zebras mating with donkeys, so I had to accept I'd been wrong, and be thankful Darwin hadn't been in the audience, or I'd have had him screaming at me as well.

There's a limit to how much impact all this history can have on a place which still exists as a town of 100,000 people. You can't expect that every time your neighbour sees you they'll say, 'Well, to think this was where Boudica took her revenge on the Romans all those years ago. Anyway, could you feed my fish while I'm away at the weekend?' Or that every time someone buys a lightbulb they say, 'Boudica never had one of these.'

I expect that in Carthage there are people who say the town is of great importance, because it's the only place for miles where you can get a decent set of trainers, and on Krakatoa people say, 'We've had all sorts happen here. One year the vicar ran off with a choirboy.'

I wonder what Boudica would have thought, as she looked across at her legions, prepared to die for the right to live and worship in liberty as they destroyed the symbols of the occupying Roman forces, if she'd known that one day, whatever the outcome, the people of this land would be united in heartfelt passion at the questioning of a fucking zedonk.

Exeter

If ever you fancy an in-depth account of the history of Exeter, I recommend the book I used for this study, *A Child's History of Exeter*. Because it was from this book I learned that in the tenth century Exeter was invaded three times by the Danes, and apparently the third time this happened, 'The people of Exeter said, "Oh no, not the Danes again, surely!"'

It's possible they went even further and added, 'Can't we be raped and pillaged by someone different?' But that's just guesswork, so it wouldn't be right to include it in a historical document.

Historians of the future might conclude that in the twentieth century Exeter was lucky to be invaded in a different way. Because a study found it was more overrun by chain stores than any other, making it the 'clone-town capital' of Britain. It was given this title by the committee that analyses Britain's towns, judging their cloneness by how many of the shops in their centres are chain stores.

At first this seems unexpected, because with the prejudice that comes from living in a big city, you can't help imagining that in the centre of a rural town in Devon the Asda is just the farmer's son selling onions out the back of his truck. I'm often caught out this way. I was in Shrewsbury one evening, wandering in a park by the banks of the River Severn near the Charles Darwin Shopping Centre, contemplating the ducks and pondering how peaceful Shropshire is compared to South London, when a teenage couple, sixteen at the oldest, emerged from under a bush beside me. The lad made a groan as if he was off his head on birdseed and Benylin, and the girl yelled in a perfect rural accent, 'How d'you expect me to say I love you when you fuckin' look like that, you fuckin' dick?' And she stomped off over the quaint footbridge as geese gently flapped in formation above her.

Because you forget that towns in the middle of large rural areas aren't rural, they're towns. And it may be that outside Exeter is a series of fields, and lanes that come to crossroads with no signposts, leaving you to guess which road winds on to Longdown and which goes three miles to a dead end by a vandalised barn so you have to reverse all the way back again. But inside Exeter is Zizzi's and Debenhams and H. Samuel, a university, an airport, and a record-breaking level of chain stores.

A wander around the title-winning city centre, though, suggests that it may have won the accolade unfairly, because between the ubiquitous shops and restaurants is a vast, majestic golden cathedral in the middle of the pedestrianised area that gives it a hint of distinction. And there are dinky alleys between the window displays, including Gandy Street, where a local artist has covered the walls in paintings of Elizabethan figures from the town.

The only thing is, John Lewis had some of them destroyed. According to *South-West Business* magazine: 'A spokesperson for DTZ Investment Management, the discretionary property fund manager of the John Lewis Pensions Fund, said, "The building is held as an investment, as part of a property portfolio, on behalf of the pension fund. The current occupier has advised us they intend to vacate the property when their lease expires. We are therefore looking to refurbish and improve the building in order to increase its appeal to potential occupiers."'

It would be almost impossible to compile a list of words more chillingly indifferent to anything beyond the demands of a property portfolio than those. Dickens would have struggled. He might have come up with a Mr Grabwall, who says every morning while shaving, 'Purchase my property, offer me stock, but paint on my wall, you can suck my cock.' But that would still seem Bohemian and riddled with hippyness compared to the prose of the good people at DTZ.

In a corner of one alley is a theatre with displays of local photos, and there are medieval passages under the High Street you can visit, stooping and squeezing through, so you feel part of an underground movement in hiding, waiting to run the town one day. And there's a prominent painting at the main station, in which an entire wall including the timetables is submerged behind two backpackers and two finely toned young men, one in shorts, gazing with intent at one another while striking poses of a Roman sculpture in what is known as the local homoerotic mural.

The cloneness of a town probably can't be measured simply by the number of shops selling the same autumn tops as their branch in Dundee. It may be more a case of how far its sense of identity is submerged.

And Exeter certainly has a unique past, that it likes to share with its children. Which must be why *A Child's History of Exeter* informs young historians that when the Romans were in charge of the town, a Roman teacher might tell his pupils, 'Leave your clothes over there and come and join me for some exercise. Let's start with some leapfrogs. We can ask a slave to clean our bodies. He'll cover them with oil and scrape it off with a metal hook. Don't worry.' This suggests that Exeter's social services department in Roman times wasn't as thorough as it should have been.

More widely known across the town is the wonderfully obscure hero figure of Bishop Leofric, who earned his place in history by compiling a book containing the first ever riddles. Like an idiot, I started reading them, thinking they'd be riddles as we understand them, with answers like 'A box of dates.' Or at least questions like, 'With my axe and my dagger I'll make you quite poorly, When I invade, folk say, "Not them again, surely." Who am I?'

Instead the Bishop's riddles are along the lines of asking what makes men incapable of performing any task but still attracts them. The answer is wine. They've been passed through folklore and were written in Saxon, so most of them would confuse people today if they popped up in a Christmas cracker, but they're a source of pride in the town, the originals protected by all manner of chunky glass and electric beams somewhere in the cathedral.

And they have a football club in Exeter, which has dropped out of the Football League and come back again, but which creates a sense of pride partly because it drags every other team in whichever league they're in hundreds of miles further than anyone else. Like all football teams it's had its moment of glory: for Exeter it was the period from 2002 to 2003, when Uri Geller became the co-chairman.

I find it impossible to hear this without imagining him being interviewed in front of logos for Lucozade Sport and Barclays, making comments such as, 'I think our problem today was when our midfield got the ball, they should have laid on the ground and breathed in the spirit of the universe to push away the demons that were allowing Dagenham and Redbridge to hit us on the break.'

Even more spectacular – and everyone I spoke to in the town mentioned this as a day Exeter would remember forever, for reasons entirely comical – was the day Uri brought his mate Michael Jackson to a match. Maybe he'd read about the games the Romans played, and decided it was a place Michael might identify with. But it's hard enough taking your football team seriously at the best of times, so who knows what that did to the psyche of the average Exeter fan.

Whatever impact it had, Michael did the town a favour, giving it something else that was defiantly, uniquely Exeter, and I suspect preventing it from deserving the title of Britain's clone-town league champion.

Portland

One of the eeriest places in Britain must be the Isle of Portland in Dorset. You get there via a sort of sea-level bridge, stretching over a vast field of pebbles across the water from Weymouth like a finger straining to reach a key that's fallen down the back of a fridge, or a passage into another world on a computer game. The road that crosses the island passes a hotel converted from a Ministry of Defence naval headquarters, cliffs covered in knee-length grass that should never ever be cut, several quarries where piles of pure white stones the size of sideboards have been randomly discarded like shopping trolleys by a canal, two lighthouses and a prison.

There's a website on which you can ask people on the island about the place. One person has asked if there's a shop that sells CDs. The first answer is, 'There are people on this island who've never seen a CD.' The second is, 'What's a CD? In fact what's a shop?' If you look up 'cinemas', it says, 'We've all got satellite TVs, so what's the point?'

I'm not sure I've ever been to a place that feels more like an island. The inhabitants even have a word, 'kimberlin', for people who come from off the island. This shows an admirable logic, to have a special word for that branch of the human race that *doesn't* come from the Isle of Portland. You could be from Paris, Ecuador or Weymouth, and you're a kimberlin. Whether you've been to the Chelsea Flower Show or to the depths of the Congo to live amongst the people and learn their customs, you've been mixing with kimberlins.

This might be a result of centuries of isolation before the road across the pebbles was built.

One historian of the area, J.W. Garren, wrote: 'At one time 90 per cent of the population of Portland had the surnames of Pearce, Stone, Comben, Attwooll, Flew or White.' So nearly everyone had one of six names. The calling of the register at school must have gone: 'Attwooll' – 'Here'; 'Attwooll' – 'Here'; 'Attwool' – 'Here'; 'Attwoll' – 'Here'; 'Attwoll – where's Attwoll?' – 'He's absent, sir.'

As a result, everyone became known by their nicknames. For example, a man called Fido Lunettes wrote in 1825 about a conversation he'd heard about: 'A gentleman made repeated enquiries after one James Miller, but his enquiries were fruitless. Meeting a man on the island he asked where Miller lived. "I don't know," was the immediate reply. "There's no such man on Portland, sir."

'The gentleman added, "He's also commonly known as Wapsy."

'"Oh, Wapsy," replied the Portlander, "That's my father."'

Yet Portland has been at the heart of some of the most innovative international modern city life, because the island is made of Portland stone. This is a result of how the land mass of Britain was apparently formed in two chunks. If you draw a diagonal line from Torquay in Devon to Hartlepool on Teesside, most of the country north of that line is made of rock that's over 300 million years old, which might have become coal or slate. But south of that line is younger, Jurassic, rock, only 140 million years old, a lot of which is chalk. And then there's limestone, made by the broken-down bones of fish and amphibians. In certain areas, especially Portland, the carbonate of lime has built up around the broken shells in tiny egg shapes, at which point it's called 'oolitic'. All this makes Portland's stone stick together in huge hard blocks, perfect for building. It also doesn't fade from that grand white imperial look that's perfect for huge columns and buildings that say, 'Take a good look at me when you walk past, won't you? Nelson attended a banquet behind these columns, you know, so don't you dare lean against me, you grubby peasant. I, if you didn't know, am oolitic.'

The Romans used stone from Portland, the Saxons used it, and in the seventeenth century six million tons of the stuff was blasted out from the quarries. Christopher Wren came to Portland to choose the stone he wanted to rebuild St Paul's Cathedral. Whitehall, the Cenotaph and the grandest buildings in New York were built from it. As you wander across this small island, past quarry after quarry, you start to imagine the prestigious buildings that were once embedded in the land before you. Surely there must be nothing left. Getting any more out must be like playing a giant version of that Jenga game, where you have to keep picking out blocks without everything collapsing. One day a crane driver will whisper, 'Right, we're going for this stone here – careful, careful, caaaareful, woooooah, oh shit, the Co-Op's collapsed.'

Everywhere you look in Portland there are stone houses, stone walls and obelisks commemorating no one in particular that were presumably built to use up some spare stone. So if your ambition is to have a statue made of yourself, it's advisable to move to Portland, do something like run two hundred yards in under three minutes or learn to say the alphabet backwards, and that should do it.

Walking through a quarry is one of the most masculine activities you can imagine. They're by necessity arenas of vast craggy ugliness, the odd digger clumping across their bases like a bored bear making its way across its pen. It would be impossible to do anything dainty in a quarry, like waltz or play table tennis. A quarryman showed me this giant hammer they use for cracking the stone out of the cliff, and there was a pneumatic drill that bores through huge rocks and cracks them in half. In effect, it enables you to beat a rock in a fight.

And that's before they use dynamite. I don't know if it's genetic or social, but no male can hear someone say 'Then we use the dynamite' without going, 'I want a go, I want a go.'

Then, as if designed according to local authority regulations which insist that all that aggression must be balanced with something tranquil, around the corner is a bird observatory. It's like a miniature lighthouse, and people climb up to a tiny platform where they can spend the night, ready to observe whatever flaps past at daybreak. The manager of the bird observatory had offered to take me on a tour of the tiny platform, but when I got there he was sat in a deckchair reading the local paper. 'Hello, I think we had a visit arranged,' I said, but he carried on reading his paper in that deliberate 'I'm reading the paper and not answering you' way that means someone isn't reading the paper at all but thinking, 'I bet this is annoying you – I'm reading the paper.'

'Hello,' I said again. 'I'm Mark Steel ...' He looked up from his paper and said, 'I know who you are, I looked you up on the internet. I don't think you're suitable for this bird observatory.' He then announced that he was therefore refusing to show me round. I don't know if something led him to believe I was from al Qaeda's ornithology department, or if he'd mixed me up with someone on YouTube breaking a world record for stamping on puffins, but getting barred from a bird observatory is possibly my proudest moment as a rebel. Stick that, Che Guevara. He might have ponced around with guns and attacks on Havana, but I bet he never got barred from a bird observatory.

Half a mile further south is the end of the island, stoically marked by the main lighthouse, beautifully chunky, industrial and determined, standing on a cliff where the wind must cause havoc for the people who compile the Shipping Forecast by blowing in every direction at once. This lighthouse isn't there to look pretty and stripy: ships depend on the thing, and it looks as if it has bacon, egg, sausage, chips, beans and two slices every morning before blowing its first fog warning, and if it has fingers they're yellow from thirty years of roll-ups. As you stand beneath it defying the swirling uppercuts of wind, you will never have felt so awake. They should take people who've been in a coma for years to the Portland lighthouse. Three minutes on that clifftop and they'll be shrieking, 'Jesus what the fuck!' and unhooking their drip.

It all felt glorious and slightly dangerous, and I had started to lose myself in thoughts of schooners and shipwrecks when a man licking a Cornetto said to his wife in a London accent with amber-alert aggression, 'That fucking foghorn's doing my head in.'

The collection of unusual buildings continues with the hotel, converted from the Ministry of Defence building. Sitting at the top of a sinister hill, it is still surrounded by unscaleable fences and checkpoints where you imagine the odd double-crossing Bulgarian was discreetly shot through the head with a bullet from a long, silent pistol during the Cold War. Maybe the council insist on retaining the original features or something, or there's a preservation order on the barbed wire, but the result is that you expect that at any moment a soldier will point a gun at you and yell, 'Put the complimentary biscuits down NOW!'

The ground floor is a series of enormous oblong rooms all connected by a concrete path, giving it the ambience and in places the smell of a hospital. The place is managed by a young Czech who somehow is always right behind you. Three times, at diverse points in the hotel, I said out loud, 'Where am I?' to myself, and each time the smiling Czech suddenly appeared and said, 'Can I help, sir?' From my room to the restaurant was a ten-minute walk, along corridors leading to corridors and more corridors, like at Heathrow when you're walking to the place where you collect your bag after landing. I decided to run along one corridor, off which there must have been fifty doors, all painted the identical blue of the blue of the carpet and the blue of the walls, so that as I ran I wasn't even sure I was going forward – it was like a depiction of an acid trip in a film from the sixties. At the end was an enormous door, the sort that might be the entrance to the head office of a major bank. I went through it and found myself outside, on a patch of grass leading to a cliff with the sea air pinching me beneath the right angles of this military structure. To my right appeared the Czech, who said, 'Are you lost, sir?' adding, 'I saw you were running.' At that point it seemed almost certain that the next person I'd see would be Jack Nicholson with an axe.

There are separate villages within Portland, but Portland is the area that people there identify with. A sentence from an islander will often start with 'The Portland people ...' and go on to describe some trait such as 'are proud of their wind', or 'don't like to be rushed in the morning'. Weymouth is a foreign power, distrusted as if it was stealing Portland's stone, with blatant disregard for UN resolutions. In the official history of Portland by Stuart Morris, there's often a diversion such as: 'The *Dorset County Chronicle* remarked of a parade in Weymouth in 1863, "Portland men were all half a head taller than Weymouthians. They are a fine, strong, healthy race, greatly superior in stature, both in person and intelligence."' See. That proves it.

There is one issue, though, that all visiting kimberlins should be aware of before they arrive. On Portland no one's allowed to say the word 'rabbit'. For example, when the Wallace and Gromit film *The Curse of the Were-Rabbit* came out, a special poster had to be devised for Portland, which renamed it *The Curse of the Were-Bunny*. This must, you think at first, be a joke played on tourists. But then someone will tell you about 'underground mutton' or, as in Stuart Morris's book, say, 'Monks introduced a furry little creature with long ears in the twelfth century.' The first time a Portlander tells you how blasphemous it is to say the word, on account of the awful luck it will surely bring, you joke along with them, and then realise they've maintained an earnest expression, the same one they'd use if they were warning you not to go past the deserted house on the hill, as the ground turns into quicksand.

Then comes that awkward moment when someone you've been chatting amiably to for a while calmly and suddenly reveals themselves as mad. You're forced to try to maintain your demeanour, and maybe even to appear genuinely keen to hear more about what you've just been told, in the way you might say, 'Oh that must be a useful talent. How often do you use this ability to turn someone into a snake?'

Nobody is sure why the custom arose, but it may have originated with quarrymen, as it's possible that the sight of rabbits scurrying was a sign of the impending collapse of some ground. Even so, I'd have thought that in those circumstances it would be unlucky *not* to say 'rabbit', as you'd be screaming at your colleagues, 'Get away quick, I've seen what-nots, you know, no not Hell's Angels, warren-dwelling mammals renowned for their sexual proclivities, oh too late everyone's buried under a heap of rubble.'

But if anywhere can get away with upholding a superstition that would seem irrational to your average medieval leper, it's Portland. The whole place is bracingly disjointed. Its beaches aren't sandy and inviting, but stony and hidden between cliff faces; not for the all-day bather, but for the smug bastard who goes swimming there for one minute at six in the morning so he can feel he's achieved something with his life.*

---

* While there I went swimming for one minute at six in the morning, and as a result felt I'd achieved something with my life.

Having warmed to the wind and the long grass, the weather that's glorious because it's on the edge of violence, the charming sense of pride in perceiving Weymouth as a domineering historic foe, I found myself accepting the legitimacy of banning the word for a species not dissimilar to the hare. After four or five people had told me that it really *really* mustn't be said, the custom seemed like a religious practice. You could no more justify upsetting them by deliberately saying it than you could go up to a tribe of Aboriginals who thought taking a photograph of them removes their soul, and locking them in the *Big Brother* house with cameras in every corner while yelling, 'We don't have souls, we're just physical organisms, you irrational idiots!'

Even so, you ought to be aware if your custom seems eccentric to those who are not in on it, and I decided to end the show I did on Portland by making that point. I talked about its origins and asked Stuart Morris his theories about it, and what struck me was how any word can acquire the power to create tension if enough people agree on it. Because each time I ventured near to a place where I might be approaching saying the dreaded word, there was a communal mini-gasp, until I became aware that to actually say it would be so perverse, would break so many rules, that a switch in my head was deleting the possibility of saying it, the same one that ensures you don't say 'cunt' to your mate's granny.

But I'd worked out an ending, which was to suggest as the show was part of a series celebrating communities, there could be no more appropriate way of ending it than with a community singalong, and the perfect song would be the Chas & Dave classic that everyone must know, so, 'Come on Portland, everyone join in: "Oh you won't stop talking, why don't you give it a rest ..."'

The tension broke, in the way a stand-off between two blokes glaring at each other in a pub for two hours finally breaks when one of them whacks the other with a pool cue. Some people laughed, some shrieked, with possibly a laughy air, some booed, and one man stood and raised his middle finger while thrusting his hand aggressively forward, in a gesture strangely modern given what was troubling him. Someone else leaned back and frisbeed a pound coin that just missed its target and hit the curtain at the back of the stage.

This was thrilling. History has recorded performers causing riots before, perhaps by singing in support of black rights in segregated states of America, or giving licence to teenage rebellion in the 1950s. Now I knew what they felt like. Bill Haley, Lenny Bruce, Nirvana, Tupac, and now my version of Chas & Dave's 'Rabbit' were in the same bracket.

The producer, at the side of the stage, looked quizzical, possibly because of the ending we'd worked out. So while the finger-thrusting and discontent continued I stopped singing and said, 'Don't worry, the last thing I want to do is upset everyone by coming to Portland and saying "rabbit".'

As I was saying this I actually felt quite tense, the way a suicide bomber might feel in the moments before he detonates himself. As with most disturbances, only a minority of the people present were actually involved, but that minority seemed quite upset, storming out and presumably thinking, 'Why do comedians these days insist on using bad language? Why can't they stick to "shit", "fuck" and "arseholes" like proper family entertainers?'

Afterwards I sat in the bar, which was in one corner of a cavernous space that could easily have been used for archery practice. In the opposite corner, away in the distance, was a grand piano. A couple in their seventies came over, and the man, wearing a precisely knotted maroon cravat, said, 'I've lived here all my life, and these buggers need telling how bloody daft they are.' He walked off with a defiant gait as I sat pondering how at last I appeared to have made a political impact, on the most unlikely of issues. I chatted for a few moments to other people who'd been in the show, then heard a chorus from the piano –

'Run Rabbit Run'. It was the man in the cravat, while next to him we could just make out his wife's expression, that said, 'Fifty years I've been putting up with him causing trouble like this.'

Motorways

Many of the great advances in civilisation have involved travel: ships, railroads and aircraft have made cities and continents accessible to people who would otherwise have had no hope of getting there. During the Enlightenment, as well as demands for rational thought and democracy, some of the most radical thinkers became obsessed with bridges. Ballooning fascinated, as did the earliest pushbikes and cars, not only because of the speed at which they travelled but of the way they offered a new view of the world, the fusion of science and art, the intricate ingenuity of the steam train, galleon or Golden Gate Bridge enabling the hitherto unimaginable exhilaration of glorious vistas of mountain ranges, oceans and plains. I wonder if it felt the same when they opened the M6.

Maybe a certain type of engineer feels a tinge of excitement as he approaches his favourite slip road, but generally the motorway is brutally functional. No one even pretends the journey itself will be fun, it just gets you to junction 34 in two hours. So when you're sat motionless in a line of motionless traffic on a concrete strip that serves no purpose apart from motion, you enter a world of unmatchable pointlessness. You can't even read or do a crossword, because every forty seconds you have to put the car into first gear, creep forward a few yards and then stop again, each little judder as you stop representing another failure. If they'd had motorways in ancient Greece there would have been myths about men who defied the gods and were condemned to spend an eternity on the M1 just south of Luton, shuffling twenty yards every couple of minutes and never finding out the reason why.

For a few minutes it's possible to listen to a CD, but eventually even that becomes a reminder of how long you've been there. A whole ska compilation comes to an end five lamp posts after you put it on, and you realise it's better to go into a trance with nothing to measure time by. In the end you exhaust all possible distractions. You've eaten all the chocolate éclairs, wriggled into every position and picked every orifice. You adjust your expectations of arriving again, writing off another birthday but hoping to be there for the birth of the second grandchild. You envy that bloke in the film who trapped his arm under a rock and had to saw it off to get out, as at least he had a plan. And you dream of the turn-off to Northampton, which is 150 miles from where you're heading, but if you ever reach it you'll be out of this queue and can start a new life there like a refugee, though there'll probably be lots of you trying the same thing and you'll be despised by the locals who complain there isn't room in their town for the roadworks community, who get whatever they want off the council and ought to get back to the M1 where they came from.

Sometimes when these queues end there's no apparent reason why they ever happened. The traffic just starts moving freely. It's almost a disappointment. At least if there was a lorry on fire or alligators in the middle lane or a crashed spaceship you'd be able to rationalise it, but off you go as if someone's been playing with you, like a torturer who doesn't even want information from you but just enjoys watching you scream, then releases you when he's bored.

Even when it's working, you don't pass anything on a motorway except numbers. You don't pass Rugby in the sense of experiencing even a glimpse of the place through the window, you pass it in the sense that it's seventy more miles to Nottingham.

While you're on a motorway your whole world – the road, the signs, the vehicle you're in, the service stations – stays exactly the same, regardless of where you are. So it's a shock when you stop for petrol and the lad in the shop has a Birmingham accent, as it's the first clue as to where you're actually at, rather than just on the motorway. This means there are places we all know the names of simply as points we pass: Newport Pagnell, Keele, Membury, Flitwick, Wednesbury. They're real because they represent another target reached, but maybe there's no such actual place. You could easily make up somewhere, add it to the road sign on junction 30 of the M1, and before long millions of people would be familiar with Iddlethorpe, and tell themselves regularly that they were always happy to pass Iddlethorpe as it meant they were only forty minutes from Sheffield.

So it's a puzzle why so many people prefer to travel this way, rather than by the motorway's main competitor, the train. One reason must be the cost. Somehow the price of a return rail ticket from London to Manchester comes to around the same as the petrol for most cars, so if two of you go together it's half the price to drive. Then there's the wonder of the peak fare policy.

Until 2010 there was a rule that the rail companies couldn't raise fares by more than 1 per cent above the inflation rate. They got round this by extending the peak times, when a return from Manchester to London costs over £300, just short of an average return fare to New York. 'This only affects a small percentage of customers,' explained the operator, the way Reggie Kray might have exclaimed, 'What's the fuss? I only shot 3 per cent of the people I met all week.'

If you turn up at three in the afternoon you'll be told in an emotionless voice that you have the option of paying a £230 supplement or waiting four hours until the next off-peak service. These alternatives are so ridiculous they might as well have fun with them and add, 'Or you can be injected with depleted uranium in a Ministry of Defence experiment, then you can stand in coach E on the 4.15 for only £137.65.'

Then there's the way many trains are now so packed that people are sat on the floor between seats, their cases piled across doorways, or standing for two hours, and a trip to the toilet is like being on *Total Wipeout* as you clamber over rucksacks and vault over distressed toddlers until you wouldn't be surprised to hear, 'We apologise to customers for the outbreak of cholera on this service,' and you wonder if you've inadvertently got on the wrong train and boarded a shuttle ferrying refugees away from a military coup in Chad.

Most of the problems with trains would probably be solved by simply having more of them. There's still a sense of destiny in getting a train to Newcastle or Glasgow, a feeling as you walk through the station, between the people rushing with forty seconds to clamber on board, amidst the traditional echoey indecipherable announcements, past the queue of taxis and the beggars and booths selling pasties, that you're doing something that matters.

The profit-driven motives of the rail companies can't entirely destroy the experience, but they have a go. One problem presented by privatisation is the difficulty of going somewhere but coming back via a different route, which entails travelling with two different companies and causes mayhem. Ask to go to Sheffield but to come back from Manchester and the poor member of staff looks at you with such bemusement you wonder if, by mistake, you said, 'And on the way back I'll need a carriage to myself as I like to have a wank as I'm going through Stafford.'

Then there's the dispiriting business of trying to contact the rail company at all, which is more irritating than the old British Rail system of there being no number to ring in the first place. Virgin seem to excel in automated chill-speak, and Richard

Branson was rewarded for this effort with the statistic that Virgin received twice as many complaints as any other rail operator, and more than all the others put together. Perfectionist that Branson is, Virgin also has the worst record for answering complaints, replying to a wonderful 36 per cent within twenty days.

I enjoyed some of this service when I rang to reserve a seat, but couldn't get through for twenty-six minutes. When I said I'd like to complain I was put on hold for another fifteen minutes. Then I was told the complaints department was very busy, so could I ring back later. Later I called the customer relations department, who told me, 'This can happen.'

'Is there an explanation?' I asked, and she said, 'I've given you one.'

I said, 'What was it?' and she said, 'I *told* you – this can happen.'

Just to make sure, I said, 'Are you telling me "This can happen" is the explanation?'

'Yes,' she said triumphantly.

So it seems Virgin is being run by philosophers from the thirteenth century. When someone rings to ask why they were stuck for two hours outside Preston they must be told, 'Ah, 'tis God's will.' The station announcements will soon say: 'We apologise for the cancellation of the 2.15 to Coventry. This is due to the fact that this can happen. It's not our place to incur the wrath of our creator by asking why.'

I can think of two ways we might restore the splendour associated with travel in the nineteenth century, while retaining today's (usually) higher speeds. Firstly, regulators of the rail networks could compel the companies to employ people to greet passengers as they arrive at their destination using nineteenth-century language. They could take their cases and say, 'Sir, I welcome you to our humble city. It is indeed an honour to be visited by one as esteemed as your good self. I trust your journey was not too arduous, and can only hope the buffet car did not suffer its customary malfunction of a faulty boiler, rendering hot liquid refreshments unattainable. Also I offer my deepest regret at the exorbitant fee which you were obliged to forfeit, and my sincerest hope that your business here is so outlandishly profitable that the fare may be covered. And you, madam – rarely has this station been graced with such beauty, which shines miraculously, if I may be permitted to say so, given that you've spent three hours squashed between a tower of suitcases, four crying toddlers and a bloke of six foot five who drank nine tins of Stella, with your back pressed against an automatic door that periodically opened and jolted shut on your fingers.'

Or they could refranchise the entire network to steam-train enthusiasts. Because a remarkable feature of Britain is that every area has a steam-train line, staffed by volunteers who spend their holidays polishing pistons and fixing gaskets so that on a Sunday they can beam with joy in their jackets with shiny buttons as families plonk half-excited, half-bewildered children on the gleaming train that puffs to a nearby village and back. The boundless glee of these characters is so infectious that they should be paid to run the national rail service properly.

Hardly anyone would still use motorways as every old train was put back into service, and thousands would arrive at the stations every day just to travel and come back, so they could enjoy buying a little cardboard ticket that gets punched by a smiley guard, who helps you onto the train and waves at you as it pulls away. Then as it thundered past Watford Junction you'd see the ticket collector in his cap kneel next to the businessman opposite as he was collating figures on his laptop, and say, 'Now then, I hear it's your birthday today. So, as a special treat, would you like to come and sit with the driver?'

They'd be so intent on making the trip as fun as possible, you wouldn't be all that surprised if a guard whispered to you, 'Just for you, because we know what makes a journey special for you, we're going to give you a carriage all to yourself as we go through Stafford.'

Yorkshire

Part of the quaintness of Britain is how it's divided into counties. There's no difference in language, culture, or identity as you
cross from Bedfordshire into Buckinghamshire or Dorset into
Somerset, because for two hundred years almost every area has
been identified either as a town, or by the town that's nearest to
it. As counties were set up as fourteenth-century fiefdoms,
someone must have decided we ought to keep them going
anyway, because these changes shouldn't be rushed.

As a result, no one's sure which counties the biggest towns
are in. Manchester is the heart of Lancashire, but bits of it are
in Cheshire, and most of it is in a district of its own in no
county, so a visiting Palestinian would assume it's a disputed
territory overseen by the United Nations. Birmingham is sort
of in Warwickshire but not really, and no one can explain what
Middlesex is, let alone where it starts. Is it a county, or the
capital, or a local authority? Someone could make a case for it
being a comet. It seems to include bits of central London,
Berkshire, Hertfordshire and assorted random areas. There's
probably a strip of land in Afghanistan where the Royal Mail
is responsible for the postal service, as its postcode is Middlesex
AF9.

It's not surprising that the institutions that cling to the county
system most doggedly are cricket and BBC local radio, institutions not known for their eagerness to embrace change.

A few counties, such as Essex, have a jokey image that defines them as an area in which the women all have artificial suntans and think chocolate milk comes out of brown cows, but in reality there's nothing that unites the place. Essex starts in Leyton, where people think of themselves as East Londoners, moves on to Chelmsford, where the town slogan could be 'Made a few bob in the building game, moved out of London, got a semi-detached with a gravelly path and a statue of something or other in the garden, I'm laughing.' Further east are rural areas with rural accents and handwritten signs urging passers-by to pick their own blackberries. And in the middle is Harlow, where the motto is probably 'I tell you what we did last night, went down Chelmsford and nicked this wanker's statue.'

Cornwall, as discussed elsewhere, has some sense of identity, and so does Kent to an extent, but the only county that instils a true sense of purpose to anyone connected with it must be Yorkshire.

You'll be told someone behaves as they do 'because I'm from Yorkshire', in a way that would be inconceivable if they were from Wiltshire or Leicestershire. Followers of Yorkshire County Cricket Club cheer their team in the way people cheer a national side, not just because they identify with the club but because they love *Yorkshire*.

There's a dialect, that might alter from Barnsley to Halifax but is still Yorkshire, in which laking is playing, snap is food and 'appen means maybe.

The Yorkshire manner is perceived to be a dour determination to 'tell it like it is'. For example, Yorkshire's record-breaking batsman Geoff Boycott is famous for his 'gruff honesty', such as responding to a question about a player who had to go home from the World Cup because he was suffering from depression by saying, 'I'm not surprised he was depressed. He must have heard what I've been saying about him, that he's not good enough.' Then he added, 'I'm from Yorkshire, we don't get depressed.'

I met Boycott once, at a Test match, and he was gloriously entertaining. I was with my son, who was twelve at the time, and Kevin Pietersen, England's star batsman of the time, was out caught. 'Pietersen's shot was bad, wasn't it, Geoffrey?' said my lad. Boycott, while delicately holding a cup and saucer, said, 'Bad? It was a pile of shit.'

Being from Yorkshire is often offered as an explanation. You could make a speech at a wedding that ends, 'I can't see it lasting, surely she could do better than this steaming ugly hideous sphincterous disfigured idle moron,' and someone would say, 'Oh well, he's from Yorkshire. They don't mince their words,' the way you might excuse someone who suddenly throws a chair out of the window by saying, 'He was in Vietnam. He has good days and bad days.'

Clearly, not everyone from Yorkshire behaves like this. There are shy people from Yorkshire and tactful people from Yorkshire and even depressed people from Yorkshire, and if someone from Yorkshire works for the Samaritans they can't spend all night barking, 'I'm not surprised thou wants to top thyself, thou's nowt worth living for, thou daft bugger.'

But there is a sense of identity, that has resulted in furious campaigns whenever an attempt has been made to redraw the county boundaries, for example. This must add to the sense of 'defending the community' when it's perceived as under attack from 'outsiders'. Sheffield was the most militant town in Britain at the time of the French Revolution, the Luddites' strongest base was in Yorkshire, miners' leader Arthur Scargill came from Barnsley, and in the 1970s the news often referred to the 'Socialist Republic of South Yorkshire'. During the 1984 miners' strike there was a sense across much of the county that Yorkshire, rather than just the miners of Yorkshire, was under threat.

But Yorkshireness doesn't necessarily drive the county's people in a socialist direction, as their distrust of outsiders can stretch to a suspicion of anything vaguely modern, and can be used to justify an earthy racism. For example, Yorkshire county cricket matches were often venues for the abuse of Asian players. Of Britain's major cities it was Leeds where the National Front had most success in the 1970s, and the same was true thirty years later with the British National Party.

But while there's a definite sense of Yorkshire, it contains multiple unfathomable rivalries, possibly more than any other county. Maybe this is because most of it is made up of small distinct towns, which grew up around a mill or a pit during the early stages of the Industrial Revolution. So there are a million semi-jokey hostilities (such as the Skipton view of Keighley as a 'sink of evil').

The book *Huddersfield Voices*, written by a local author, tells us: 'Huddersfield is as it was, not as elegant as Leeds but at least not as ugly as Bradford.'

There are probably academic tomes, considered as seminal works among Yorkshire professors and published by university presses for eighty quid, that go, 'In comparison with Pontefract, Rotherham's shite. And if thou's reading, Professor Whitworth CBE, Dean of Leeds University, work of thine on cotton exports int' 1830s were double shite, and I'll tell thee that to thy face if thee dare come near Ponty.'

Huddersfield seems classically Yorkshire, especially when approached from the west across Emley Moor, past the fields where *Last of the Summer Wine* was filmed and a huge telecommunications mast that's visible from all West Yorkshire.

The greatest Luddite battle took place near Huddersfield, when stocking-makers threatened with unemployment shot dead one of the wealthiest mill owners, William Horsfall. After this incident there were more troops sent to Huddersfield than had been at Waterloo.

Another consequence was that shortly before going to Huddersfield for a show, I asked on Twitter if anyone had a comment they'd like to make about the town, and a few people from the area mentioned the Luddites. Then someone wrote on Twitter, 'Go on Mark, you slag off the Luddites as much as you like, it's not like they'll be following you on here.'

Now, there's one thing the town seems proud of above all else, which is its role in inventing rugby league. Rugby was originally played in the public schools only, and it was considered a fundamental rule of the spirit of the game that no one should be paid for playing it. Then in 1895 a meeting took place in the George Hotel in Huddersfield, at which representatives from twenty-two northern clubs formed a different style of rugby, with payment allowed, to attract working-class men to play the sport.

This meeting seems to be known about by every resident of the town. They refer to it with gleeful enthusiasm, and seem astonished that you didn't know about it, as if you went to Calvary and said, 'Did anything of note ever happen here?'

The hotel itself has been moved, and is now opposite the station, by the much less revered statue of Harold Wilson, who was born in the town. Inside it is a shrine to rugby league, so much so that it's officially recognised as a museum. The walls opposite the reception are covered in huge framed photos of generations of men diving through mud, and you're directed to a room full of trophies and newspaper cuttings of classic matches from *Daily Mirror*s and *Daily Sketch*es over the last hundred years.

Amongst these snippets are a framed front page of the *Daily Mirror* depicting VE-Day, and one of the moon landing. So it looks as if someone's put together their top two hundred events of the twentieth century, which in their opinion were VE-Day, the moon landing and 198 games of rugby league, including a scrappy win for Castleford at Widnes which just edged out the First World War.

Then there are more rooms and corridors and staircases, all packed with mesmerising framed jerseys and photographs, so you find yourself thinking, 'Ah yes, dear old Bobby "Battleship" Armworth,' before remembering you've never heard of any of these people before. But it's beautifully captivating, like being shown pictures of an extended family by a proud grandparent. It's pride from below. Any town might be lucky enough to provide a Prime Minister, but to invent a sport and then sustain it for more than a century takes the dedication of thousands of people.

The influence of rugby league is also evident in *Huddersfield Voices*. For example, there's an account by David Gronow, Secretary of Huddersfield Rugby League Players' Association, with some charming tales, such as, 'In a match against Wigan they singled out Tony Johnson, a police officer and the only coloured guy on the pitch. They gave him some stick; every time he ran they clobbered him with a forearm smash. Tony laughed about it afterwards, it was just good-natured violence.'

As you're pondering the implications of this, he says that his favourite coach was Maurice Bamford: 'Maurice wasn't too fond of his mother-in-law, who'd had a pacemaker fitted. Maurice found out that microwaves, in the early days, could interact with pacemakers. So he offered to poach her an egg in one and within no time she wasn't well and had to go home. Maurice said the microwave was worth every penny.'

She probably laughed about it later, saying it was just good-natured attempted murder.

About twenty miles north is Keighley, and then Skipton, which is so dominated by cattle-farming that the theatre is a cattle market. In the daytime the cows are paraded and sold, then the farmers depart and a hose is brought out to wash away what the beasts deposited and you do the show on the platform where a few hours earlier the auctioneer was taking bids for cattle. So the shows are accompanied by the sweet but all-encompassing aroma of a thousand cowpats. It would be comforting to think the cattle are aware of this, thinking, 'I may be off to slaughter, but a bit of me will still be here. Let's see if they can concentrate on Chekhov while *that's* wafting past.'

Around the backstage area, instead of the usual signed posters for *An Evening with Bill Beaumont* and a one-man show about the life of Dr Goebbels, there are huge photos of prize-winning bulls, and trophies for '1986 Friesian of the Year'. Just outside the auditorium, where you would normally expect a little café and maybe some exhibits from a local artist, there's a shop selling fishing rods and wellington boots.

The area where you wait behind the curtain to go onstage is the start of the pens where the cattle go once they've been bought. So you'd have to worry if a panto was on there – the poor sod in the cow costume would only have to take a wrong turning and he'd end up in the abattoir, forlornly screaming, 'Don't mince me, I'm Keith Chegwin.'

You get some idea of the dominance of farming in the town's history from a local book that explains the impact of the Road Traffic Act of the 1930s: 'The Act took much of the fun out of buses. No longer could operators accept calves, crates of hens and piglets on their buses, when the driver's reward might be a brace of rabbits.'

So even the bus fares were paid in animals. You imagine the conductor saying, 'Have you nowt smaller? I've no change for an ox.'

Back in 1877 animals were held in higher esteem than now. A travelling circus advertised: 'For the first time in Britain come and see Tipster, the world's first clairvoyant educated talking horse.' Which suggests how hard to please they are in Yorkshire – it has to be an *educated* talking horse, otherwise they'd go, 'That horse ain't worth seeing. I asked it if it'd read much Russian literature, and it said, "I can't say as I have." Well, I don't call that conversation.'

Now, with delicate green barges drifting along the canal, the High Street has a market running its whole length, and at the end of it there's a castle. There seem to be about forty butchers, one of which has two huge smiling cartoon pigs on the front, who seem to be in a chirpy mood considering all their mates have been hacked to pieces and laid out to be sold indoors.

It feels as if everyone should be talking in Yorkshire ITV Sunday-night drama language. For example, although there's a curry house, you expect it to be full of farmers resting their arms on the table and saying, 'I tell 'ee what, Betty love, I'll have a bowl o' your piping hot dopiaza if you don't mind, to warm me toes.'

Even in a brothel in Skipton, you imagine, the clients take off their mud-spattered overcoats and say, 'Hello, Elsie love. I shan't be after full session tonight if thee don't mind. I've to be up at dawn to take lamb to vet's at Otley. So just hand relief'll do me fine, if that's a'right with thee.'

Recently Skipton's Yorkshireness has helped to retain the town's independence, keeping out almost all the chain stores and being declared 2008 High Street of the Year by whoever decides these things. Everyone seems aware of this achievement, and its implications.

The main streets feel constantly busy. The market's open almost every day, and there's a constant gentle flow of Yorkshireness in all directions. The chatter of people who've met unexpectedly or gathered round a market stall seems almost quaint, because it couldn't happen in the same way in a pedestrianised precinct.

And yet it isn't contrived to attract coach parties and American tourists (although the Brontë sisters lived nearby in Haworth, and Jim, who runs one of the canal-boat rides, told me he enjoys saying in his commentary, 'See that tree there, that's where Emily Brontë lost her virginity,' because Americans believe him).

For the genuine twee, effete, fake-cosy Yorkshire experience you must embrace the delights of Harrogate. Wander round the town centre there and you have to assume that in the local diet, when you need something quick and wholesome to sustain you through a day of physical labour, nothing beats a jar of asparagus chutney garnished with locally-produced satsuma curd in a jar with a frilly bit of yellow cloth tied over the lid. When someone in Harrogate rolls out of the pub in need of some late-night starch to soak up the beer, I imagine they queue at the late-night deli for a slice of stilton that takes forty minutes to wrap in chequered paper with a ribbon tied round it.

Harrogate developed into this sort of place when it became a spa town in the late seventeenth century, after local entrepreneurs convinced wealthy people that the water from the town's mineral springs had healing powers, and that if they bathed in them their vacuous lives might last a bit longer.

The novelist Tobias Smollett wrote an account of a visit to Harrogate in 1766. He described how the visitors spent their time at exquisite balls and playing cards, adding: 'The water is said to have effected so many cures. I drank it once, and it cured me only of the desire to ever do so again. Some people say it smells like rotten eggs, others compare it to the scourings of a foul gun. The only effects it produced were sickness, griping and insurmountable disgust. I can hardly mention it without puking.'

Bathing in this natural stinking steaming sulphuric potion regularly made healthy people feel ill, but somehow the local tourist board marketed the spa as an attraction rather than a punishment for witchcraft.

So it was visitors from outside the county who fuelled Harrogate's prosperity and secured its image.

But nowhere is one-dimensional, and Harrogate has also been the centre of militant protest. In the 1930s the council approved a change to the town's main park, in which some of the grass would be replaced by a flowerbed. The local population were at last driven to take up arms. A committee was formed to coordinate the opposition to this breach of human rights, and angry meetings were held across the town. When these were ignored the movement developed a guerrilla wing, and invaded councillors' squash matches. Still the elitist fascist flowerbed went ahead, and there were probably marches with demonstrators chanting 'Rhododendrons OUT!' and carrying placards that read, 'They say hydrangea, we say don't put the simplicity of the park in danger.'

This was Harrogate's Civil Rights movement, but the campaign seemingly went down to defeat when the flowerbed was finally installed. But then came a dramatic development, when a local businessman who'd funded the campaign got his chauffeur to drive his Rolls-Royce across the flowerbed, ruining the whole thing. Maybe this is what the protest movement needs more of, employing staff to carry out guerrilla activities. Direct action would be so much more convenient if you could simply tell the servants, 'Once you've swept out the scullery could you nip into Harrods and do in a couple of windows to oppose cuts in public services, there's a good chap.'

Harrogate's history allows it to retain an independence from cloned chain-store dominance, but in a less attractive way than its neighbour Skipton. A traditional jazz band stands by the unfeasibly immaculate green and plays 'When the Saints Go Marching In' all day on a Saturday. I suppose they must play other tunes as well, but it always feels as if that's what they're playing. Opposite their pitch is the famous Betty's Tea Rooms, where the queue in the morning generally takes an hour to get to the front of.

The reward once you've been admitted is the opportunity to buy a scone for £4. You might think that would be an unlikely candidate as one of the things people are prepared to queue that long for, but for some reason it's up there with seeing the dentist on Christmas Day and voting in a country's first election after thirty years of military rule. When people queue to buy something it's usually to get a bargain, but the long line at Betty's seems to have misunderstood the jubilant types who appear on the news on Boxing Day with their new coat, so that if a news reporter was around they'd screech, 'I waited outside all day, but it's worth it because I got this AMAZING toast and marmalade and it's normally ninety pence but I got it for EIGHT POUNDS FIFTY, so I'm THRILLED.'

To add to the surreal nature of Harrogate, it now has a major conference centre, so living there must feel a bit peculiar, because every time you'd pop out for a pint of milk you'd find yourself surrounded by huddles of carpet salesmen or orthopaedic surgeons wearing name tags and carrying folders.

This is all part of the complex and contradictory nature of Yorkshire, which at least would never be fooled into paying to be dunked into its own stinking cauldrons, as the whole county would say, 'Healthy, is that? It's a pile of shit.'

Nottingham

One of the most surprising starts to any book I've read is the opening lines of *A Centenary History of Nottingham*. It's a six-hundred-page academic study, with graphs depicting matters such as the growth of lace exports from the city, but the first words of the introduction are: 'Visitors tend to come in search of the people's hero Robin Hood, to buy the famous lace, and to stare at the pretty girls.'

Does that really happen in Nottingham? Do coach parties arrive, take pictures of Sherwood Forest, buy a gift in the lace museum, then have two hours set aside for going 'Wahoooooor, you don't get arses like that in Luton,' before light refreshments and the return journey?

I felt it would be hard to take anything else this book said seriously. Maybe a table of average incomes in each parish in the 1950s would be followed by, 'I tell you what's not average though, the tits on the barmaid in the pub by the station. Anyway, let's get back to post-war wage rises for the semi-skilled.'

This seems to be part of a pattern. William Cobbett, the radical reformer of the early nineteenth century, wrote that his interest in Nottingham was stirred by 'Tales of Robin Hood, and rumours of its sprightly and beautiful women'.

As well as this, it seems to be believed by many people in the town that there are several women in Nottingham for every man. When I first heard this, in the 1980s, I was told the ratio was eight to one. Since then I've been informed by people from the city that it's a variety of figures. When I asked for comments from Nottingham residents, one poor sod sent me a message saying, 'I moved to Nottingham because I heard there were three women for every man, so now some bastard must be going out with six women.'

The claims are so obviously untrue that you feel like dragging anyone who makes them to the main square, and making them count the numbers of each gender as they go past. In fact the percentage of women in Nottingham must be lower than in any other town, because the rumours about how many women there are must have attracted thousands of single blokes.

This myth of the town as an East Midlands version of a South Sea island full of unfeasibly stunning women where all the men have perished at sea, might be part of a thread, in which somehow Nottingham has combined being pivotal to Britain's industry, from the days of the earliest mills, with being possibly the most romantic city in the country. Thus the tale of a gallant outlaw robbing the rich to pay the poor is based there, and one of the main streets is called Maid Marian Way.

One of the greatest romantics of the industrial age, Lord Byron, Europe's first pin-up boy, spent much of his youth at Newstead Abbey, near the town centre, of which he became lord. It's probable that he learned his passion for valuing the fascinating and beautiful over the functional there, from his mother. Because when the family was almost bankrupted, she had to compile an account of expenses, and one entry reads: 'Garden labourers £156. One gamekeeper £39. One servant £30. One bear £20.'

Wouldn't that have been a wonderful moment, when that was handed to the accountant, and after studying it several times he tried to say calmly, 'Is there a reason why the bear is entirely necessary?' Maybe she saw it the way destitute pensioners sometimes think of cigarettes, and said, 'I couldn't give up the bear, it's the only pleasure I get.'

There's a romance to the history of Nottingham's radical movement as well. In 1799 the chaplain of the Loyal Nottingham Volunteer Infantry mentioned, 'I have lived 17 years in the town of Nottingham, and in that time there have been 17 riots.' The politician Charles James Fox said the town contained an 'uncontrollable spirit of riot'.

In 1811 Nottingham stocking-makers who were put out of work following the introduction of new machinery formed the Luddite movement, eventually pledging to destroy the machines that were destroying their crafts.

And there's the account of the incident in 1812, when a businessman in London lost all his money on a bad share deal, so he did what anyone would do in those circumstances, and shot dead the Prime Minister, one Spencer Perceval. Where Nottingham plays a part is in its reaction: according to E.P. Thompson in *The Making of the English Working Class*, 'The town crier ran through the streets of Nottingham leaving joy and glee wherever he went, shouting "The Prime Minister is dead. Hurrah hurrah."' It's a shame there wasn't twenty-four-hour rolling news back then, as a clip of an expert in the studio saying glumly, 'This is a tragedy that will unite the whole nation in deep mourning, respect and grief,' followed by the presenter going over to Adrian in Nottingham, where the crier was shouting, 'The Prime Minister is dead. Hurrah hurrah,' would have been shown every Christmas for a thousand years.

The city's sentiment must have been partly due to the destitution inflicted upon thousands of craftsmen by the new industries, and the Draconian punishments imposed on anyone who complained. But this was the time when the country was becoming ruled by the functional, when the new rules of economics meant that mills and factories must be packed with workforces operating machinery at all times, when eating was to be undertaken while operating the machine, when children were units to operate machines and whistling was punishable with a fine, presumably because it made the whistler human, rather than a thing that operated a machine.

Figures such as William Blake and Byron, through to the Pre-Raphaelite painters, despised this process, and sought to promote imagination and beauty as a protest against a world in which everything needed an economic reason for the right to exist. And Nottingham seems to have been in the middle of both the artistic and the political wings of this protest.

Byron is buried in Hucknall, a village eight miles from the centre of town. Despite his mother's slight extravagance on deadly carnivores, he seems to have learned to identify with the poor during his time in Nottingham. He used his seat in the House of Lords to make a speech about the vast operation by the state to defeat the Luddite movement, and in 1816 he wrote his 'Song for the Luddites', quite an act of bravado for an international pin-up, the equivalent now of Justin Bieber recording a song called 'In Support of Bob Crow and Transport Strikes, and Industrial Action by Other Key Workers Including Gravediggers'.

If Byron was influenced by the radicalism of Nottingham, the town in turn seems to have followed his inspiration. In 1831 there was a national campaign that would lead to the Reform Act of 1832, which went some way towards giving most men the vote. One of the most strident opponents of this reform was the fourth Duke of Newcastle, who owned Nottingham Castle. So in pouring rain a mob set fire to it and burned it to the ground.

Thousands stood in the rain cheering, apparently, but while it's always tricky to know what to do next after a spectacular stunt, the Nottingham campaign for reform went down an unusual route. The next day the rioters went to the house of Dr John Storer, another strong opponent of reform, and according to *A History of Nottingham*, 'After an acrimonious exchange they stole his carrots.'

Can there ever have been another movement that's travelled, in one day, from a strategy of burning down a castle to one of nicking a local doctor's carrots? Was there a feeling that the local establishment might say, 'All right, we give in. We could put up with our castle being reduced to ash, but please, please don't start swiping our root vegetables'?

Nottingham doesn't look much like a pinnacle of romance and rebellion. Today the centre consists of a one-way system that swirls round the castle, to the extent that even members of the UK Independence Party must grunt, 'I wish the French had invaded us and demolished that bloody castle, it's impossible to get round.' The main reference to Byron in this area appears to be Byron House, which looks like the sort of building in which at least two floors are dedicated to the offices of insurance companies.

The Holiday Inn dominates one half of the centre, though there is a giant sculpture, created by Anish Kapoor, called *Sky Mirror*, that's tucked up a one-way street by the theatre; there are no signposts for either, as if a deal was struck, with the mayor saying, 'All right, we'll have a theatre and some of this here "art", but only as long as no bugger can find them.'

But the quest for romance has seeped through. Can it be coincidence that one of the most romantic sports stories of all time took place in Nottingham, when the charismatic phenomenon that was Brian Clough took over the ailing local football team and within six years they'd won the European Cup twice? Or that people in shops call you 'duck'? Or that one of the moments often revered (though it's not really my thing) as a great landmark in the history of romance was when Nottingham's Torvill and Dean kissed at the end of their day out ice-skating? Or that one of the town's main tourist attractions appears to be the opportunity of staring at the beauty of the four-fifths of the population that isn't male? So fuck Paris, book a honeymoon in Nottingham. Ride through the tunnel of love in a rowing boat under Trent Bridge, hold hands as you stroll through the turnstiles into Forest's home match against Cardiff, and make love to the gentle purr of the traffic that after several circuits of the one-way system has given up and is heading in the wrong direction up the Alfreton Road.

Coventry

The most endearing sense of identity in a town is often when it becomes doggedly irrational. Salford, for example, is obviously part of Manchester: it's where Manchester United play, and its station is one stop from Deansgate, which is in the centre of Manchester – but it's a separate city, so it has to tell itself it isn't sodding Manchester. The official council website describes its geographical position as simply as possible: 'Salford is a city that can be found just two hundred miles north of London.' So if you're looking for it, that's the easiest way to find it. With regard to its distance from other major cities, if they were explaining to someone who'd never heard of Salford where it is they'd say it's also two hundred miles south of Edinburgh and 5,800 miles west of Tokyo, and quite a trek from Melbourne, and if you pointed out that it was surrounded by Manchester they'd go, 'Are we? I'd never really noticed.'

Coventry doesn't have Salford's excuse, but it does have a series of touchingly contradictory reasons for being proud. Its people can claim, and this is especially true of anyone who was between fifteen and twenty-one in 1979, ownership of the Specials, which would be a glorious cry of civic pride, except that in effect they're saying, 'You know when they sang "This town – is coming like a ghost town"? That's *here* they were talking about. How about that?'

The Coventry Council website has a section that proudly announces the top one hundred prominent people of Coventry. So it says 'Billie Whitelaw – actress', and 'Frank Whittle – engineer', and so on, which seems reasonable. Then I noticed 'Number 21 – Cat bin woman'. This is the woman who was filmed on CCTV putting a cat in a wheelie bin, which certainly made her prominent for a while, though it didn't quite make her a national treasure like Judi Dench or Henry Cooper. But she was from Coventry, so that's the main thing.

There may be a sense of defiance flowing through Coventry, because it was bombed more thoroughly than almost any other British city during the war. But there's a joke they tell there, which is sometimes told in other cities but which applies more solidly to Coventry, that the Luftwaffe tried to destroy the place, but the city council did a much more professional job.

Because, given the opportunity to rebuild the town almost entirely from scratch, they opted to hollow out the entire city centre and insert a ring road that's mostly flyovers, so it's impossible to walk anywhere without feeling encased in concrete, and so complicated it's even more impossible to escape from if you're driving round it, as if it's a motoring version of a religious cult, and it's possible there are motorists stuck on it while their families cry, 'We were worried when he joined it five years ago, and now we have no contact with him and don't know if he'll ever ever leave.'

If you disbelieve me, I refer you to a website set up by the Coventry police called 'How to Drive Round the Coventry Ring Road', featuring 'PC Adam Irwin's top ring road tips'. This is a serious film, in which PC Irwin drives round the ring road, giving advice such as, 'When coming up to exit at junction 6 check nearside mirror, nearside indicator, move into lane one cancelling nearside indicator looking for traffic coming up nearside slip road, indicate again to move out, nearside shoulder check, move onto slip road and indicate right for next roundabout.'

As long as you do that, you'll be fine. If you think you can't remember it all, why not take your laptop with you and check PC Irwin's film as you're driving, for extra safety.

There can hardly be a town of Coventry's size that's more submerged under a maze of flyovers, retail parks and the inevitable shopping malls, yet underneath it fizzes with a unique Coventricity. It was the town that began the process of twinning, when it tied the knot with Stalingrad after the war, identifying with the Russian city as somewhere Hitler had reduced to rubble. People there love to tell you that much of the car chase in *The Italian Job* was filmed in Coventry's sewers.

And it's the home of one of the most celebrated tales of history, the place where Lady Godiva rode naked through the city centre, most impressively without the aid of a police website telling her how to get across junction 12 without colliding with a stagecoach from Kenilworth.

Lady Godiva was the brother of a Saxon Lord called Theoric who lost all his land when William the Conqueror invaded. She was married to one of William's people, and complained to him about the amount of tax demanded of the city. Then, 150 years later, some monks wrote an account of how her husband agreed to cancel the tax as long as she rode naked through the streets on a horse.

The monks' version enters the realm of the story told by a bloke in a pub who rocks backwards and forwards when it adds that 'No one saw her ride,' apparently due to a miracle. But what definitely did happen is that in 1839 the procession was revived for the local fair, when a local lady was chosen and thousands came to watch. In 1842, according to a local account, 'Godiva wore a body stocking, but caused such a sensation that fights broke out amongst those trying to get a better view.'

The mayor and the Church tried to ban the spectacle, the bishop writing: 'I cannot believe this custom takes place in a civilised country, that every third year a common prostitute is hired at Birmingham, to be paraded through the streets, followed by a mob of the lowest rabble in Coventry.'

To which I imagine the people of Coventry said, 'Birmingham? You cheeky fucking bishop.'

A compromise was reached, that the procession could continue, but with Godiva clothed. The result was that in 1845 'Godiva was dressed in a tunic of white satin, a girdle of some kind, scarves thrown over her shoulder, sleeves, a mantle, an ostrich-feather plumed head-dress, and as she entered St Mary's Hall she said, "Why, bless you man, I have never worn so many clothes in my life."'

By then the city was on the way to becoming a magnificent, bustling, vibrant heart of transport, after the Rudge company began making penny-farthing bicycles in the 1880s. How proud Mr Rudge would have been if he'd imagined that from this humble beginning, within a few decades his trade would have grown to an industry so important the Germans would take the trouble to destroy the entire city.

Another result of this industry is that Coventry has one of the most compelling museums in Britain, full of majestic motor-bikes, buses and assorted vehicles instead of the usual glass cabinet full of bent coins. And it was also within the trade unions at the car factories that the radical movements connected with the city emerged.

In the 1990s Coventry's labour movement developed a wing that was independent of the Labour Party, with several councillors being elected. And the engineering unions were at the centre of the anti-racist movements of the 1970s, of which one result was the Specials.

All this makes Coventry a delightful series of contradictions. Its most exuberant export was in response to the dourness of its environment, the success of its industry led to the annihilation of the city, and the whole place revolved around building vehicles, but whatever vehicle you're in you can't get anywhere except round and round in a bloody great pointless circle.

Walsall

Whoever it is that arranges towns has worked hard to make an example of Walsall. Every generation of soulless, grimy uniformity has been poured onto the place: the concrete and tower blocks of the sixties, the ring roads of the seventies, the identikit pedestrianised precincts of the eighties, and the pre-packed retail parks of the nineties, all competing to be the true ugly face of the town.

It's also the point at which the M5 and M6 converge, so everywhere seems as if it's under a motorway. It feels that if you were in someone's house and asked the way to the toilet they'd say, 'You take the M5 to junction 19, come off at the third exit and come back on yourself to the kitchen and it's on the right.'

The onslaught starts at the point of arrival, as the station is moulded into a gloomy shopping mall which even the official illustrated history of Walsall describes as 'a soulless structure built amid much protest'. Translated from the rosy-speak of these guides, that means, 'Please, dear Lord, don't make me go to this shithole again.'

The writer Theodore Dalrymple wrote, 'It's possible there are uglier towns in the world than Walsall, but if there are I don't know them. It's like Ceaușescu's Romania with fast-food outlets.'

To be fair, poor Walsall's plight can't just be blamed on the modern era. Benjamin Disraeli referred in a novel to one part of

Walsall as 'the ugliest spot in England', and Dickens described the area as 'the journey's end, and it might be the end of everything else, it's so ruinous and dreary'.

Every writer seems to have joined in. There's probably a story by Beatrix Potter that begins, 'One day Jemima Puddle-Duck wanted to make some delicious apple crumble for the summer fair. But she had no apples and had to walk all the way to the woods in the pouring rain to collect some. "Not to worry," she smiled, "at least I don't have to go through fucking Walsall."'

Efforts to change the town's image haven't always worked. In 2000 a sculpture of Princess Diana was commissioned to go in the bus station, but before it was unveiled it turned out that the granite made her black. There were headlines like 'Black Diana Gives Her Majesty Displeasure', and it was never put up.

The most ambitious attempt to provide Walsall with some individuality was the decision to build an art gallery in the town centre. The lift has a voice telling you which floor you're on that belongs to Walsall old boy Noddy Holder, which gives a local flavour as you hear it telling you, 'SECOND FLOOOOOR!!!'

But the building itself is as unartistic as it could be, oblong and colourless; you'd imagine it's where you have to go to apply for a Ukrainian work permit, or a licence to keep dolphins.

On the other hand, Boy George was brought up in Walsall, although he now denies any link with the town. That's not complimentary, as it means he's saying, 'Yes, I was a heroin addict, I accept that. And sure, I invited a stranger back for sex, handcuffed him to a hook on the wall and beat him with a metal chain. But I did NOT come from Walsall.'

There is, however, one icon in Walsall that is adored by all local people: a concrete hippo. It is in the central square of the main pedestrianised precinct, and for several years has served as the main meeting point in the town. Of the eight Walsall residents I spoke to before visiting the place, prior to recording an *In Town* show, every one of them implored me to see the hippo.

There's a Walsall Hippo Statue Appreciation Society on Facebook, with 1,644 members. The council's cultural officer, who took me on a tour of the town, explained that only after we'd been round the leather museum, the town hall and the art gallery would we finish off with the treat of the hippo.

By now I was expecting a glorious giant marble hippo in mid-yawn, hippo calves playing at its feet, with meticulously crafted sheets of bronze to represent the gurgling, enigmatic mud. Instead, there's a two-foot-long vaguely hippo-shaped slab of concrete that is – and no other word would do it justice – pathetic. At first I thought it was a bin. 'There she is!' said my guide, as if we'd turned a corner to see a Pyramid in a deep orange sunset. I tried, but I knew I was failing to hide my disappointment. 'Oh, er, right. Well, er, is this it?' I said, the way you'd react if you discovered your Christmas present from your wife was a jelly baby.

Maybe it was especially disappointing because of Walsall's history. This was a town that oozed heavy industry. The region was given the name the Black Country because it was so full of smoke from the ironworks that everything was turned black. Offshoots of the iron trade include Britain's largest locksmith industry, and companies used the iron to make stirrups, which led to the saddle trade and a leather industry that eventually boasted that it supplied the Queen's handbag.

This industrial image is supplemented by the treacly drawl that is the barely plausible Walsall accent, which, once you're used to it, has an ugliness that's actually quite beautiful, like the disused Battersea Power Station, or a scrap-metal yard in a thunderstorm.

The joy of the accent is summed up by the joke about the bloke from Walsall who joins the army, and on the night before a battle the general makes a speech: 'Now then, men, I'm sure you didn't come here to die,' and the Walsall man shouts, 'I didn't sir, I came here yesterdie.'

There's a snobbery directed at the accent. It's inconceivable that anyone from Walsall could present *Newsnight*, as there'd be such horror at them saying, 'So minister, did yow know about this when yow made the statement or did yow not, and are yow going to resign?'

In a way the accent suits the town, as there's a hint of defiance in it. There's no compromise, no lightening of the fully adenoidal twisted vowels as you get in Birmingham, no attempt to give it a tune or make it palatable to the untrained ear; just a message conveyed with the insistence of a stroppy young film director who won't allow subtitles on his documentary about an Eskimo village, that 'This is what we sound like, and if yow don't like it yow can piss off somewhere posh like Stafford.'

Maybe it was this attitude that led to Walsall being home to the most famous anarchists in British history. In the 1890s there was a Socialist Club in Goodall Street, but some of the members became anarchists. They met two Frenchmen who said they wanted to join the group, and were then contacted by a man called Auguste Coulon, the leader of a group of anarchists who met in Tottenham Court Road in London. When Coulon found out that one of the anarchists in Walsall, Fred Charles, worked in a foundry, he wrote a letter saying, 'Then he will do to make bombs for us.'

Coulon persuaded his followers to form a chemistry class and to 'worship the great God dynamite'. He wrote in favour of anarchist bombs across Europe, and the editor of the Walsall anarchist newspaper wrote that – and I promise this is true – 'Coulon sent me an article celebrating the blowing up of a cow in Belgium as a great and revolutionary act.'

And that, I propose, is surely the most magnificent sentence in the history of anarchism.

The police started following members of the Walsall Socialist Club, and then raided its premises, where they claimed to find plans for a bomb sent by Coulon. Five of the anarchists were arrested and jailed for five or ten years, despite a national campaign to release them led by William Morris. Later it was discovered that the plan for the bomb was useless, so the police altered the design to make it for one that *would* blow up. The only anarchist involved who wasn't arrested was Coulon, who it turned out was a police spy. Inspector Melville of the police recommended him for a post teaching French at a private school for girls. I suppose he stood there going, 'Il allume la vache Belgique – He explodes the Belgian cow. Nous allum*ons* la vache Belgique – *We* explode the Belgian cow.'

But the best-known representative of the town is Sister Dora. She was a sister of the Anglican Church in the 1850s who became a nurse because 'The hospitals consider men as men, and not just hands to work.'

Sister Dora came to Walsall, which was considered a 'difficult' place to do nursing because, as one book about her says, 'Furnacemen and miners were the heaviest drinkers, and the butties, who controlled labour below ground, drank on a Homeric scale.' Dora became a nurse for the poorest people in the town, and set up schemes to improve the health of beggars, drunks and prostitutes. She made a point of nursing the Irish, who were under attack at the time. As a result of her labours she said, 'There's hardly a poor man or woman in Walsall I don't know personally.'

Dora questioned why so many patients became sick while they were in hospital, from what were called 'hospital diseases'. She worked out that it was because the places were full of filth and dirt, and organised a cleaning system that almost eliminated 'surgical fever'. Isn't it extraordinary how stupid we were back then – not to realise that hospitals are healthier if they're not filthy. The hospital in Walsall was so proud of its new cleanliness that it was opened to the public for a day to show it off.

In 1875 there was an explosion at the Walsall Iron Company, and dozens of ironworkers were killed or maimed. Dora organised the treatment for the survivors, and collections throughout the town. She became such a heroine that her picture was put up in thousands of homes across Walsall.

Sister Dora died at the age of forty-six, and her statue in Walsall was the first in Britain of a woman who wasn't in the royal family. So it's easy to see how they must have thought, 'How do we top that? I know, we'll do a statue of a woman who *was* in the royal family, and make it black.'

Today the statue stands in the middle of the central square. Around it teenage girls chew gum and shout insults at boys on bikes, but everyone knows it's Dora, knows she was a nurse who looked after everyone, and that she's *Walsall*. A few yards away is the hippo, proudly unique, a symbol of the survival of the town's individuality. When I was recording the show, the mere mention of the hippo provoked a disconcertingly exuberant cheer, of the sort a reference to Usain Bolt would with an audience of Jamaicans. Because they don't have a hippo in Wolverhampton or Dudley, and in Redditch they probably arrange to meet somewhere tediously unimaginative and clichéd, like a clock tower. But in Walsall there's affection, even love, for the concrete beast that defies the decades of soulless structures, a reminder that a town will always retain some history, some charm, to remain its own place.

Lewes

Towards the Sussex coast, amidst the rolling majesty of the South Downs, is the seemingly pedestrian town of Lewes, a sloping High Street with delis and cafés that serve twenty-seven varieties of tea, a pub with a courtyard and a carvery, and second-hand bookshops so rickety that as you walk between the shelves it feels as if you're at angle, like in a house of fun at the fairground.

But Lewes is a cauldron of stroppiness, not because of one campaign or issue, but in general. This is summed up by the town's slogan, 'We won't be druv', which is medieval for 'Oy, you wanna try something, DO YA?' It's an attitude most prominently displayed each Guy Fawkes Night, when the town becomes a pyromaniacs' carnival that would leave Al Qaeda organisers yelling, 'Steady on, that's *too* dangerous!'

The attitude seeps out in other ways. For example, in 2004 the town tried a novel car-parking policy, which involved the council installing a series of parking meters in the High Street, while the residents blew them up. To quote an article in the *Independent*: 'The respectable-looking lady in the tea shop was an unlikely advocate of urban terrorism. But she said, "Everyone I know is secretly pleased about the attacks. Good luck to them," in a hushed tone.'

At the bottom of the town is Harveys brewery, nestled by the river and looking like the sort of brewery they'd have if everyone drank beer in Toytown. Most of the pubs in Lewes serve Harveys, including the Lewes Arms, a tiny locals' pub with no music or quiz machines. When I went there one lunchtime someone pointed out a regular at the bar, saying, 'You see that old boy? He's called "The Incredible Dancing Man". Wherever he is, as soon as the music comes on he starts dancing. So because there's no music in here he comes in to get a rest.' In 2008 the Lewes Arms was bought by the Greene King brewery, which removed Harveys from the bar, and this provoked a boycott of the pub. A picket line was set up outside in a protest that lasted over a year.

As causes go, it might not rank alongside the deepest, and you can only imagine what someone from Burma might have felt if they'd wandered past and said, 'I must give you solidarity and greetings, my comrades. In my land we too face injustice and must protest with untold courage. What is the nature of the outrage embodied in this "Lewes Arms" which you are resisting? Have they kidnapped your families and held them in the cellar? Is it the headquarters of the brutal and sadistic local secret police? Oh, they've replaced your favourite beer, have they?'

Nonetheless, after months of boycotts and picketing, the campaign began earning publicity, with articles in several national newspapers. When the German magazine *Der Spiegel* ran a feature, Greene King reinstalled the beer, sold off the pub, and the managing director resigned.

Lewes has become a popular town to emigrate to from London, and people brought up there refer to the immigrants as 'DFLs', meaning 'Down from Londons'. You can detect a smugness from some who've moved down, who might boast that 'It's wonderful because there's a direct route to Victoria that takes only thirty-four seconds and it's *so* much better to bring up kids here because the air's so fresh and everyone's an expert in explosives.'

Some parts of the town appear to cater exclusively for this constituency, such as 'Bill's', the organic café and grocers where you seem to hear comments like, 'The fruit here is amazing, the apples are £9 each but they've all been naturally pecked by crows.'

But the attitude of refusing to be druv must be part of the attraction, so the intake enhances the town's independent spirit. When you look at the history of Lewes, it seems that process may have been taking place over several centuries. By 1800 it had a reputation as a home for the deliberately awkward, including Tom Paine, possibly the stroppiest Englishman of all time. Paine was a corset-maker, born in Norfolk, who ended up among the leading figures of both the American War of Independence and the French Revolution. But where did he learn his stroppiness – Lewes?

He went there when he was offered a job as customs officer, and joined the Headstrong Club, a debating society that met every week in the White Hart, still there on the High Street. Each week the debater judged to be the best would take the Headstrong Club trophy to keep at home for the week, and the winner was always Tom Paine. Imagine how historically unlucky that was for those other poor sods. It would be as if at one point in history there was a weekly wine-making race, and every week the judges said, 'Well, once again the prize goes to Jesus.'

While Paine lived there he said of the women in Lewes, 'Every one of them falls victim to my charms and good looks.' One of these must have been Elizabeth Ollive, as he married her, though it may have been mostly for business reasons, as it meant he could set up a shop with his new wife selling tobacco and spirits. His employers told him this might create a slight conflict of interests, given that he was a customs officer, whose main duty was to stop the smuggling of tobacco and spirits.

Paine seems to have written his first pamphlet in Lewes, on why customs officers should have their salaries increased, and he finally got the sack for taking days off in London. It was there that he met the American radical Benjamin Franklin, who suggested he go to America, where he wrote the pamphlet that inspired the American troops as they went into battle with the English.

You can tell the nature of a town from how it commemorates its association with Tom Paine. In Thetford, where he was born, an argument about whether a statue should be erected in his honour led to the mayor stating he would only allow it if there was just a single word inscribed on it: 'Traitor'. But in Lewes the White Hart has a cardboard Paine inviting you in for Sunday lunch, and Harveys produces a beer called Tom Paine ale.

Most spectacularly, though, Lewes is famous for burning stuff. Thousands of people are active in the many bonfire societies, who spend months planning their celebrations, each of them choosing someone they can build an effigy of so they can blow them up.

In some ways it must be like living in a town full of schizophrenics. Perhaps there should be a scheme across Britain whereby if someone says to his doctor, 'The man in the corner keeps telling me to burn things down,' instead of prescribing strong medication the doctor will say, 'Why don't you move to Lewes?'

The origins of the custom lie in the events following the death of Henry VIII, when Queen Mary set about trying to make England a Catholic country again. In her enthusiasm she burned Protestants. One third of the victims were from Sussex, and the biggest concentration of fires took place in Lewes.

For example, Deryk Carver, a brewer from Brighton, was arrested for saying prayers in English. He confessed, was told not to do it again, but carried on. At his second trial he said to the prosecutor, in the spirit of compromise, 'Your doctrine is poison and sorcery. If Christ were here you would put Him to a worse death than He was put to before. You say that you can make a God. Well, you can make a pudding as well.' Following that magnificent combination of defiance and surrealism he went up in flames at the Star Inn, which is now the town hall. Over the next two years there were sixteen other executions in Lewes, for crimes such as refusing to attend mass conducted in Latin, or to believe a priest had the power to absolve your sins. Huge crowds gathered at these burnings, but rather than terrifying them, they made them quietly furious.

When England settled into being Protestant after Elizabeth I came to the throne, there were constant rumours of plots and conspiracies to make the country Catholic again, of which the most famous was the one involving Guido Fawkes. The year after the plotters were captured on 5 November 1605, the government passed an act called 'For public Thanksgiving to Almighty God every year of the fifth day of November'.

In some places the locals celebrate this festivity by writing their names with sparklers, but in Lewes each year the towns-people would build a model of a priest sprinkling holy water, and set fire to it. The custom continues; every year they still burn a Pope, while 'No Popery' banners hang overhead, so it looks as if Lewes is the only genteel Sussex town whose council has passed directly from the Liberal Democrats to the para military Loyalists.

I spent Guy Fawkes Night in Lewes in 2010, arriving in the town around five o'clock, which I naïvely thought would allow time for a meal before it all started, because no firework nights start earlier than seven. But twenty yards from the station we had to stop at a crossroads so that around three hundred people dressed as drummer boys, carrying burning torches and push-ing wheelbarrows full of blazing wood, could pass by under a street-wide banner. Then the first bangs started. Not distant kabooms and crackles as a circle of purple stars cascade above. Lewes bangs are sudden dull cracks, that sound as if something's exploded right by your feet. Then you look down and realise that's because a banger has exploded right by your feet. So you yelp, 'What the fuck shit bollocks!' but despite this complaint they carry on exploding, like musket fire, and you can't hear what anyone's saying, but presumably it's 'Evans has bought it, sir,' and 'Perkins, take Amy this letter and tell her I love her.'

But within a couple of minutes you get used to these minia-ture bombs blowing up all around, and it becomes part of the background noise, like the bubbling of a fish tank. No one even comments on an explosion unless it goes off extremely close to them, and even if it caused an injury they'd chuckle, 'Look at that, my middle finger's sheared clean off, that should get me a discount off a manicure, ha ha.'

As well as bangers there are rook scarers, that crack like the background gunfire on a news report from a war zone, sold in their millions for bonfire night. Anyone looking at the sales figures of rook scarers who wasn't aware of the parades would assume that Lewes must have the hardest rooks in Britain, sat on roofs on their own while other rooks tell the young ones, 'Always be polite to Charlie there, he done three years in Lewes.'

By six o' clock everywhere smelled of sulphur, burning wood, and a dozen varieties of smoke. Every street was full of crowds that might suddenly shift in one direction, as if an enemy has been spotted and must be pursued. Then another procession, of sailors or pirates, would march by, before a race took place in which burning barrels of tar were rolled across a bridge and into the river. Then came the effigies, the first one a giant David Cameron emerging from the House of Commons as a puppet-master with a frail Nick Clegg dangling from his strings. It was two storeys high and covered in holes packed with explosives.

The most compelling thing about the spectacle is the ragged-ness of it all. None of it is choreographed, or announced by a presenter from local radio. There are no ropes to stand behind, no advertising or banners boasting that the council works to make things better. There are no speeches from a mayor or a representative of the sponsor in which they hope you have a wonderful evening but should remember the safety code.

Sometimes the air seems to be completely smoke, although it's colourful smoke. At one point I heard what I assume must have been a chemistry student say, 'That Society's smoke is purple, which indicates their fireworks contain phosphorus.'

Most people who live in Lewes are members of one of the five main bonfire societies, which spend the year raising money, preparing costumes and building their arsenal of firepower, and choosing someone to build an effigy of, so they can burn it in a field. The crowds cross each other as they head towards the bonfire they've chosen to watch this year, which seems to be a huge decision, the equivalent of where to spend Christmas.

The one I ended up seeing was a huge construction, maybe four storeys high. The field it was in was so packed I thought I couldn't see a single space where anyone else could fit, at which point a couple of hundred more squeezed in, each holding a can of beer as the flames danced in the wind, sometimes suddenly turning and bolting our way like an actor in one of those plays where they run into the audience. Everyone would cheer and laugh, which is healthy, because it is quite funny to feel that one unexpected gust in the wrong direction could kill four hundred people in an instant.

In fact the whole thing seems to be designed as a deliberate affront to the world of health and safety. You wonder if there's one society that says, 'To add to the gaiety we set a rhino loose amongst the crowd.'

The most astonishing challenge to modern precautions comes with the arrival of the Cardinals. Each society selects three people each year to dress as Cardinals for bonfire night. Your prize, should you be lucky enough to be chosen, is to stand on a platform for ten minutes while fireworks are aimed at you. Apparently it's a huge honour to be picked, and the candidates sit at the planning meetings thinking, '*I* want to be deafened, *I* want explosions all round me with a 70 per cent chance of being maimed for life, pick *me me me*.' The lucky winners prepare for their big moment like girls in an American beauty pageant, probably with members of their family sewing patterns on their cassocks and saying, 'I don't want the doctors who attend to your burns to think you've got a scruffy outfit.'

About fifty yards to the right of the bonfire was a scaffold, and that year's three Cardinals made their way up to the platform to a mighty wave of derision. They waved defiantly, the crowd booed more violently, and then the fireworks started. The whole scene had seemed surreal enough when I'd first heard about it. But whatever your expectation, the reality is more dramatic. The boos rise in a crescendo, winding up for action like a jet engine, then a flurry of assorted fireworks are hurled, the bap-bap-bap of countless bangers merely a drumbeat for the melody of rockets, fizzing fountains and blazing objects that rain down on the three proud Cardinals from all directions. Every few moments one of the Cardinals has his mitre knocked from his head by a flying hissing sparkling thing, that probably has huge letters on its side warning you to light it carefully and then retreat fifty yards, and on no account ever to let anyone pass near it again for two years. The crowd cheers the direct hit, and the Cardinal politely bends down to retrieve his headwear.

For around fifteen minutes this spectacle goes on, and every time the torrent subsides to a flurry and you assume the ammunition is running out, a renewed surge takes place and the Cardinals disappear once more inside a pall of gunpowder. I can honestly say it's one of the funniest things I have ever seen. I kept thinking there must be a trick, that with cameras and computer graphics they can do all sorts of stuff these days, but no, the truth was that three men dressed as cardinals were being bombarded with lit fireworks.

When the process finally winds down and you're giving thanks to the town for such a display, the Pope is wheeled out, a thirty-foot-high hunched-up pontiff who crackles and pops in the flames until they reach the fireworks embedded in him and he splats and fizzes to wild cheering before eventually exploding in all directions.

As I turned to go back to the centre of town I saw something behind the hedges that I chose to disbelieve. By now it felt like being in *Alice in Wonderland*, in that as soon as one adventure with something impossible was over, something just as baffling would replace it, so if we'd all been handed a potion that made us shrink it would have seemed reasonable. But at one side of the field there appeared to be another effigy, that looked like Barack Obama. It must be a trick of the light from the flames, I decided. Either that, or the evening had played games with my mind, and now I could see the shadow of a hot-dog stall and imagine it was an effigy of a black man. Someone might hand me a Twix and I'd chuck it in the road expecting it to explode.

Or it was someone else, and I'd looked at it wrong. Perhaps it was supposed to be Chris Moyles, and only looked like Obama from a strange angle. But as I walked along the path next to the bonfire, the height of which was now reduced to two storeys, a giant kneeling Barack Obama was pulled towards the crowd and set ablaze. It was a sight to get the section of America who scream at rallies that Obama is a crazed communist un-American African with a terrorist middle name waving their bourbons in the air and yee-haaing across Kentucky.

The decision of who to burn each year is taken in the summer, as it takes three months to build the giant models, and in the summer of 2010 Obama had been seen by some as an enemy of Britain for his criticisms of BP when its oil was leaking across the Gulf of Mexico. I presumed that was the reasoning behind setting him alight, but this vision would have been cheered most enthusiastically by Sarah Palin and her colleagues, should they keep a close eye on the Lewes annual bonfire night.

That's the contradiction of the festivities: they're a giant and blazing snub at authority, but that doesn't mean they're driven by liberal values. In Victorian times the night used to celebrate the victories of the British Army throughout the Empire, and according to one local book, 'When Brighton councillor W. Evans tried to hold a socialist debate at the top of School Hill he was greeted by a crowd who taunted him with shouts of "Bum him."'

I've spent a while wondering about this quote, and reckon it's a misprint, and they were shouting 'Burn him,' which might not be as interesting, but makes it even less likely that they meant it in a friendly way.

Conversely, in the 1850s some bonfire society members went to America to work on the railways, and were so appalled at the way the Native Americans were treated that when they came back they set up the Commercial Square Bonfire Society, one of the rules of which is that everyone has to go to the bonfire dressed as a Native American.

Recent effigies have been of Blair and Bush, following the invasion of Iraq, and, with a slightly less liberal tone, a family of gypsies in a caravan. And while there's an argument to be made for burning Popes in a town where Protestants were executed, I can see why you might feel slightly uneasy about cheering along if you were a Catholic.

Insisting you won't be druv can be a gesture of solidarity against the powerful, but it can also express a refusal to be part of a wider community. What is exhilarating about the Lewes bonfire celebration is that it's planned, arranged and executed by the people who take part in it. Whether you agree or not with some of the choices they make, they have at least been made entirely by those participating.

Even if you arrive from out of town, when you follow the parades you feel you're taking part rather than merely watching. You become part of the procession, part of the chaos, which is one of the reasons the event is vastly popular, with two-hour queues for the trains that leave the town after midnight.

So the stand taken by the martyrs meant that in the town where they perished there remains, 450 years later, a commitment to an evening not decided by sponsors or councils, or the demands of celebrities or their agents, but remaining the product of immense imagination and organisation, of a culture formed from the bottom up. It may not be quite what Deryck Carver was hoping for as he clutched his Bible amidst the flames, but his line about the pudding suggests that he was capable of thinking outside the box.

In 2008, in an act of wonderfully confident stroppiness, Lewes issued its own currency. Only a few years after much of the rest of Europe had merged its currencies, Lewes came up with one that isn't even accepted up the road in Haywards Heath. Maybe the hope was that eventually the financial reports at the end of the television news would go: 'The dollar was up three cents against the pound this morning, and the yen up by 2 per cent, but again the strongest rally is from the Lewes pound, which rose against all major currencies following excellent quarterly figures from Percy's fishing-tackle shop and Bill's the organic grocers.'

On one side of the Lewes currency is the face of Tom Paine, with his line 'We have the power to build the world anew.' It's as if they love trouble. I bet the whole town gets called in to see the government every few weeks, to be told, 'Always the same faces, isn't it, Lewes?'

'Yer.'

'WHAT?'

'Yes, sir.'

'Now what have you done?'

'Made own pound, sir.'

'Why can't you be like Eastbourne, eh? THEY don't make their own pound. Nor does Seaford, or Hurstpierpoint.'

'What about Hastings, sir?'

'You know full well, Lewes, that Hastings was expelled long ago.'

By seeing the world from the bottom up, the town has quite an impact on it, to the extent that Barack Obama concluded his inauguration speech in 2009 with the words: 'With hope and virtue, let us brave once more the icy currents, and endure what storms may come. Let it be said by our children's children that we did not turn back nor did we falter as we carried forward that gift of freedom and delivered it for future generations.' This was a quote from Tom Paine, written shortly after he arrived in Boston from Lewes.

In any normal place they'd emblazon the tourist brochures and the council's headed paper with the fact that the new US President came into office quoting lines by a man from their town. Only in Lewes would they build a model of him, and blow the fucker up.

Gateshead

Sometimes, when I visit a new town for the radio show, I'm given a tour by someone from the museum, or who runs the local historical society, who's about sixty-eight and has written a book about a steamroller that was often seen in the area until 1965. And I feel woefully guilty, because they've spent four days putting together an itinerary including the collection of pepper pots at the old vicarage and a VIP visit to the basement of the town hall to see plans of the original plumbing. Then they show me the corner of a church that, if you look closely, you can see was rebuilt after the great gale of 1685, before asking me if I'd like to see the guttering, which is similar to the type we saw at the disused abattoir, and I risk breaking their heart by confessing I probably won't have time to fit all this into the show, although I will make room for the story in the local paper of a tramp who walked into a pet shop and was sick on a goldfish.

But in Gateshead things weren't like that. It was unlikely that they would be, as Gateshead is renowned for being the smaller, less notable, almost insignificant forgettable other side of the river from Newcastle. Its image worked in its favour only once, as it made it the perfect setting for the 1970s film *Get Carter*, in which Michael Caine trudges through two hours of relentless grime and misery, and when they finished filming the producer probably said to the mayor, 'Thanks so much for making the place absolutely perfect for our requirements. It must have taken a huge effort making *everything* so shit. I hope it doesn't take you too long to get the place back habitable for your citizens.'

I was met by Mark, whose dad had worked in a local pit. Mark was employed by the council to promote the area, which he did with disturbing enthusiasm. 'I can't wait to show you how Gateshead's changing,' he said, and recited quotes from European committees about the efficiency of the transport system while cantering to the Baltic Art Gallery, a recently converted flour mill on the bank of the River Tyne. We passed through the vast glass doors and into the vast glass lift to whirr past the empty shiny wooden floors. He didn't seem entirely at home as he made comments such as, 'They've got all sorts of like, art and that, in here like.' Strangely, there was a chemist's on one floor, and I made a vague mental note that there wouldn't normally be a chemist's in an art gallery. Then I thought, 'Hang on, that isn't a work of art, is it?' And there was indeed a little board saying 'Damien Hirst's *Pharmacy*'. We went inside and it was just like a chemist's, with hundreds of glass cabinets containing jars and plasters and tubes of cream, and Mark kept changing his expression as he tried to think of something positive and chemist-related to say, and I felt he was going to blurt out, 'According to the *Lancet* we have more Nurofens per head in Gateshead than anywhere else in western Europe.'

I looked around for something about this chemist's that might make it at least as interesting as a normal chemist's, and said to Mark, 'If these jars here were swapped with the ones on this shelf below, would Damien Hirst see it and scream, "Noooo the whole effect is *ruined*"?'

As I did this I lightly touched the glass cabinet, and within a second a huge security guard had taken three strides across the pharmacy floor and put his nose right up to mine, like a sergeant major about to bark at a private. In perfect Geordie he growled, 'DON'T you touch that. This art's worth TEN MILLION POUNDS.'

This was so ridiculous it somehow wasn't intimidating, so I said, 'It's not any more. Now I've touched the glass it's only worth nine million.'

'Oh, you think you're very fucking funny you, don't you?' he said.

Mark looked at the floor, but he shouldn't have worried, because all I could think was what a magnificent effort the area puts into living up to its stereotype, when even the pretentious art galleries are hard. One wrong word in an exhibition and you'll get a security guard yelling, 'Ay, come here and slag off Botticelli's perspective to ma face, ya prick,' while his girlfriend implores him, 'Leave it, Darren, it's not worth it. It's from his later orange period.'

Like most regeneration schemes, the one in Gateshead has created a series of buildings alongside water that have won architectural prizes and have open-plan cafés where you can buy mushroom soup for eight quid a bowl. For example the Sage Centre, the new waterside venue for theatre and concerts, is shaped like the back of a snail.

But a minute's walk from there towards the centre of Gateshead is the start of the unregenerated tower blocks, boarded-up pubs and very old women struggling with bags full of shopping past places with 'We change your cheques' above the door and off licences in which the staff sit behind reinforced glass as if they're awaiting a nuclear attack. Some pubs are still open, including the Metropole, though to get in I had to clamber across two men slumped in the doorway, each holding one crutch, as if Gateshead runs a crutch-pooling system so the disabled of the town don't waste energy. Or maybe one of them wasn't drinking, as he was the designated crutch-bearer.

Inside there were four people in the far corner, including a man in a scarf and gloves who kept yelling, 'And that was only the fucking parrot!' then cackling, not unlike a parrot in fact, so this was presumably the punchline to a joke. The others stared straight ahead, so unmoved I felt like someone who can see people no one else is aware of, like the boy in the film *Sixth Sense*. A few seconds would pass, long enough for general laughter to die down if there had been any, then he'd yell, 'And that was only the fucking parrot!' again, and cackle again.

Eventually one of his audience, a short man in a red jumper, left the parrot man and came to stand next to me instead. He asked if I liked jazz. I told him I loved jazz, and he said, 'I love jazz, me,' and asked who I liked in particular. I told him I always enjoyed hearing Dexter Gordon in Paris, but he hadn't heard of him, so I tried Miles Davis, and he didn't know him either. I asked who he did like, and he said, 'I don't know any of the names but I love the jazz.'

Then he told me something very personal about himself. 'What I do,' he said, applying himself carefully as if it was essential I got all the details, as I'd need them on a mission once I was behind enemy lines, 'is I drink a pint of Scottish & Newcastle. But then, for my next pint, I like change, to a different ale, could be anything, but not Scottish & Newcastle. Then I go back to Scottish & Newcastle, and then – after that, after the second Scottish & Newcastle, then I have a different ale. It might be the same ale as after the first Scottish & Newcastle, or it might be a different one again, a third one like, it doesn't matter, as long as it's not Scottish & Newcastle. Then I go back to Scottish & Newcastle, and then, after that, I have a different ale, could be anything, one I've had before or maybe not, and keep swapping about like, all night, a different ale and then Scottish & Newcastle. And that way I don't get bored.'

He sat back down with his friends, the jokester having given up with his parrot line, and for a few minutes there was only the sound of five people supping. Then, at about twenty past ten the landlord suddenly stopped washing up glasses to yell in the direction of the four people opposite, 'Right – that's it! Now FUCK OFF you Irish CUNT!' And the four of them got up and left, as if accepting that they did indeed between them comprise an Irish cunt, although there were four of them and they all seemed to be from Gateshead.

The pubs of the High Street are considered tourist attractions. The council website boasts: 'It is often claimed it's not possible to walk the length of the High Street drinking half a pint in each pub.' This is followed by: 'Well excuse me but there are 32 pubs so that's only 16 pints!'

Moving further away from the River Tyne, the next landmark after the Metropole is the Dunston Rocket, a thirty-floor block of flats shaped like a rocket and hailed for its innovative design. For example, the book *Gateshead Architecture* describes it as 'supported by large concrete fin-like flying buttresses, a design unique in Britain'. All of which is accurate, but avoids the detail that it was condemned in 2005 as uninhabitable, and is now surrounded by wire and covered in hardboard.

Apparently there's a name for this sort of architecture, which is 'brutalist'. Which is to say it's brutal on purpose. So at some point in the construction maybe it was marginally more appealing, and the architects grimaced and said, 'Hmm, not quite brutal enough.' Maybe the original plans pushed the boundaries of brutalism by including concrete windows and spikes that sprung from the living-room walls at random intervals, until these were rejected by some bureaucrat at the Housing Department who pointed out that it contravened EU regulations to kill all the tenants.

Brutalism originated in the Soviet Union of the 1950s, so it must be one of the few concepts to have come out of that time and place to be joyfully adopted by English inner-city local councils. At some point someone must have stood up in a meeting at Gateshead Town Hall and said, 'In place of all the grime in this area, we should make the place livelier by introducing the values of Stalinist Russia.' He probably added, 'Furthermore, I propose the installation of gulag kiosks, situated on each street corner, in which residents can be incarcerated in freezing conditions for several years and then shot as dissidents, providing an exciting and innovative approach to the demands of human resource distribution within a context of modern urban accommodation.'

So now the Rocket sits there, the dominant sight for a community of thousands, a tower which the people of Dunston have to circumnavigate if they want a bag of chips or a pint of milk, the pride of the sort of people who compile *Gateshead Architecture*, a crumbling, empty, astronomical monument to failure.

Gateshead has a supplementary problem challenging its self-esteem: that it's the much lesser-known sibling of famous relative Newcastle, which everyone's heard of and which has a famous football team, and which has threatened to swallow Gateshead for almost a thousand years. The earliest example I found was in 1080. Before I began reading about the history of the town I made a conscious decision that in my show I wouldn't resort to the stereotype of Geordies wanting to fight all the time as a source of jokes, as that would be clichéd and lazy. Then I opened my first book, called *Around Gateshead*. And the second sentence on page 1 went: 'St Mary's church was on this site many centuries ago, but in 1080 it was burned down by locals, with the Bishop of Durham inside.'

Throughout the twelfth century there were constant feuds between the two towns about where the border between them should be. In 1322 Newcastle merchants burned down Gateshead's fisheries. In 1383 they built a tower at the Gateshead end of the bridge, declared it a bit of Newcastle in Gateshead, a sort of Geordie Gibraltar, and refused to tear it down until 1416.

In 1552 an Act of Parliament officially annexed Gateshead to Newcastle, the introduction saying: 'The quiet ordre of the corporacon of the Towne of Newcastle upon Tyne hath bene not a little disturbed and hindered, by the men of Gatesyde. In the said town of Newcastle, they daly comit manyfolde disorders which escape unpunished.'

According to *The County of Durham*, 'The feud grew to a frenzy when the wicked Newcastleites passed the act to amalgamate the two towns. Gateshead rose as one and declared, "The town of Gateshead is good and wholesome. It is known that the South side of the river is deep and more clean than the side towards Newcastle. If we are united with Newcastle, Gateshead would be replenished with evil-disposed persons and thieves."'

You have to wonder whether some of this was written by the leader writers from the *Daily Express*, as only they could argue, 'Now foreigners threaten to make our half of the river shallow!!!'

And so, through history, the relationship persists, not just about rivalry but about one side battling not to feel insignificant, so that being from Gateshead must feel like being Muhammad Ali's flatmate.

But there is something unique about the town, making it distinct even from its neighbour. One reason why Gateshead has been consistently pilloried as a den of squalor might be that it had an unusually early start at being a centre for industry. The first mines were sunk there in 1344, the first railway started in 1620, and the first house ever to be lit by electricity was in Mosley Street.

Gateshead also exhibits a love for the bridges across the Tyne, which have no interest in seeming picturesque, but demand human activity, as if this is where the life is, and the land is the tranquil part, because they're clanky and chunky and together seem joyously unplanned and uncoordinated, but ready for action like a gang of builders leaving a greasy-spoon café at six in the morning. There are the domineering girders of the main bridge, an effete, delicate swing bridge, and a mischievous little road bridge with a red light on the top, so it looks like the main bridge's impish son, and you don't want to upset it or the big bridge will clobber you with its rivets.

There's an underground system that clunks under Newcastle and Gateshead, that's big and yellow and rattles and feels industrial, as if it ought to be carrying girders, or that to get off you have to be unloaded by a docker.

Gateshead was also the home of the Blaydon Races, the famous annual fair commemorated in the Geordie anthem, with its chorus 'Ganning doon the Scotswood Roooooad – to see the Blaydon Races'. The races were eventually cancelled in 1916 after a riot following the disqualification of a horse, but a few years later a painting of them exhibited in Shipley Art Gallery was still able to attract a huge crowd. Unfortunately a fight broke out in the queue that was so violent the gallery had to be shut down.

And Gateshead has a sporting hero, Harry Clasper, a local miner who became a world champion in the 1840s, his performances regularly attracting crowds of between 50,000 and 100,000 people. The unlikely sport that dominated the scene at that time was rowing, which now has connotations of Oxford and Cambridge and rowing lakes at Eton. You don't think of the Henley Regatta as something 100,000 rowdy people would turn up to.*

Harry redesigned the rowing boat, and invented a new rowing style in which the rower slides back and forward during the stroke. He won the world coxed championship in a boat with his three brothers, and was seven times winner of the Thames Regatta.

Everyone in Gateshead seems to know about Harry Clasper. When I asked the audience if they knew who he was there was a

---

* Unless the Eton boys had their own version of 'The Blaydon Races' that went, 'Howay the lads, you should have seen us punting, Sipping Pimm's and finding ways to beat the ban on hunting, All the lads and lasses you can see they're a disturbance, Walking down the private drive to sack two of the servants.'

bored collective 'Yees, he was a rower,' the sort of tone you'd adopt if a teenager asked if you'd heard of Jimi Hendrix. He's theirs, a link with the industry and overcrowding of the past, not just any Victorian industry and overcrowding but Gateshead's, whose mines, river and concentration of people could combine to make a hero out of a rower.

Equally theirs is the Angel of the North, a seventy-foot-high statue by the A1, weighing two hundred tons, and perched on the edge of an ex-council housing estate. I went there twice, each time it drizzled and each time a sequence of visitors strode up to its sturdy ankles, smoking or pushing a pram or walking a dog, having decided that this activity would be more pleasurable if undertaken by a seventy-foot-high metal angel. Everyone I spoke to said they visited it regularly, although it's a work of art, and none of them said they'd ever been yelled at for touching it.

Harder to explain is the attachment much of the town has to its other most famous monument, the *Get Carter* car park, the location for the scene where Michael Caine carries out the most famous murder in the film, throwing the actor who played Alf Roberts in *Coronation Street* off the roof. It was perfect for that purpose, an unforgiving, dismal structure, another shining example of the tribute to concrete that is brutalism. But it was theirs. Instead of 'Gateshead – you know – the other side of the river from Newcastle,' they could say, 'You know the film *Get Carter*? Well, you know that car park where there's that murder? Well, that's the main square in Gateshead.'

It was known as the *Get Carter* car park, and the butcher's opposite one corner of the car park is called the *Get Carter* butchers. Then the site was bought by Tesco, which promised to demolish it. So a campaign to save it was set up by the *Get Carter* Appreciation Society. This made for the most unique of preservation campaigns.

Graffiti was sprayed on the boards erected by Tesco around the condemned brutalist car park, with slogans such as 'We will never forget' and 'You can demolish a building but its spirit will live on'. You could imagine a nightly vigil being held there, with candles across the floor and folk singers singing, 'Its floors may not suit all but it's beautifully brutal,' and a guest speaker from Chile saying, 'You must remember, the digger may knock over the concrete, but it cannot knock over the spirit of struggle within our hearts. Whatever the outcome, if we fight for this cause, our children and our children's children will remember we stayed true to the spirit of the building where Alf Roberts was thrown from the roof.'

In the days before the demolition, *Get Carter* car park tea towels went on sale. The final destruction made it onto the national news, a spokesman for the campaign telling reporters, 'It's as if Gateshead's front teeth have been knocked out.' And this was for the loss of a building that became famous because it was so horrible it was an ideal setting for a film that needed somewhere as horrible as possible. The campaign was yelling, in effect, 'You can't get rid of that – it's horrible!' But it was theirs, in a way a branch of Tesco won't be, no matter how horrible it turns out to be.

Kent

There's something lurking beneath Kent. I spent the first eighteen years of my life there, and I still don't know what it is. Sometimes you'll get a shifty look from a stern, silent and slouched pair of smoking stubbly blokes, as if they're thinking, 'I reckon that arsehole knows about our illegal bear-baiting club that starts every night at two in the morning in Farningham Woods.'

The town I was brought up in – Swanley – specialised in petty crime, the way Luton made hats or Sunderland made ships. But Swanley had the last laugh, because its industry is still booming. Maybe that's because it always emphasised the 'petty' part of the trade, making every effort to nick the most worthless tat, so lads with curly hair would look both ways as if they were in an amateur production of *Oliver!*, then mutter in your ear, 'I've got a box of Welsh-Portuguese dictionaries – three quid the lot.'

When I was seventeen I teamed up with a mate to start a business buying useless cars, polishing them and selling them for a profit. We bought a Ford Corsair for £12, gave it a wipe and advertised it in the newsagents for twenty-five. We got a call from Nobby, one of a family of hundreds who all lived on the same estate, who were regularly mentioned in the *Dartford and Swanley Chronicle* when they were convicted of burgling each other.

Nobby came round to look at the car. We assumed he was going to use it for some ill-fated felony. 'Can I have a look inside?' he asked.

'Of course,' we said, as any car dealer would.

So he got in – and drove off.

There was a pathetic forty seconds or so after we watched him turn the corner, before we looked at each other and mumbled, 'It doesn't look like he's coming back.'

The 30,000 people of the town are served by one pub, the Lullingstone, which must be among the most dangerous buildings in the world to enter. Going in there if you're not familiar with most of the regulars is suicide. Those people who go all the way to Switzerland are wasting their money: all they need to do is buy a one-way ticket to Swanley, then pop in the Lullingstone and say, 'I'm not from round here.' That should do it.

My friend Linda Smith was from Erith, a few miles from Swanley, and after she died I saw an article about her in which she was quoted as saying, 'I often used to argue with Mark Steel about which was worse, Erith or Swanley. I'd make a good case for Erith, but in my heart I knew he was right.'

There's a Roman villa just outside Swanley, beautifully preserved, with a mosaic floor and plenty of columns, that's the only reason for anyone to visit the area. If you take a peek at the town itself you'll understand how the Romans made it all the way to the edge of Swanley, but not to the actual centre, and probably returned to plead, 'Caesar, their legions poured forth from the Lullingstone with many thousands of pool cues and a mighty cry of "Fuck off up to Sidcup."'

Between Swanley and Erith was Dartford, the metropolis we looked on with envy, for here was a town so important it had a Pricerite *and* a Co-Op. It even trumped our major enterprise, as illustrated in a poem written by Edward Cresy in 1857 about the main occupations of towns in the area. It went: 'Sutton for mutton, Horton for beef, South Down for gingerbread, Dartford for a thief.'

I found myself lost in nostalgia when I revisited Dartford, because so many shopping malls and TK Maxxes have replaced the old city centre that I could hardly figure out where anything I remembered used to be. A local historian was trying to explain the new layout to me when I suddenly felt a soothing glow of security as I recognised a building that brought back warm memories. 'Ah,' I beamed, 'there's the magistrate's court. *Now* I know where I am.' Its dull municipal brickwork reminded me of the day I was done in the juvenile court for nicking records. I recalled that with some affection, probably because it meant I got to spend a rare weekday with my dad. If only I'd known about the town's poetry, I could have told the magistrate when asked if I had anything to say before sentencing, 'As Edward Cresy said, Dartford is for a thief, so I'm only upholding the town's tradition, sir.'

The tragedy of Dartford is that if you return after many years you find yourself in a recurring exchange. After noting that the old cinema where I saw *Papillon* and the film version of *On the Buses* had closed, I was told, 'That's because there's a cinema complex at Bluewater.' The old record shop where I bought – actually paid for – the first Clash album had shut, as there was an HMV at Bluewater. Clothes shops, restaurants, all had succumbed to the giant Bluewater complex three miles up the A2. When I saw that West Hill Hospital had shut down, I thought, 'Oh no, I suppose now if you have a heart attack you have to go to the Bluewater Cardiac Complex, between Gap and River Island'.

To get to Bluewater you turn onto a slip road and descend between cliffs, as if you're being driven into the headquarters of an evil genius. Then you enter the sparkly, spacious monument to shirts and bracelets and muffins, and wander round and round, not sure where to gaze until you lose concentration and start wondering whether you've been past Monsoon already maybe twenty minutes ago or was it two hours and your legs start to feel weary but you feel you must keep going and maybe you've been here several days now and you tell the same woman for the fourth time you wouldn't like her to demonstrate how your skin can feel vibrant and energised once she's cleansed it with soap made of natural salts from the Dead Sea combined with walrus whiskers and then it occurs to you no one appears to leave this place so you have a panic attack and yearn for the moment when you might emerge like the prisoner who escapes at the end of *Midnight Express* and begin the process of reacclimatising to society and to natural light.

On one visit to Dartford, by train, I was sat opposite two guards in uniform who were discussing Bluewater. One said he never ever went in, as he knew it was impossible to get out of it without losing a whole tortured day. His mate smirked with pride and said, 'I went in just before Christmas – three presents, twenty minutes and straight back out again. I was like the fucking SAS.'

Once you've managed to get outside, you find yourself in the eerie emptiness that stretches through places such as Northfleet and Swanscombe. I bought a book called *Who's Buried Where in Kent?* Kent is probably the only county for which it seems fitting that there's a book detailing the locations of corpses. It tells you that Henry IV is in Canterbury and Malcolm Campbell is in Chislehurst, and I expected the next page to say: 'Big Tony – shallow grave in Swanley recreation ground.'

Maybe it's the look of Kent that creates a sense of hidden murkiness. The patches of glorious greenery that earned it the title 'the garden of England' are interspersed with scenes of compelling ugliness, leaving you unsure what you're supposed to think. You gaze through the Eurostar window and try to process the sights that go: 'Rolling hills cement works delightful village orchard fucking great smoky funnels oast house oast house greatest concentration of electricity pylons in universe oast house lush green fields lorry park three hundred diggers in excavation site where motorway's in four hundredth year of being rebuilt abandoned quarry church spire unspoilt since 1342 five miles of concrete and cables leading to Eurotunnel.'

Some of the towns plonked between the foliage are places that appear to have been entirely forgotten. I know there is a place called Sittingbourne, because you can see the cranes there from the train to Canterbury, but when's the last time anyone checked to see what goes on there? One day a civil servant looking through some old folders will exclaim, 'Hang on – there's a town here called Sittingbourne whose file must have slipped down the back of a cabinet, because there's no record of it in any official papers since 1927.'

Or someone might squeal, 'Oh my God, we've forgotten we put a place at Sittingbourne,' the way you suddenly remember you left a pie in the oven, and they'll rush down there to find all manner of mutant underground activity before fencing it off and having the military patrol the perimeter, while signing an order that no one must ever be told of what took place.

Then there's the Isle of Grain. This is a marshy piece of land that sticks out into the Thames where it meets the end of the Medway. On maps of Kent it's left blank: just a grey patch, the way a road map of the South Pole would be. There's one thin lane that creeps tentatively up there, to an estate of portable homes that look like chalets in a holiday camp, except it would make more commercial sense to set up a holiday camp in a hospice. In 1995 a leisure company *did* convert the place into a holiday camp, the Allhallows Leisure Park. I looked at its website, assuming the area must have undergone a major transformation since I last went there in 1980. The first review to appear began, 'NEVER AGAIN!!! The beds were wonky, the shop was empty, the food was awful – will never be going back.' Then there are four more scathingly awful reviews, before one seems at first to break the trend: 'Great place. Great food. Shame then that someone set fire to my caravan. Burnt to the ground.'

I returned there for a day, and there it was, a lumpy stretch of mud sloping down to the Thames Estuary opposite Canvey Island, with Kingsnorth power station a mile to the right, and another power station to the left, as if a power station salesman had convinced the local council that their beauty can only be appreciated if they're kept as a pair. And there are chalets and the sort of outdoor pool that looks as if it would be freezing even in a heatwave, and a bar from which a steward emerged as I was walking nearby and shouted, 'We're SHUT!'

But it was strangely, disconcertingly beautiful. Hundreds of seagulls bobbled about looking like litter, and a family on a walk through the marshy grass kept shouting at their teenage son for lagging behind. It was blustery, as it should be, and made me feel that in genuine countryside there should always be a power station and a view of industrial Essex. Like one of those landscapes by artists at the start of the industrial era, in which the barley fields were flanked by a mill in the background, Allhallows seems to make a statement that this is *genuine* countryside, not the twee, unblemished meadows that appear in framed prints in charity shops, the pastoral equivalent of a model who's been photoshopped to create the perfect figure.

Kent is forever punctuating its 'garden-ness' with its industrial, poor and urban side, as if it's embarrassed to be thought of as cute. Round the corner from Sandwich, where the Open golf championship is sometimes held, is the debris of Kent's coalfields. These were opened in the 1920s, the four pits attracting unemployed miners from across the country, many of whom had been blacklisted for militancy during the 1926 General Strike. So you can dreamily gambol across an orchard, turn into a dainty lane past a blacksmith, and suddenly find a bloody great rusting black winding wheel above a dilapidated depot, grass reaching its broken windows.

Even more startling are the villages that housed the miners. Between the sort of towns that get called 'picturesque', with names like Tenterden and Nonington, from where you could probably be exiled for being caught going to bed without wearing a blazer, are settlements such as Aylesham, which was attached to the pit at Snowdown. Aylesham is a series of classic semi-detached houses like a council estate from the 1950s, the sort that get covered by lights in the shape of reindeer at Christmas. At one end of the village is a statue of some miners, and there's a welfare club with bingo and forty-year-old couples who sing 'Quando Quando Quando' as double-acts with names like Melons and Cream.

Even when you've been there many times, you're still amazed that it's there. Mining villages, even ex-ones, aren't supposed to be in Kent. They're supposed to be in Yorkshire and South Wales and Newcastle, not a mile and a half from a village where the mayoress writes to Ann Widdecombe to ask if she'll speak at the Townswomen's Guild.

But there's also something about Kent that makes it a definable county. I was brought up eighteen miles from central London and eight miles from Essex, but rarely went to either before I was sixteen, whereas Maidstone, Folkestone and Margate, while much further away, were part of my patch. There was BBC Invicta radio. There were words that only made sense in Kent, such as 'chore' for stealing and, ahead of its time, 'chavvy' for a mate, that came from the Romany influence in the area. (This must also account for Gipsy Tart, a sickly pudding made from evaporated milk and brown sugar, served once a week at school, that no one outside Kent has ever heard of.) And there was the county cricket team, that won a trophy practically every year between 1970 and 1978, and the grounds were always packed and expectant. Everyone in Kent supported the cricket team, creating a bond from Swanley to Dover and making us distinct from shitty pointless places like Surrey and Essex.

I go to a match at the Canterbury ground once a year, partly because it's the only place I can still go where I'm half the average age. Rows of the retired sit with blankets on knees, the men occasionally peering into their Tupperware to investigate the rolls oozing with Branston pickle packed by their resigned wives. Limping stewards wobble by the members' bar, causing their blazers to bobble up and down, revealing curious lumps on their necks. One group of retired spectators told me about the life-time season ticket, available to over-sixty-fives, saying, 'It costs the same as seven annual season tickets. So basically, Mark, it's a gamble.'

At five o'clock one of them left, with an hour's play still to go. 'I always leave at five,' he said, 'because my wife has her bath around now, so when I get home I can share her water.'

My annual Canterbury pilgrimage is an essential part of my calendar. I can inhale the yeasty whiff of the Shepherd Neame beer tent, walk between the fold-out canvas chairs, around the military-green BBC Radio Kent van and the old man in a tiny wooden hut selling scorecards and *Daily Telegraph*s, savour the applause so sparse you can make out each individual's clap, and the air of pride that the spectators exude in dedicating so much time to the sheer unnecessariness of the modern County Championship.

Because a day at the cricket is a quirk of time. There are six hours of play, plus lunch, plus tea, so there really is no rush. Even the way people greet each other pays homage to this lack of urgency. Instead of the normal 'Hello, Jack, how you keeping?' delivered with a standard beat of quaver quaver crotchet crotchet crotchet quaver quaver, they'll sigh, nod, take a breather from the exertion of sighing and nodding, then manage an elongated 'Jaaaaack—, you keeping well?' which, written as a musical score, would show a semibrève followed by three pages of rests.

And Kent is so close to France. 'Oo, there it is,' my parents would say about France when you could see it clearly from the beach, but it would never occur to them that it might be fun to go there, any more than they'd think we might go to the sun because we could see that. Now the proximity to Europe provides thousands of jobs, and day trips to Calais for cheap shopping at the complex of warehouses and malls built at the end of the tunnel. It was during the days of Napoleon that the first plans for a tunnel were drawn up, when maybe the world's finest engineers would gasp, 'Consider it, my good and learned friends, that there may come a day when folk from Faversham shall pack cases of screwtop bottles of Amstel for their barbecue in their boot for to save themselves fifteen quid.'

The mentality of Kent is shaped by this geography. From Dover downwards along the coast are Martello towers, mini-fortresses built as stations from which to fire on Napoleon's invading navy. And in 1940 Kent was twenty-one miles from the edge of the empire of the Third Reich, the Spitfires that fought off Hitler's Luftwaffe in the Battle of Britain doing so over towns such as Folkestone and Greatstone.

So one of Kent's best-selling beers is called Spitfire, and Kent's limited-overs cricket team is called the Spitfires, and a randomly selected copy of the *Folkestone Herald* from October 2009 contained three articles with 'Spitfire' in the headline, although Kent can hardly claim credit for the success of the battle on account of having been underneath it.

But in other ways there isn't enough made of the county's place in history. Folkestone's museum consists of one room above the library with some of the customary old axes, and barely a mention of the impact of war. In any case, when I was there two girls were shouting at each other, 'You fucking did fancy him!', 'I fucking never!' next to a stuffed otter, so it was hard to concentrate.

Folkestone also seems to be stuffed with tattoo shops, the way other towns have cafés. Maybe they're *instead* of cafés, and after a morning's shopping the people of the town meet up with a friend for a relaxing chat and a snake round the ankle. There's a harbour from which you can buy cockles from a variety of fish stalls, an intriguing view of a viaduct, and a tiny station with a ramp to a road that leads gently to a giant Lidl that takes thirty minutes to walk round and makes you lose all sense of where you're facing or where the sea is, so if anyone does ever invade us they'll get no further than the Folkestone Lidl before all their regiments collide with each other and walk back into the harbour, asking, 'How can we be *this* side of Dixons again?' as they're taken prisoner.

Along the coast is upmarket Hythe and the magnificence of the Romney, Hythe and Dymchurch railway. I first went on this when I was eight, during a day trip to Greatstone, and now I must have been on it twenty times. Maybe that's because you need to be an adult to fully appreciate its beauty. The journey starts as any miniature steam-railway experience would be expected to, with a slightly-too-enthusiastic volunteer of sixty in full railway uniform and cap, who you know could get a discussion on child abuse round to the gauge settings on the 1934 Great Western Line to Taunton, selling you an old cardboard ticket, slightly rough to the touch, that makes anyone of a certain age think, 'Ah, that's when tickets were tickets.'

You have a proper cup of tea in the proper station café that sells purple cakes with a green sweet on the top, then squeeze into the little wooden cabins, wait for a magnificent climate-changing cloud of steam and the dramatic throaty whistle, and chug-chug away.

At this point anyone unfamiliar with this railway would expect it to toodle through a village or two and pass some ducks, on the way to the seaside to be greeted by jolly tubby men dressed as elves. But this is Kent, remember. So it leaves Hythe and enters Romney Marsh, where you peep and chundle through miles of desolate wasteland. On your right are endless miles of neglected fields full of long shabby grass, punctuated by hundreds of electricity pylons that seem to have disobediently fallen out of line to create maximum random disorder.

And on your left are everyone's back gardens. You're so close you feel you can lean out and dip your fingers in the paddling pools. But everyone waves at you, as if you're toddlers in a fairground teacup. This is impressive, as eight of these trains go by every day, and have done since 1936. So the owners of these houses must have to wave and wave and wave – perhaps it's a condition of the leases. But they do it with such enthusiasm it feels as if they're genuinely thrilled and slightly surprised to see you pass by the bottom of their garden in a miniature railway carriage. You find yourself waving back, despite being in your fifties, to other people in their fifties, wondering whether if you didn't you'd break a spell and everyone on the train would turn into a lizard.

As you trundle past more gardens and pylons and the sort of craggy fields where you expect a boy's dog to discover a corpse, you get a sensation alien to the modern traveller, that the purpose of this journey is the journey. The train *is* used by people as the only public means of getting between Romney, Hythe and Dymchurch, but its ludicrous nature literally makes you laugh. At some point, as you pass a particular garden or pylon, you will just start laughing. In its seventy years I can't imagine there has ever been someone sat on the train going, 'OH BLOODY TYPICAL – what are we slowing down for NOW?' Or, 'Hello Trudy, I'm going to be late for my 10.15. This fucking thing should be at Dymchurch by now, and we're not even at bloody Littlestone.'

But the miniature railway did have more urgent demands placed on it when the area became the first line of defence against the Germans. The cheerfully tatty sand dunes of Littlestone were covered in scaffolding from where gunners would try to shoot down doodlebugs, and the trains were armoured as protection against German rockets. That sounds so exciting I think I'd have gone on it every day, steam blowing over the armour as we passed the gardens, from which the families would all pop up and wave from their Anderson shelters.

The train was used to secretly carry supplies to Greatstone in preparation for the Normandy landings. Most exciting of all, in 1942 a Luftwaffe pilot crashed right next to the train, just as it belched out a huge cloud of steam that killed him stone dead. You'd like to think that when the letter arrived home saying, 'We regret to announce Herr Schröder was killed by the steam from the Romney, Hythe and Dymchurch Railway,' even his own family had the decency to snigger.

After the train passes Dymchurch, things get more eerie. The marshland becomes pebbly, the houses more spread out, then you see in the distance the compellingly spooky Soviet-looking gunge machine that is Dungeness power station. You never see anyone go in or out, you just hear it belch with a booming baritone horn once a minute, as if it's a giant snoring robotic alien. Eventually you're past all the gardens, and chugging across a plain of pebbles towards this beast. Right next to it are two lighthouses, which may be in case the power station eats the one nearest to it. Nothing else is in sight except for pylons and rusty abandoned boats.

The power station is the end of the line. Of course it is. So here you are in this twee little carriage with a chirpy railway enthusiast blowing a whistle, and you're cranking your way towards the most frightening-looking building in Europe, like plummeting into a volcano in a pedalo. Yet its ugliness is seductive, almost beautiful, like a hunchback. And it's not just the power station, it's that expanse of pebbles, way back past the beach and inland, and then dozens of random dwellings plonked on the pebbles higgledy-piggledy, so their addresses must be 'along from the power station and right a bit and past a rusty barrel and along a bit'.

The most famous of these is called Prospect Cottage, and belonged to the film director Derek Jarman. If anyone famous was going to live there it would be him, and probably not Amanda Holden. The cottage is surrounded by rusty wire and cable that's been bent into shapes and shoved in among the pebbles, and the whole area is wonderfully unsettling. I've never been to Dungeness with anyone who hasn't said, despite all they'd heard about it, that it isn't more disconcerting than they'd anticipated.

So it's right that it sits at the very end, of the miniature railway and of Kent. There is nowhere to go after that. I could in theory sneak round the back of the power station and traipse across miles of pebbles past a military base towards Camber, but I doubt anyone's ever tried that and lived. Instead I bask in the weirdness, the permanent twilight, the lack of bearings, and reconnect with what I love about Kent: it's – unsettling. Something's going on underneath, but what is it? It's like a brilliantly disturbing play, or an East European brandy that leaves a lasting, unidentifiable, strangely industrial tang, or a bedroom painted entirely bright purple. It's probably wrong, but it's certainly not bland. You're not sure what you feel, but you know you're alive.

Bristol

The difficulty for poor Bristol is, no matter how well it maintains its waterways and pretty Victorian ships, and displays its bridge and its association with Isambard Kingdom Brunel, it's hard to skirt round the embarrassment that the modern city was built on slavery.

It tries its best to ignore it. In 1996 it held a Festival of the Sea, but made no mention of the slave issue at all. This must have made for some entertaining exchanges between inquisitive tourists and the guides, such as, 'So where did these ships go then?'

'Well they went to Africa, and then across the Atlantic.'

'What did they take?'

'Oh, this and that, but the main thing is, isn't that mast a beauty?'

The 'Visit Bristol' tourist website mentions all the glory of the city and the sea, while slavery passes it by. But there is a section called 'Bristol History'. Amidst the prose is one sentence that refers to the issue. It goes: 'Bristol's strong links with the ocean, and its key role in the profitable trades of slavery and tobacco, inevitably led to the city's involvement with piracy, and Britain's most famous pirate, Blackbeard, was allegedly born in the city.'

It might be fascinating to see whoever wrote that delivering a lecture at a conference on the history of black people and the slave trade, as they say, 'I found the Reverend Jesse Jackson's lecture on the long-term impact of slavery most informative, and thank you for that, Jesse. But I feel the main thing is that slavery led to piracy, and Blackbeard, which is rather jolly. So everyone join in, "Yo ho ho and a bottle of rum, fifteen men on a dead man's chest …"'

As well as Blackbeard, Bristol also provided 2,000 ships for the slave trade. When William Wilberforce's first Bill to abolish slavery was defeated, the bells rang out across the city in celebration. In 2006 a debate was held across the city about whether Bristol should formally apologise. I'm not sure what good this would do, two hundred years late, and it might seem slightly awkward if the local mayor was to go to Jamaica, get off the plane and say, 'Well, er, sorry about all that, you know, chains and that. Anyway, er, take it from me, it won't happen again. Well, er, hope that clears things up, bye.'

Even so, in a poll by HTV over 90 per cent of those who responded said they thought an apology ought to be offered, which suggests that Bristol's population isn't quite as coy about the past as its tourist industry.

Maybe the issue leads more people in Bristol to display a feeling for their history than in other towns, because when I performed there the audience was meticulous in correcting anything they considered below PhD standard. For example, it seemed odd to me that the city had a series of canals, given that it was already blessed with a river, a sea and a major international port. I imagined these poor Irishmen in the early nineteenth century digging and sweating for sixteen hours a day to build the canal, then finishing it, leaning on their shovels and saying, 'Years of backbreaking toil, but at last we've brought a means for water to flow through this city.' Then turning round and going, 'Ah, for fuck's sake, there's a fucking great river, we're fucking eejits.'

But I was corrected almost as soon as I'd begun. 'Oh no,' said a concerned man in the second row. 'Oh no, Mark, it's not a canal.'

'But it's called the canal, and there are signs all over the city imploring everyone to go on a ride up the canal, so if I was Sherlock Holmes I might be forgiven for thinking, "Hmmm, the clues suggest there's a canal," I told him. Then the whole room started. 'It's *called* a canal, but it's actually a "new cut", said several people, while everyone else nodded.

Then one man, with the exasperated look of a mechanic who's had to break off from his work to explain to his apprentice which bit's the engine, told me the 'canal' was built to divert the existing river, and enables the harbour to float, apparently.

As comments to ruin a joke go, this was fairly effective, but like an idiot I carried on, to be interrupted a few seconds later by several people calling out that the Irish didn't build the canal that isn't a canal. As I should have known, it was built by French prisoners during the war with Napoleon. I couldn't help wondering if too much education is a bad thing.

There was something else about Bristol that suggested a unique attention to detail. Two weeks before the show, which in part was a tirade against the strangling of towns by the chain companies, most obviously Tesco, there was a riot against a new Tesco store in Bristol that became national news when protesters set fire to the place. Sometimes in a pompous moment, as a performer you get the idea that you have some minuscule influence, that a couple of people in the town might be affected in some small area of their life, if only to think, 'He's right, you know. Bono *is* a wanker.' But for a moment I wondered if I had undiscovered powers, if all I had to do was announce I was coming somewhere to rant about chain stores, and two weeks before I arrived the locals would burn down the Tesco.

In the Stokes Croft area of the city, Tesco had been granted permission to build its thirty-second store in Bristol. Several hundred local people objected, one of them by painting a mural on a wall, and in a poll of the area 90 per cent opposed it. A demonstration was called, which seems to have involved neighbours playing guitars on bus shelters, and a generally convivial and orderly display of Tesco-hatred. But the situation was complicated by a nearby complex of squats, which the police viewed as a problem area, so riot vans were sent in, just around pub closing time, which probably wasn't a strategy the finest military minds would have opted for. While the details are disputed, one way or another the result was Britain's first anti-Tesco riot.

My own influence was probably limited, because the next time I was in Bristol the Stokes Croft Tesco opened, with what the newspapers called 'a heavy police presence'. Even so, it's not the company's ideal scenario, to extend the franchise by setting up militarised Tesco Express stores.

Or maybe it's planning a private army for the next stage of its quest for greater domination, with soldiers stood at the checkout with their guns loaded, yelling, 'Goods in the bag NOW! Come on, MOVE IT! No, DON'T put cold meats in the same bag as raw onions, do you WANT TO GET SHOT?'

As with all protests that become riotous, the reasons for the tension were more than the immediate demands. But there is a pattern of opposition to Tesco, and nearly every application it now makes for a new store provokes controversy and some sort of campaign to stop it.

In almost every town I've visited in the last three years, I've been told that one of the major local issues concerns the building of a Tesco. It's as if it's even managed to make protest movements the same in every town.

It's often suggested that there's a class divide in the attitude towards a new Tesco – that the working class are grateful for a cheap, convenient superstore, but the middle class think everyone should shop at the quaint little deli and live off slices of Roquefort cheese. But in almost every case, hundreds or thousands of people sign petitions objecting to the store, and only a few of the proposed sites are in places where the complaint is that a Tesco might lower the tone of the area.

For example, near to where I live, in a fairly poor area of Croydon, a new Tesco was successfully stopped by a campaign that included a petition signed by four hundred people from the few streets around the proposed site.

The idea that opponents of Tesco are the worried posh is a new version of the myth that all protest is the work of 'outsiders', or is at least propelled by them. There must be another reason why a shop should provoke such a reaction, when it isn't selling heroin or Semtex or taser guns tested on badgers.

There are many accounts of the practices of Tesco, the impoverishing of farmers, the low wages, the aggressive marketing that forces local competition out of business, but those things are probably only in the background of most people's minds when they sign one of the petitions. It's more likely that the issue most concerning them is the indefinable but steady way in which every Tesco that emerges robs an area of a bit of its soul.

Because the thing is plonked there by people from afar, not just in distance but in spirit. They'll have looked at a map on Google Earth in their regional head office and seen a mile and a half between two other stores, with the potential for selling 54 per cent of the milk and all the Sellotape necessary for the area, especially if the existing shops are put out of business. And then there will be a building identical to all the others, with its staff in stripy uniforms with badges telling you not to ask for beer unless you're eighteen, and unworkable self-service machines and the woman on the Tannoy saying, 'Why not try a spicy Friday with a Mexican ready-cooked meal, *hmmmm*, the *ideal* way to get your weekend off to a *frying* start,' in a voice that sounds as if she's a manic depressive at the apex of her 'up' phase, and any minute she'll crash and mutter a barely audible, 'Or there's lasagne. Fucking lasagne. But what's the point of pasta, what's the point of anything?'

Then on the way up again she could have been in the Stokes Croft branch when the riot was on, and she'd still have been

gasping, 'Why not take advantage of ready-sizzled flaming packets of Jaffa Cakes, a *scrumptious* treat and a whopping *ten pence
off* for all packets that have been melted by a petrol bomb.'

The staff seem generally cheery, and it's handy if you run out
of mushrooms at half past eight in the evening, but a Tesco
Express still feels like a whirlwind of gloom, like an occupying
force that's implanted itself in your manor, and somehow this
vague eeriness is enough to instil active and increasingly successful opposition from wherever they seek to land next.

There's also a widespread sense that Tesco is heading towards
world domination, to the point that soon when we see some
roadworks and assume it's something to do with gas or water,
when the hole's filled in there'll be a Tesco Express there, in the
middle of the road. If they're not stopped, you'll wander behind
the bins at the back of a council estate and hear a chirpy voice
beaming, 'Or how about giving yourself a well-earned treat after
a hard day's work, with our hand-picked ready-rolled spliffs of
skunk, *three* for the price of *two*, come on, you *deserve* it.'

I used to think that unless it was stopped Tesco would apply
to the United Nations to become a country, and within five years
it would have the world's third largest army, and be turning
countries like Spain into giant stores, with Gibraltar set aside as
the 'eight items or less' aisle. But now I fear its plans may be
grander than that, and that it will try to become a religion, with
paradise assured only for followers who earn over 20,000 loyalty
points.

They'll stand in high streets on Saturdays singing 'Every little
helps' while clapping in a shopping trolley, and claim that the
first ever Tesco was a miracle, built by followers who had only
sand and polystyrene but who did it in two days because they
had faith.

But the most powerful and seemingly invincible dynasties
can crash at great speed if there's enough underlying resentment
against them. From the Medicis to the Murdochs, the powerful

have assumed everlasting dominance right up to their demise. Maybe one day Tesco stores will be turned into music venues and cinemas, old people's homes and adventure playgrounds for kids, who will shriek and giggle as they chase each other past the toiletries and hide behind the cat litter.

And then Bristol will be remembered for its vital role in history, as the town that made up for its earlier *faux pas*, by starting the battle against the greatest threat the human race has ever faced.

CONCLUSION

Karl Marx predicted the Wetherspoon's pub. While the industrial society was in its infancy, he wrote that in time the bigger companies would swallow the smaller ones, until the world was dominated by vast global outfits, so eventually the individual and local companies would be overwhelmed by these multinationals. And somewhere, I think, he proved this by illustrating how mv>x results in chain pubs that open at 9 a.m. so customers can take the edge off by sipping cheap bitter while staring out of the window with the blank expression of a serial killer.

And this process is gradually becoming international. Most major airports are indistinguishable from each other, as if the virus of uniformity spills off the planes and seeps out from there. So travellers go from London to Melbourne and have a night out in Nando's, or arrive in Buenos Aires and exclaim, 'Oh, that's handy, they've got a Gap Kids.'

This isn't the fault of 'people', as we can't help the attraction of familiarity. But the rewarding experiences are when we're jostled out of this comfort into the unknown, into a world of difference. Even Vincent Vega in *Pulp Fiction* finds the most fascinating aspect of his trip to France is that in McDonald's the Quarter Pounder with cheese is called a Royale with cheese.

A town is a public space. It should be shaped by those who inhabit it, either permanently or for just that day, or who have inhabited it in the past. The hopes, fears and loves of all the

267

people who've passed through it should be embodied in its customs, its streets, its bars, its smell. Then it becomes fascinating. Remove the bustle of the crowds and replace the markets with units imported from an executive office, then turn the centre into a series of logos, and you're left with a sterile vacuum, of no interest because there's no difference.

The modern British town is still a long way from this extreme, because despite the efforts of the multinationals to remove the uncertainty of humanity from their domain, humanity insists on staying put. In every area, no matter how grubby it may appear, an affection for what makes it distinct will break through.

There's often an assumption that fighting to retain local, individual quirks is to stand against an inevitable tide, as hopeless as buying vinyl records or keeping a donkey in the house. But it's the young who make the most strident efforts to retain individuality. For example, hip-hop is almost designed to comment on a local area, and almost every town has rappers on YouTube, ranting about the precise places and people that piss them off there. Almost every town has a Facebook page set up by the youth of the area, combining utter frustration with a veiled affection.

It's the young who work tirelessly to create a local dialect, somewhere between their traditional accent in Gloucestershire and one they've borrowed from the Bronx, and it's the young who cherish the endearing awfulness of the club in their town that everyone goes to, such as Boston's Eclipse. And it's the memories of youth that make it hard to abandon a place entirely, as you recall the parks where you played and fought, the pubs where you could drink under age, and the days when it seemed to you to be the centre of the universe, though later, in adult life, you find yourself describing it while someone looks at you blankly and says, 'I think I may have gone past it once.'

The sports teams, music venues, film nights and tales of local history are almost, without necessarily realising it, a scream of defiance against a world that reduces everything to a franchise. Most towns have a museum and a theatre run by delightfully pedantic volunteers. I have yet to find a town in Britain, no matter how nondescript it may seem, in which there isn't a collection of people who will fall over themselves with enthusiasm as they convey the stories of their manor. Often this applies to the entire population. Everyone in Gateshead knows of the nineteenth-century rowing champion Harry Clasper, and everyone in Walsall knows the radical Victorian nurse Sister Dora.

Like a soldier who writes a poem, a factory worker who slips to the toilet to read a novel, or a prisoner who learns to paint, these are expressions of staying human in the face of imposed uniformity. So activities and an outlook that is localised and spontaneous grate against the sponsored corporate world. Any event, such as the Lewes bonfire night, that attracts a community without sponsorship, is a missile aimed at the assumption that society can only function if it pleases big business for it to do so. Like a butcher who stays open despite the efforts of Tesco to close him down, they've broken the rules and made the gods angry.

Even if Tesco were to establish a giant store that covered the whole planet, and to convince us that anyone venturing beyond the shopping trolleys would suffocate, there would be muttering and little acts of rebellion, secret festivals in the corner behind the children's clothes, and guerrilla fighters jamming the absurdly jolly Tannoy announcements to make revolutionary statements.

In the nineteenth century a series of movements reacted against the functional culture of the mills and factories by cherishing the imagination, and promoting the individual. Poets and musicians were classified as Romantics, and later in the century people such as the Pre-Raphaelite painters and William Morris defied the smoke and the obsession with production to promote what was simply beautiful.

Now we need an army of Romantics for a new century, not just to cherish the village church and dry-stone walls, but to preserve the flair and passion, the imagination and history, the anecdotes and eccentricity, the madness, the wit, the grime, the rebellion, the music, the poetry, the boundless fascination of human existence, that under the ring roads and the retail parks are the heartbeat of a town.

BIBLIOGRAPHY

I've now read so many books about one town or another, with titles such as *The Pavements of Burnley* or *The Week the Lamp Posts Didn't Work in Southampton*, that I recommend you read a novel, or a biography of a film star, or anything other than a book about a specific town. But if you really want some, drop me a note and I'll pop half a dozen in the post.

ACKNOWLEDGEMENTS

Firstly I'd like to thank the BBC for allowing me to make the programme that led to this book. Obviously that doesn't mean everyone at the BBC. Huw Edwards can take little credit, and Sue Barker didn't lift a finger. But Jane Berthoud, Julia McKenzie and the comedy section of Radio 4 made the show possible. Otherwise I'd have had to record it in my bedroom like Rupert Pupkin.

Natasha has been marvellous in many ways, script-editing, suggesting jokes and spending every weekend for years coming with me to places like Dorking and Dungeness, and never once yelling, 'Why couldn't you write a book called *Mark Steel's in Brazil* or *Mark Steel Stays at Home and Does Something Slightly Fucking Useful*?'

Equally tolerant have been Elliot, Eloise, Maddie and Bridget, for putting up with demands such as, 'No, you can't stay in watching *The Mighty Boosh*, we're going to walk round Wigan.'

Pete Sinclair has been invaluable as ever, and without him this book would be called *A Random Load of Thoughts* and be written in biro.

Nick Pearson and Louise Haines at Fourth Estate turned the idea into a book. Nick's method was impeccable, as he spent the entire meeting in which we were supposed to discuss the idea talking about sport, and I knew straight away we'd get along.

Robert Lacey's notes have been captivating, as in between corrections of grammar he's written miniature essays putting me right on the history of rugby league and other issues.

And in every town I've mentioned, and several I haven't, there have been people who've gone to vast lengths to show me round, lend me books, enthuse about the history, the architecture, the geology and layout of the town. So I'd like to thank them for their wonderful enthusiasm, and even more I'd like to thank the people in the towns who were rude and unhelpful, as it's much easier to be funny about them than the kind ones.

Thanks to so many of the nation's cafés, in which much of this book has been written.

Lastly, I'd like to thank the people who've put the book together for getting my name right, which isn't as easy as it might seem. Once before, with a previous book, the publishers sent me their blurb for the back cover. I read it through, until I got to the last line: 'All in all, this is Mark Thomas's funniest book so far.'

I put my head in my hands, and my daughter, who was very young, said, 'What's the matter, Dad?'

I said, 'Read that and see if you can spot a mistake.'

She read it, and said, 'But Dad, Mark Thomas might buy this book, and he'll be reading it and he'll say, "It's funny, I don't remember writing this."'